THE CHILD AND SOCIETY

Essays in Applied Child Development

THE CHILD
AND SOCIETY

Essays in Applied Child Development

DAVID ELKIND

New York
Oxford University Press
1979

Copyright © 1979 by Oxford University Press, Inc.
Printed in the United States of America

Library of Congress Cataloging in Publication Data
Elkind, David, 1931–
    The child and society.

    Bibliography: p.
    Includes index.
    1. Child psychology.   2.   Socialization.
3.   Cognition in children.   I.   Title.
BF721.E35   155.4'18   78-2758
ISBN 0-19-502371-4
ISBN 0-19-502372-2 pbk.

To David Rapaport,
who taught me to read and to write
and much, much more

CONTENTS

THE CLINIC

THE CHURCH

INTRODUCTION

In this book, I have brought together several essays that were written over the past ten years. All of the essays deal with issues in applied child development. As I view it, the field of applied child development is a broad domain which includes not only the application of research findings to the home, classroom, and clinic, but also the use of pratical experience as a basis for conceptualization and theory. The essays in this book reflect this two-directional approach to the field. Some of the papers move from research and theory to practice, while others move from practice to research and theory.

Before introducing the essays in more detail, it might be well to say something about my own involvement in the field of applied child development. My interest in the interaction of theory and practice has roots in my childhood. My father was a gifted machinist who had had little formal schooling. Many times he would come home with blueprints that had been drawn by college-trained engineers. My father brought them home because, while they were beautifully drawn, *they could not be machined*. The engineers who drew up the plans did not really understand what could and what could not be done on a lathe or milling machine. Consequently, my father had to redraw the blueprints so that the pieces could be machined and still do the job they were designed to do.

The issue of relating theory to practice has been an abiding interest of mine ever since those early experiences. When I moved into psychology, I was very much interested in learning theory—which was in great vogue at the time—and did my dissertation with rats. But I also undertook clinical training and received a degree in clinical psychology. Throughout my career I have worked in both academic and applied settings and have always been concurrently involved in research and teaching as well as applied work. My applied work has been in psychiatric hospitals, mental hygiene clinics, family courts, schools, and some private practice and consulting.

Although this occupational pattern is surely not the one that everyone should follow, it has distinct advantages. To my mind it puts research and teaching in perspective and does not permit them to become too esoteric and removed from concerns of everyday life. In the same way, applied work that is in touch with current research and theory is likely to be innovative, open, and flexible and not mired down in entrenched habits.

I am aware, of course, that this model of the practitioner/ scholar was advocated by clinical psychology as a discipline and that it has largely failed to be realized. Clinical psychologists in the university tend to become academicians, and clinical psychologists in practice tend to become practitioners. This bifurcation is reflected in the burgeoning movement towards professional schools in clinical psychology. Apparently, the practitioner/scholar route is harder to follow than either direction taken singly.

If the practitioner/scholar path is not the road for everyone to take, I do not believe that it should be abandoned. There should be training opportunities and jobs for those persons who feel comfortable moving between research and applied settings. In my opinion, such persons are particularly needed in child development where the gap between what we now know how children think and learn and how we use this knowledge in schools and clinics is very wide indeed. I hope the work reported here will encourage more young people to enter this difficult terrain between research and practice.

If we turn now to the essays themselves, they may seem disparate because, in part at least, they were written for different audiences at different times. On rereading them, however, I found that they reflected a few central themes, hinted at in some of the essays and more fully elaborated in others. One of these themes is the role that society plays in the emotional disturbance of young people. This theme is suggested in the lead chapter, "Culture, Change, and Children" and is developed more fully in the chapters entitled: "From Ghetto School to College Campus" (Ch. 3); "Choosing to be Gay" (Ch. 5); "Middle-Class Delinquency" (Ch. 15); "Borderline Retardation in Low- and Middle-Income Adolescents" (Ch. 16); and "The Curriculum-Disabled Child" (Ch. 18).

Another theme that runs through several of the essays is the enormous distance between public policy and the actual and unmet needs of children. This theme is taken up in the discussions: "Day Care in America" (Ch. 2); "Ethnicity and Reading" (Ch. 4); "Humanizing the Curriculum" (Ch. 11); and "We Can Teach Reading Better" (Ch. 14). Although the immediate focus of each essay is different, in each case I have tried to point out the discrepancy between child need on the one hand and societal priorities on the other.

Some of the other essays are united by a common explanatory construct. One such construct is that of the "frame" which is borrowed from anthropology and sociology and which I have tried to employ in the understanding of parent–child relations in "Cognitive Frames and Family Interactions" (Ch. 6) and in the understanding of teacher–child interactions in "Observing Classroom Frames" (Ch. 12). Another construct, again more current in sociology than in psychology, is that of the "contract," conceived as an interpersonal understanding. I have used this construct in trying to understand: "Middle-Class Delinquency" (Ch. 15); classroom conflict in "Teacher-Child Contracts" (Ch. 10); and the generational conflict in "Exploitation and the Generational Conflict" (Ch. 7). In employing the concepts of "frame" and "contract," I have had to extend and modify them to suit the phenomena being dealt with. This is a necessary, but speculative, aspect of applied work in child development.

Although I dislike writing "How to's" because children and families are just too variable to be dealt with by simple formulas, I have written papers addressed to parents, teachers, and practitioners that do have a practical aspects. In each of these papers I have tried to present the young person's point of view in the hope that if we really understand a child's perspective, the "how to's" will follow as a natural consequence. These more applied discussions are to be found in the chapters entitled: "Understanding the Young Adolescent" (Ch. 8); "The Early Years: The Vital Years" (Ch. 9); "Piaget and Montesorri in the Classroom" (Ch. 13); "The Active Classroom and Children with Special Needs" (Ch. 19); "The Study of Spontaneous Religion in the Child" (Ch. 20); and "Life and Death: Concepts and Feelings of Children" (Ch. 22).

The remaining two essays are more general and more speculative. The essay on "Cognitive Development and Psychopathology" (Ch. 17) is an attempt to show how our knowledge of cognitive development can broaden and deepen our understanding of psychopathology. The other speculative essay has a somewhat different aim. In that paper, "The Origins of Religion in the Child (Ch. 21)," I have attempted to show how the various components of a social institution, namely religion, meet the emerging cognitive needs of the growing person.

In addition to these several themes and constructs that unite some of the essays, there is an underlying theme that unites them all. This is the need for a greater respect and concern for the young people with whom we interact at home, at school, at the clinic, at church, and in society at large. There is no better investment for the future of mankind in general and for the future of democratic society in particular than children. They are our most precious, our most important but, unfortunately, our most vulnerable natural resource. It was in the hope of helping to protect and to conserve this all important human resource that these essays were written and why they were brought together here.

SOCIETY

1
CULTURE, CHANGE, AND CHILDREN

Social change affects children indirectly, through the alterations it produces in parental attitudes toward children. Some illusions that prevent us as adults from appreciating our role as mediators of social change introduce this chapter. A description of three changed attitudes operating in contemporary parent-child relations follows. The chapter closes with a discussion of some of the problems produced in children by these changed parental attitudes and some possible directions that mental health professionals might take in solving them.

How do the almost revolutionary changes taking place in our society impact upon children and adolescents? In my opinion, the force of these changes is much more indirect than it is direct. That is to say, social change affects the attitudes that adults hold toward themselves, toward children and toward society in general. It is largely these changed attitudes that communicate social change to children. But it is not always easy for us as adults to fully appreciate our role as the mediators of the social changes that affect children.

Accordingly, in the first section of this chapter, I will describe some of the illusions that block our appreciation of our role as

Social Casework, 1973, 54, 360–66.

mediators of social change. Then, in the next section, I will describe three contemporary parental attitudes and the effects that they are having upon today's children. In the final section of the paper, some of the problems created by these changed parental attitudes are presented along with some suggestions as to how those of us in the helping professions might go about solving them.

SOME ADULT ILLUSIONS

In general, growing up means giving up one's illusions and coming to view the world as it is, rather than as we want it to be. But adulthood brings with it its own illusions. One of these false beliefs is the *generational illusion*. Parents whose children reach adolescence come to think of the young people they know as different from the young people of their own generation. Contemporary youth appear to be wilder, freer, more boisterous, and more disrespectful than parents remember themselves to have been.

Like most illusions the belief that our own offspring constitute a unique generation stems from a failure of differentiation. What we do, in arriving at such illusions, is to mistake what is new for us as individuals for what is also new for society and for mankind. When we are middle-aged for the *first* time, and the parents of adolescents for the *first* time, we mistake our first experience with adolescent rebellion and disaffection for something new *on society's* horizon. In fact, of course, the young people of today are much more like us, when we were adolescents, than they are different. The generational illusion has often caused us to exaggerate the uniqueness of contemporary youth to the point of distortion.

A second illusion to which adults are prone has to do with time and might be called the *immediacy illusion*. As we grow older, short-term time intervals often seem to pass slowly, whereas long-term time intervals seem to have passed, in retrospect, quite quickly. When we stand in a line at the bank or at the airport, or while we wait in traffic, each moment seems so excruciatingly long. And yet when we look back at the years during which our children grew up, we marvel at the rapidity of the passage of time. So, when we think of social issues such as pollution, crime, energy resources and so on, we have a tremendous sense of urgency—of time fleeing by and of the need to do something *now*. We believe, and thus is the immediacy illusion, that young people share this sense of urgency.

By and large, they do not. For the young, short time intervals pass with amazing rapidity. Waiting in line is not a terrible burden when we are young. Even when children are bored and say they have nothing to do, it is the lack of activity rather than the dragging of time which distresses them. When we are young and the world is full of novelty and charm, short periods of time pass quickly. And yet, in contrast to adults, a year in retrospect seems very long ago and a year in prospect seems very far away.

One consequence of this immediacy illusion is that there is considerable discrepancy between what young people and what adults regard as urgent. Adults see the dangers of pollution, energy depletion, and overpopulation as imminent and as requiring immediate action. Young people appreciate the same dangers but do not feel the same urgency for remedial action. Rather they feel the need for an immediate expression of their appreciation of the danger. For example, in the early 1970s after a massive antiwar demonstration in Washington, D.C., the mall in front of the Lincoln monument was covered with litter.

Of course the difference is only relative and many adults express dissatisfaction without doing anything about it while many young people work very hard for causes which they believe in. It is true, nonetheless, that young people in general have a tremendous need to be heard and to be listened to. Perhaps they still believe that if right and reason could only be heard, then these values would have to prevail. Adults are more cynical about the efficacy of expression and are on the average more resigned to working long and hard for the ameliorization of social ills.

The immediacy illusion probably helps to explain some aspects of the generational misunderstanding. For example, to the adult, for whom problems such as pollution seem imminent, youth's cavalier attitude toward littering seems callous and hyocritical. To young people, for whom personal expression seems the most pressing issue, adult unwillingness to listen and to hear them out seems pretentious and unfeeling. The misunderstandings arise because each generation assumes that the other should share the same immediacy priorities. In fact, however, there is no real reason why the generations should share the same priorities. It is only when we assume that the generations *ought* to share the same priorities that conflicts ensue.

A final illusion I want to mention migbt be called the *homogeneity illusion,* the illusion a homogeneous adolescent group exists. As adults, we are in the habit of talking about the "youth culture" or the "drug culture" or the "adolescent society" or the "generation gap" as if young people constituted a uniform, self-conscious group. We assume that young people all share a common outlook and a common set of values which are at variance with those held by adults. This is clearly a misconception.

It is rather amazing, as one travels about the country, how much values and outlooks vary among the young. Adolescents in Berkeley are quite a different group from those in Indiana. In the Northeast, college women often wear jeans and sweatshirts whereas at Southern schools many of the girls wear dresses and makeup. Even within the same community there will be groups of young people whose social life centers about the church, or about scouting while the social life of other young people centers about the corner store or the local drive-in. The diversity in outlook and values among the young is every bit as great as it is among adults.

When we look at young people as a homogeneous group, we are responding to a stereotype. Unfortunately, the mass media contribute greatly to such homogenization and stereotyping by constantly publicizing one or another group of young people as if it were representative of the whole. This is clearly not the case. Effective intervention and interaction with young people means, first and foremost, that we appreciate their individuality.

SOCIAL CHANGES THAT AFFECT CHILDREN

The generational, immediacy, and homogeneity illusions suggest that we, as adults, often misinterpret how social change affects children. Social change affects adults directly, in the frus-

trations, anxieties, and tensions it produces, and in the opportunities and challenges it presents. Children and adolescents,
however, tend to be affected by social change indirectly,
through the ways in which social change affects the adults who
deal with children. Children are influenced by social change
primarily as it is manifested in adult attitudes toward children
and toward child rearing.

This is not the place to discuss the historical circumstances
which have produced contemporary attitudes toward children
and child rearing. What I want to do here is to cite a few of the
contemporary trends in adult attitudes toward children which I
believe to be new and which seem to me to have significant
consequences for the emotional health of young people.

DEMAND FOR EARLY COMPETENCE

First of all, let us accept the fact that the era of Freudian-inspired
parenting is at an end. My impression of the parents of young
children today is that they feel their own parents were overly
concerned about emotional health and personal adjustment.
They feel they can assure their children's emotional well-being
and are much more concerned with nourishing their children's
intellectual abilities. The phenomenal growth of schools for
young children that offer academic programs (e.g., from a dozen
to over a thousand Montessori schools in the last decade) is but
one indication of this new parental emphasis upon early intellectual stimulation.

Schools too have focused more and more upon making
academic achievement, rather than personal adjustment, their
primary goal. Tool subjects are being taught at earlier and earlier
ages and new curricula in science, reading, math, and social
studies are constantly being introduced. School systems are
demanding that teachers work toward specified behavioral objectives and that they be accountable for children attaining these
goals. Currently, the back to basics orientation of many school
systems reflects this same concern. And even the "affective education" programs are intellectualized. Witness the "values
clarification" and "moral dilemma" procedures used in many of
these programs.

8

SOCIETY

One consequence of this new emphasis upon academic achievement is that children are under pressure to become competent at an early age. This is true, not only in the academic arena where the early attainment of reading and math skills is highly valued by most parents, but also in the extracurricular arena where organized sports are now commonplace at the elementary school level. Organized sports for both boys and girls demand a level of competence that in the past was not expected until high school years. Such demands indicate that we are moving back to the notion of the child as a miniature adult.

While the encouragement of early competence can have beneficial effects, say by enhancing self-esteem, it can have negative ones as well. The pressure for early competence is tied up with competition. And competition entails failure as well as success. Children are not always prepared to deal with the ups and downs of competition, and parents who urge their children to compete may not be sensitive to the frustrations and anxieties a child may suffer in the vagaries of competition. The demands on children for early competence thus confront them with the potential for an array of emotional problems that we in the helping professions must begin to recognize and respond to.

DEMAND FOR EARLY EMOTIONAL INDEPENDENCE

It is not only Freudian-inspired parenting that is at an end; so too is the child-centered orientation that held sway until a decade ago. Child centeredness implied that the child's needs (and too often his or her wants as well) took precedence over the parents' needs and wants. Mothers stayed home with the children because it was what they were "supposed" to do. Working mothers were looked down upon with pity if they worked of necessity, and with hostility if they worked out of choice. Implicit in the child-centered home was the belief that the role of the parent, particularly the mother, was one of self-sacrifice to family and children.

Without going into the manifold reasons for its demise, the child-centered approach to child rearing is rapidly disappearing. Young couples today are planning their families with an eye to their careers. The willingness of mothers to put young children into day care centers and full day preschools reflects a new middle-class attitude toward children and child rearing. Parents today, particularly women, see themselves as having personal rights, particularly the right to self-realization through meaningful, productive work. In such a family, the child's needs have to be given equal, not superordinate, priority.

A major consequence of this parental emancipation and democratic attitude toward child rearing is that children are increasingly expected to attain *emotional independence* at an early age. In a family where both parents work, a child soon learns that he or she is not the center of the universe no matter how hard he or she contrives to be. Such emotional independence can have positive benefits for both parents and children. Adolescence is less tumultuous when both parents have interests other than children and home. Emotionally independent adolescents need not feel guilty about preferring friends to parents. And emotionally independent parents need not feel that losing the children is losing the reason for living.

The early emotional emancipation of children can, however, have negative consequences as well. Divorce is a case in point. When parents regard children as emotionally independent, they weigh their needs and their children's needs differently from when they regard the children as dependent. Many contemporary husbands and wives feel that their emotional needs are as important as those of their children and are more willing to break up a marriage than in previous generations. The divorce rate (about three out of every five marriages) probably does not mean that contemporary unions are less made in heaven than they were before. It may mean only that today marital partners are more ready to move out of unhappy unions than they were before.

In any case, the number of children who come from broken homes has increased twofold over the past decade. Despite this fact, there are few studies which deal with the effects of divorce and separation upon the children. The relatively few studies of father absence which do exist do not really give us a picture of what it means to a child to be part of a marital breakup. My own impression, after more than a decade of working with delinquent youth, is that family disruption is still the outstanding proximal cause of middle-class juvenile delinquency. On the other hand, for some young people, the emotional turmoil of the divorce can serve as a spur to striving and to high levels of achievement.

The point I wish to make is that the pressure for early emotional independence can take its toll. Chidren are never as emotionally independent as they seem to be or as parents would like them to be. The real danger in contemporary society is in taking the child or the adolescent's emotional maturity for granted. For example, in my clinical experience, I have often found that divorce can be more difficult on the teenager than on the younger children of a family. We in the helping professions must recognize the new burdens that contemporary values and divorce place upon children. In particular we need to counsel parents who are moving toward divorce to take heed of and to attend to the emotional needs of their offspring.

THE LOSS OF FAITH

A third factor which affects adults, and through them children, is what might be called, for lack of a better phrase, *loss of faith*. It was often said, when Freud first became popular, that his work destroyed man's faith in reason. The discovery of the unconscious put the rational mind, so cherished by the nineteenth century, in a new perspective. It suggested that reason was the slave and not the master of man's more primitive impulses. But Freud saw the unconscious as but another challenge to reason, not its natural dictator. Freud hoped that, "Where id is, there shall ego be." He had faith in the strength of reason to overcome the challenges of the inner as well as the outer world.

But today we are undergoing a genuine loss of faith in reason and its handmaidens, science and technology. Our belief in an ever better world has been badly shaken by what has been done and what continues to be done to the environment. The threat of a nuclear holocaust is still a very real possibility and continues to be hardly more than a phone call away. In short, we have lost that messianic faith that we were leaving a better world for our children and for all future generations.

As adults, I think that we are for the most part unaware of this new loss of faith. We have our work, our families, and some immediate purpose in life. Yet we do have a sense of having lost something, some hope for the future, and the evidence for this loss of faith appears in our children who often reflect our unconscious aspirations. In effect, children learn as much from parents by unconscious instigation as they do by conscious imitation. The tuning out with drugs, the communal living, and the search for alternate life styles among young people reflects parental, as well as their offspring's, frustrations and unconscious longings. When society gets sick, young people take the medicine.

It may be presumptuous of me, but I would like to venture the opinion that the most endemic problem of young people today is not so much a crisis of identity as it is a *search for faith*. Identity formation presupposes a more or less stable world in which there is a predictable future and where there are adults who believe in certain values which guide their lives. In such a world one can rail against the future or against the adult values to find out where one stands as an individual. But when the future is problematical, when adults have abandoned the values that formerly guided their lives, the matrix of identity formation is shattered. Under these circumstances, the need to establish a personal identity is subordinated to the need to find something solid to hold onto, something to believe in that is permanent, true, and beautiful.

The evidences of this new search for faith abide in such phenomena as the new fundamentalist revival in the religious activity of youth. Although the Jesus movement started as a therapy for drug addicts, it has become a fast-growing religious crusade. Other fundamentalist religious groups on campus, such as Inter-Varsity, have also swelled their ranks in recent years. Interest in the more academic facets of religion has been so great that new courses and programs are now being offered on many campuses around the country.

But the search for faith has gone in other directions as well. The current addiction to magic, to the occult, to astrology, and to witchcraft all attest to a need for people to believe in something. Unfortunately these young people who search for faith in these directions may get more than they bargained for. I heard recently of a student who was convinced by her peers that her convulsive attacks were caused by "a devil" which had to be exorcised. After the exorcism she was told to throw away her medicine. The next day she had a convulsive attack and experienced a severe concussion when she fell. Sadly, the need to believe is easily exploited and is the real danger in the contemporary loss of faith.

WHAT CAN WE DO?

In the preceding sections I described three culturally related changes in adult attitudes toward children and youth. These changed attitudes include the new demands for early intellectual competence and emotional independence on the part of children (demands associated with the new achievement orientation in child rearing and education and the new emancipation of parents), and the new lack of faith that science and technology actually promotes human progress. While none of these changes are entirely negative in implication, each is a potential source of new types of interpersonal and intrapersonal conflict in children. Accordingly, these changes confront those of us in the helping professions with problems we have not previously encountered, and challenge us to find fresh conceptualizations and therapeutic strategies. The next section will describe some of these problems along with suggestions as to how they might be approached.

INTELLECTUAL COMPETENCE AND THE ACHIEVEMENT EMPHASIS

One consequence of the new intellectual competence and achievement emphasis in child rearing and education is that we are likely to see many more children than before whose emotional conflicts are school related. We have to recognize that the chain of causality is not always from emotional difficulty to learning disability. I am afraid that we are going to see more and more children whose emotional problems are the result rather than the cause of school failure. When a child is given to understand that his or her worth resides in what he or she achieves rather than in what he or she is, academic failure becomes a severe emotional trauma (cf. ch. 18). (Incidently, this situation is likely to worsen even more, because with smaller families the proportion of competitive first borns in the population will also increase.)

My impression is that in clinical work we still rely heavily on dynamic formulations and do not give sufficient weight to the role of social pressures in the etiology of emotional disturbance. While I would not want to deny the role of such factors as the *Oedipus complex* and *castration anxiety* in the problems of children, I am convinced that young children's problems cannot be reduced to such factors alone. Harry Stack Sullivan and Erik Erikson, among others, have made it very clear how the cognitive components of the personality, the ego, and the self are affected by interpersonal and societal pressures.

In my own work I have seen many troubled young people whose difficulties had their primary origin in societal value rather than in parental pathology. Young people with low average IQs (in the high eighties and low nineties) experience perpetual failure in the classroom which is often unrelieved by any success experience (cf. ch. 16). No wonder such young people hate school and become truants or worse. The slow maturing boy and the unattractive girl also have problems which originate primarily in the social values of their peers.

What I am saying is that we have to look at emotional conflicts more broadly and recognize that not every conflict arises in parent-child relations. In treating some young people, we have to work with the schools and with peer groups and not just with parents. While I think most of us do this to a certain extent, our training still makes us believe that the root of the problem lies in the parent-child relationship. What we have to be open to is the possibility that the parent-child difficulty is itself conditioned by social pressure. The family is a link in the chain of causation in emotional illness; it is not necessarily the anchor from which that chain ascends.

EMOTIONAL INDEPENDENCE AND PARENTAL EMANCIPATION

Social change has emancipated parents in two related ways. Women have been liberated from the social pressures to stay home and tend babies. Men and women have been liberated from the social pressures to stay in unhappy and unrewarding marriages "for the sake of the children." The emancipation of parents necessarily affects children, and we have already looked at the need to study the effects of divorce upon children in a more systematic way. In addition, we in the helping professions will need to take a leading role in educating parents about the kinds of emotional trauma precipitated by separation and divorce. Parents contemplating divorce should be encouraged to seek counseling, not just to save the marriage, but also to prepare themselves and the children for the breakup should it occur. Parents, as well as children, have to learn how fragile is their claim to emotional independence. Many fathers discover, after the divorce, how much *they* need their children.

But parental emancipation has consequences over and above an increased divorce rate. Even in stable marriages parental emancipation can present problems for children. For example, in the past a frequent complaint of child care workers was that the father did not spend sufficient time with the children and that it was difficult getting him to participate in a treatment plan. The emancipation of wives could produce, as a consequence, a comparable pattern of behavior for mothers. Women who are working at their careers will have less time for their children too.

Obviously, the ideal solution would be for the father to make up some of the time with the children which the mother now devotes to other endeavors. This ideal, however, is far from being realized, at least in part because the pressures for male achievement have not lessened in proportion to the number of women in the work force. In any case, the emancipation of parents will probably result not only in more frequent divorce, but also in less parental commitment to children. This trend is aided and abetted by television whose misuse by parents, as a way of avoiding involvement with children, is every bit as negative in its consequences as the most violent TV show.

In short, parental emancipation offers adults new options and freedoms that were hardly possible before. But these options can, though they need not, be taken at the expense of children. As individuals in the helping professions, we can and should do our part in educating parents about the new parental responsibilities inherent in their new personal freedoms. We need to reiterate to parents the emotional needs of children. The recognition of these needs should not deter parents from going to work or getting a divorce, but they should keep parents from dismissing as trivial that which is of great importance to children.

LACK OF FAITH

I have argued that the lack of faith in the future, in something genuinely permanent, true, and beautiful to believe in, is perhaps the most pervasive problem among adults and young people today. The search for faith among the young is also the best evidence for the lack of faith among the middle-aged. While I don't have any solutions for this problem of faith, I do think it would help young people if we acknowledged that such a problem exists. It is an interesting commentary on our society that we adults are more willing to discuss sex than we are to discuss faith with our children. As professionals, too, we are likely to sidestep the issue of faith as being irrelevant to our practice.

Please understand, when I speak of faith I do not mean simply religious faith. One can believe in the perfectibility of man, the infinite adaptability of mankind, or some other value that gives sense and meaning to living and doing. Indeed, what is important is to have some idea what it is we *do* believe in. I am sure that young people will not want to accept our personal faith, no matter what it is. But they do need to know that we believe in something. Adult faith is, after all, the only hope young people have that they may eventually find something to believe in too.

SUMMARY

In this chapter I have argued that social change affects children and adolescents indirectly through its effects upon the adults who nurture them. The first section of the chapter described the generational, immediacy, and homogeneity illusions that make it difficult for us as adults to appreciate our roles as mediators of social change. These illusions make young people appear to be much more divorced from us then they really are. The next section presented three contemporary parental attitudes: the demand for early intellectual competence, the demand for early emotional independence, and a pervasive loss of faith in society's capacity to solve its own problems that are new and which are affecting the lives of children. The final section described some of the problems these changed parental attitudes have created for children, and offered suggestions for finding solutions to them.

2
DAY CARE IN AMERICA

Day care is a huge, multi-faceted contemporary problem whose solution will reflect our society's valuation of young children. Some dimensions of the problem and a possible course of action are presented in this chapter.

Peter, age three, gets his own lunch every day. He has to. No one else is home. . . . he eats what he can reach and what his still uncoordinated hands can concoct if he can get the refrigerator or the cabinet doors open. Some day it might be poison. . . . Peter is anything but alone in his plight. The City (Chicago) Welfare Board estimates that seven hundred children less than six years of age are left alone each day without any formal supervision when their mothers leave for work.

Unfortunately, Chicago is not unique and there are hundreds of Peters in every major city and urban area in America. In this paper we will look at day care in America in broad perspective. We will look at some of the reasons why it is so widely used and needed, what constitutes quality day care, how day care should be provided, who should be served, and who should pay. After dealing with these issues we will give our own suggestions as to how best to cope with the day care issue in America.

By David Elkind and Donald J. Cohen

17

DIMENSIONS OF DAY CARE

Currently there are more than six million children under the age of six whose mothers work full or part time. About half of these children are cared for by relatives in their own homes. An additional thirty-five per cent are cared for in homes other than their own, an arrangement usually called *family day care*. Only about ten per cent of the children are cared for in rooms or buildings specifically set aside and provisioned for children— what is usually meant by a *day care center*. The remaining children are cared for in a variety of ways. Some accompany their mothers to work while others, like Peter, are left to their own devices.

The willingness of contemporary parents to share the responsibilities of rearing young children with relatives and strangers (and unhappily as in the case of youngsters like Peter, with the children themselves) is a relatively recent phenomenon. Hardly a decade ago it was regarded as a sign of financial destitution or callous parental rejection if a mother worked and her young children were cared for by others. How far we have come in a decade is shown by a yearly survey of college women which indicates that from the middle sixties until the present there has been a regular increase in the number of women who said that they would go to work and leave their young children in the care of others.

A Stanford University survey is even more impressive. In 1967 some ten per cent of the coeds said they would work when their children were young. In 1972 some seventy per cent of the women stated that they would work when their children were of preschool age. These data imply that out-of-home care of young children has become an acceptable part of middle class as well as of low income family child rearing practice. But the demand for day care by parents has far outstripped the growth of facilities to provide it, and recent surveys indicate that large numbers of children are currently receiving substandard care.

The widespread need for quality day care is now recognized at all levels of governments as well as by businesses and by religious organizations of all denominations. The task of providing quality day care for all those children who need it, however,

presents a wealth of problems that reflect the bureaucratic com-
plexity and socioeconomic and ethnic diversity of our society.
There are no easy and simple answers to the question of what
constitutes "quality" day care or how it should be provided or
for whom it should be provided. Nor is there any clear consensus regarding who is to bear the major share of the costs of day
care. The current status of day care in America, where we stand
on these questions and where we seem to be going, is the focus
of this chapter.

QUALITY OF DAY CARE

The problem of defining quality day care illustrates the complex-
ity of the day care issues. Programs for young children can be
described on a continuum from "developmental" to "custodial"
care. Total developmental care would include the provision of
well-balanced meals, opportunities and equipment for physical
exercise and recreation, arrangements for medical or nursing
attention, directed learning experiences, and constructive social
interactions with other children (such as "show and tell"). As
the number of these components decreases, the program moves
from total developmental to barely custodial. (A program that
provided only hot meals and some exercise would be called
"custodial.")

Where on this continuum does quality day care lie, and how
much developmental day care do children need to realize their
full physical and intellectual potential? The question is important because total developmental care, which requires the services of professionals, is clearly more expensive than custodial
care, which does not. It would be relatively simple to answer
this and other questions about day care if there were some hard
and fast evidence on the questions at issue, but unfortunately
there is not. Day care and family care programs differ so much,
one from the other, in the populations they serve, in the adequacy of their facilities, in the quality of staffing, that it is
virtually impossible to generalize from the effects of one day
care program to the effects of another. Results of studies that
have been carried out are more suggestive than they are definitive, and the conclusions reached are determined as much by the

investigators' theoretical biases as they are by the data. It is not surprising, then, that child development specialists are themselves in disagreement as to how much of a developmental program is essential for healthy physical and mental growth as a standard for quality day care.

Among those who suggest that full developmental care may not be essential to healthy growth and mental development is Harvard psychologist Jerome Kagan. In a study carried out in Boston, Professor Kagan found that children enrolled in a developmental day care program rich in programmed learning experiences did not do much better on tests of mental ability than children who had been reared at home. For these children, anyway, developmental day care did not produce any intellectual gains over and above what children got from staying at home. It should be said, however, that the children in the study were Chinese American and were all living in a close-knit Chinese American community.

In contrast to Kagan's findings are those of Rick Heber of Milwaukee. Heber undertook a very intensive and extensive program with infants whose mothers' IQs were below seventy, i.e., who would be regarded as mentally retarded. For each child the program began almost immediately after the infant was born. Project personnel made daily visits to the child's home and spent several hours with the mother and child. When the infant was three months old, the child began to spend several hours a day at Heber's Childrens' Center. At the Center the children were involved in a variety of "stimulation" experiences on a one-to-one basis with trained adults.

When the children reached two years of age, they attended center classes for a full day. The program for the children two years of age and older included language-learning sessions, science and art periods, communication and language problem sessions, excursions, and field trips. In parallel with the experience provided for the children was an enrichment program for the mothers which included instruction in both homemaking and vocational skills. The children who participated in the study demonstrated many gains not shown by a comparable group of children who did not participate in the study. The children in the trained group scored an average of thirty-three IQ points higher than children who were not in the training program but who came from comparable backgrounds.

There is concurrent evidence, then, that developmental programs can be exceedingly beneficial or not beneficial at all. In part the differences may be due to the extent and the intensity of the Heber intervention. But it may also have to do with the children and families in question. There is probably an optimal amount of developmental stimulation requisite for mental growth. When children receive close to that amount in their homes, additional stimulation does not have much value. But if the children are receiving less than the optimal amount of stimulation, then an enrichment program will show startling results. There is a close analogy with diet. Children receiving an adequate diet will not make additional physical gains if provided with dietary supplements, but children who are receiving an inadequate diet will show significant physical changes once they are given adequate nutrition.

These diverse findings point up how difficult it is to decide what is quality day care and what is unacceptable. Clearly children differ greatly in terms of their needs, and no one type of day care program will fit the patterns of needs of children coming from diverse ethnic and socioeconomic backgrounds. Bilingual Puerto Rican, Cuban, and Mexican American children may need a different kind of program from low income white children. For example, they may need bilingual teachers and menus different from those for other groups of children. It is also true that programs for infants and young children have to be different from programs for preschool and school-age young people. Although quality day care programs will share some components, they must be flexible enough to adapt to the varied needs of children from out pluralistic society.

DAY CARE CENTERS

Like the question of day care quality, the question of how child care should be provided cannot be answered simply. There are both advantages and disadvantages to many of the day care arrangements currently used by parents. Nonprofit day care centers are one example. Such centers are usually supported by a combination of federal and local funds and are often located in such rented quarters as church buildings. Because the centers are subsidized, they can provide developmental care at low cost and usually charge parents on a sliding scale according to income level. For all day, five days a week, some parents may pay as much as forty dollars per week per child whereas another parent may pay as little as five dollars per child.

In many day care centers the directors are trained professionals who have degrees in early childhood education. Salaries for center directors are, however, generally less than they are for city school teachers. One of the directors we talked to spoke about what she liked and didn't like about her job. She was proud of the education program at the center and was enthusiastic about her young staff and about the cooperation of the parents. But the perpetual uncertainty of funding was an ever present anxiety. Perhaps the hardest part was getting and keeping a competent staff. Salary scales for day care personnel are abominably low, running about three to four thousand dollars a year. Consequently, most of the staff are young people who may spend a year or two at the job until they get into college or graduate school, or until something better comes along. Most of these young people are untrained when they are hired and by the time they get trained on the job, many of them decide that it is time to leave. As one young woman said, "I love the children and working with them, but I don't want to stay here forever, especially not at this salary."

The parents we spoke to were most enthusiastic about the center, particularly those who had had bad experiences with family day care. "My child wants to come here in the morning; it is her second home." And another said, "It is such a relief not to have to worry about Harold all day when I am at work. When he is here I know he is well cared for. When he was with that woman, I had to call every hour to make sure she hadn't left the children alone." For some parents the center was rather far from where they lived and worked, and this meant that they and the children had to get up earlier and get home later than if there were a place nearby. Although parents and children were willing to put up with the travel, it did occasionally work hardships. Well-run, well-furbished day care centers, despite the rapidity of staff turnover and the distance some parents have to travel to use them, appear to answer most of the parental needs and concerns. And from what we could see, at this center the children were busy, happy, and well-looked after.

Proprietary day care centers are more variable in quality than the nonprofit centers. Around the late sixties a number of companies planned to set up franchised child care centers. Most of these efforts came to naught. Although there were many reasons for these failures, the basic reason, which most companies eventually discovered, is that it is impossible to provide quality day care at fee levels parents can afford and yet still make a profit. And they also discovered that providing a human service is different from selling a product. One company we know about billed parents as they did their other customers and sent dunning letters if tuition was not paid on time. Parents got angry at this impersonal and hostile treatment from a company they thought was on their side, and many quit the program as a result.

One exception to franchise dropouts is the Singer Company which supports the Singer Learning Centers. Perhaps because Singer had some experience in providing services (the Singer Sewing Centers), they took their time in setting up programs. Early-childhood specialist and University of Illinois professor Bernard Spodek designed the educational program and modelled it after the informal methods of some of the British primary schools. The buildings are of the open-space variety with easily accessible play areas. In-service training is provided for the staff. The five centers that are in operation provide good developmental programs and are fine models of what proprietary care can be. But not all of the centers are profitable: they are more of an educational success than a financial one.

Other proprietary programs are less exemplary. One of these centers that we visited was run by an accountant as a sideline. The building was acceptable but small, and on a main business street. The rooms were rather stark and cold and there was not much in the way of play or educational materials. The teachers, mostly high school students, kept the children busy, but there was no sense of a well-thought out program with any definite direction. It was an elaborate baby-sitting operation and, as such, was not bad. At least it was safe and clean. It was convenient for the parents and relatively inexpensive at only twenty-five dollars per week.

All day care centers, whether nonprofit or proprietary, encounter problems with state licensing laws, which may be sound in principle but difficult to comply with in practice. Another reason the franchise schools can never really get off the ground is that the cost of meeting state rules regarding facilities and teacher-to-child ratios are often not included in the cost-accounting projections. Some of these problems are illustrated by the experience of a Dean at the University of Michigan who wanted to set up a day care center for the children of university students. The building chosen to house the center was superior in quality to that in which the student parents lived, but it did not meet the state's safety standards. When an effort was made to obtain federal funds to improve the building, it was discovered that to receive such funds the program had to meet the Federal Interagency Day Care Requirements. And one of these requirements was that the program meet the state's requirements for licensing!

An added irony was that when the Dean tried to discover who was responsible for the federal legislation, he found his own signature at the bottom of the regulation. The document dated from his days as acting head of the Department of Health, Education and Welfare. Somewhat abashed he said, "Things look different in Ann Arbor than they do in Washington." The Michigan Day Care Center was thus confronted with the four different types of regulation that most nonprofit day care centers must contend with, namely, state licensing, building safety inspection, federal funding requirements, and the administrative accountability to the University. For many nonprofit centers the administrative agency is the state or local education department.

FAMILY DAY CARE

The form of day care which accommodates more children than any other is family day care. Although there are licensing laws for day care homes in most states, only about ten per cent of the homes are actually licensed. There are many different reasons for this, and they speak to some of the pros and cons of family day care facilities. One of the reasons that family day care centers do not apply for licensing is that the buildings would not meet state building codes without extensive and costly renovation. In addition, most state licensing laws limit the number of children a home can look after, ranging from two or three to eleven or twelve. Many day care proprietors take in many more children than the state laws permit. Finally, if the home were licensed the fees would have to be reported as income, and a careful accounting of expenditures and income would have to be kept. All of these reasons militate against the day care proprietor applying for licensing if his or her prime motivation is monetary.

The small proportion of day care proprietors who do get licensed illustrate what good family care can be like. In some parts of the country, family day care proprietors have gotten together to provide in-service training for one another and to disseminate information about programs and materials. Many of these people have raised their own families and thoroughly enjoy the children they take into their homes and provide with excellent care. This type of family day care proprietor has often obtained licensing at considerable expense, and in many cases makes little if any profit. Family day care homes run by intelligent, caring men and women provide a healthy complement to day care centers. They cannot provide the range of activities, materials, or play things, but they can provide a continuity and intimacy of care which may be equally valuable. And they are usually close to the parents' homes and thus do not require much travel on the part of parents or children.

The quality family day care facilities have to be kept in mind when we report some of the horrors in this category. We were not able to visit any homes ourselves, but here are some reports taken from "Windows on Day Care," a national survey of day care facilities conducted by the Jewish Council of Women. First, a report on one of the quality homes for purposes of contrast.

> This day care mother is doing an outstanding job. She attends conferences and applies herself diligently to using what she gains from these meetings. She had just completed a workshop at college and already the children were reciting poetry she had read to them. She remarked that when she attended a conference, the children cried when

she left and hesitated to accept a substitute. Her family is also dedicated, as her husband, daughter and son all assist her. She is a remarkable woman who is truly helping in every way she can.

Such women are unfortunately in the minority as these reports of other family day care placements indicate:

This interviewer can still recall quite vividly one particular home she visited where she counted a total of eleven children—five infants and six other small children from about one to four years old of both sexes and almost naked, running and screaming in the four room house. The strong urine smell, the stale odor of uneaten food everywhere and the bugs crawling around made one nauseous. There was one very obese, sullen unpleasant woman in charge.

Here are some more examples:

When Mrs. —— opened the door for us, we felt there were probably very few, if any children in the house, because of the quiet. It was quite a shock, therefore, to discover about seven or eight children, one year old or under, in the kitchen; a few of them strapped to kitchen chairs, all seemingly in a stupor.
It wasn't until we were in the kitchen that we heard the noise coming from the basement. There were over twenty children huddled in a too small, poorly ventilated, cement floor area. A TV with an apparently bad picture tube was their only source of entertainment and stimulation.
When we went to look at the backyard we passed through a porch, where we discovered again, children, children and more children. The children were literally under our feet. Pathetically enough, it was necessary for Mrs. —— to reprimand one child for stepping on another. Mrs. —— takes care of two families—six children—which the Bureau of Children's Services subsidizes. The other children (forty-one for a total of forty-seven children) she takes care of independently, receiving two dollars per day per child. She told us she has been doing this for twenty years and seemed quite proud to be able to manage alone and without help.

Most of these horrors were in states where the laws limit the number of children to be cared for in a single home and which say something about the quality of care to be given. Clearly many family day care operations are in violation of the law. We spoke to a state welfare representative responsible for inspecting and licensing day and family care centers in Rochester, New York. He said, "There are a lot of places that I would like to close down, including some day care centers. But the licensing laws don't have any teeth, we can't enforce them. We can take away a license but we can't close a place down."

There are advantages and disadvantages to all of the day care delivery systems, including nonprofit and proprietary day care centers, family care settings, and programs in high schools and at factories. It is probably a virtue to have a variety of alternatives to accommodate the diversity of day care needs and finances. What seems necessary and most urgent is the establishment of mechanisms for the enforcement of minimum standards for all day care facilities. The existence of horrors such as those described above is a state of affairs that this nation simply should not tolerate.

WHO SHALL BE SERVED?

Still another question imbedded in the day care issue is, Who should be served? Actually the question has two parts. The "who" can refer to parent or child populations. With respect to parents, the question is whether parents of all socioeconomic levels should have access to publicly supported day care or whether this should be provided primarily for low-income families. At the 1970 White House Conference on Children, the consensus was for "comprehensive child care programs, which will be family centered, locally controlled, and universally available, with initial priority to those whose needs are greatest." But day care was also to be made available to "all families who seek it" and was not to be the sole province of families who required it for economic reasons.

It appears that we are moving towards a philosophy of publically supported day care that is analogous to that which underlies publically supported education; namely, that it is a government responsibility. But that has inherent dangers despite the obvious benefits of financial support. The danger is that the government can try, through legislation, to set values and child-rearing standards. When Nixon vetoed the comprehensive Child Development Act of 1971 he said, in part, "All other factors being equal, good public policy requires that we enhance rather than diminish parental authority and involvement with children." Nixon, however, was willing to provide minimal custodial support for children of mothers who would participate in work training programs. In effect Nixon was saying that middle-class families have to be cemented (hence no comprehensive day care), but low-income families do not! If day care is to become a full government responsibility, then there must be safeguards written into the legislation that prevent government from dictating life styles and values to families.

The question of which age groups are to receive day care is also not easily answered. It is generally accepted that the greatest need for day care services are for infants and young children below the age of three. But there are almost no places in the United States for the training of caretakers for infants. And there are professional disputes as to whether infants should be cared for by strangers, about what the optimal ratio for careperson-to-child should be, and whether it is important to provide intellectual stimulation or whether good old TLC (tender loving care) is all that infants require. It is not possible to go into all of these disputes here. The research does suggest that infants cared for in quality settings outside the home do not suffer untoward effects and that the parent-child relationship is not impaired by such an arrangement. The success of the Israeli kibbutz child-rearing programs provides additional evidence on this point. What is badly needed are training programs designed to prepare carepersons for working with infants and for arranging environments and experiences beneficial to healthy growth and development. Ways must be found, too, of paying such individuals salaries large enough for them to want to stay in the capacity of child care professional.

At the other end of the age spectrum are school-age children whose parents are not at home when they leave for school or when they return. It is estimated that some eighteen million young people over the age of six and under the age of eighteen have parents who work full or part time. Many day care centers provide before-and-after-school care for children of working parents. But facilities of this sort fall far short of the need, and a large proportion of these eighteen million children are left unsupervised for a good part of the day that is not spent in school. As one mother said, "Before I got them into this program (a before-and-after-school day care center program), I never knew where they were or who they were with or who they were bringing into the house. Now they have their friends at the center and even want to come here on Saturdays." Provision of part time day care for children of school age is another part, and an important one, of the day care problem.

There is another group of children, perhaps two or three million who should also receive some form of day care. These are the retarded, the physically handicapped, and the emotionally disturbed children who cannot be cared for adequately in their own homes and by their own parents. Although many parents do a remarkable job with these children and have infinite patience and love, they would often do better if they had periodic relief. One set of parents with a brain-injured child exhausted themselves in caring for him and were forced to send him to a state institution. With adequate day care facilities in the community, the child might have been kept at home and not have had to be institutionalized. Provision of day care for such children should be part of any comprehensive day care package.

WHO SHALL PAY?

We come now to one of the most difficult issues regarding day care, the question of who should pay and of how day care funds should be expended. To get some general ideas about the extent of the problem, it has been estimated that developmental day care would run about three thousand dollars per year per child while minimal custodial care would cost about a thousand dollars less. Thus to provide minimal custodial care to about six million children, the cost would be about twelve billion dollars. The provision of developmental day care would approach twenty billion dollars per year.

Currently, the government is spending about $1.5 billion on day care per year. This money is dispersed by many different agencies and in a variety of ways. Among the agencies that support day care, eithe directly or indirectly, are the Departments of Agriculture, Labor, and Interior, the Appalachian Regional Council, the Community Services Administration of the Department of Health, Education and Welfare (H.E.W.), the Office of Housing and Urban Development (H.U.D.), and the Small Business Administration. Through income tax provisions that affect both parents and day care agencies, the Internal Revenue Service also contributes some $200 million annually to day care.

Because the money is distributed in different ways, it goes to support both developmental and custodial day care services. For example, in the Work Incentive (WIN) program supported by the Social Security Administration, parents are given direct grants which allow them to purchase day care services while they work. Generally these grants are only sufficient to purchase custodial care. In contrast, Headstart, which is sponsored by the Office of Education, provides money directly for the support of the center and its staff. Headstart provides a model of developmental programming for children, but the cost is about eight hundred dollars more per child than for the WIN program.

A MODEST PROPOSAL

The issue of paying for day care is a knotty one, but we feel it should be looked on as comparable to the issue of who should pay for public education. It is a burden that most low income parents cannot afford. To be sure, those who do not have children or those who have few children often bear a disproportionate share of the cost. And those who voluntarily choose not to use the service (like parents who provide their children with private or parochial school) also pay a disproportionate share of the school burden. More equitable ways of distributing the costs of education should be found. But we feel that day care should not be singled out as something separate and apart from public education. Indeed, from one perspective, public education might be looked on as a form of day care. And from another, day care for young children can be seen as the provision of public education for young children.

In our opinion, the best way to quickly and efficiently implement quality day care service around the country is to make it part of the public education system. In particular, day care programs could be run in high schools, as is already being done in some places around the country. Placement of day care facilities within high schools would have several advantages. The building would have passed the necessary codes for safety and hygiene and the existing licensing and certification rules could be used to cover teachers working in the day care setting.

There are other benefits as well. Students could work in the day care program as part of a course in child development. This would provide adolescents with practical experience with young children before they themselves become parents. It would also provide teacher aides at relatively low cost. Such programs would of course require teachers trained in working with infants and young children, but programs to train such teachers could easily be set up by any one of the Federal agencies concerned with education and training. It could easily be made part of the job training and retraining programs already sponsored by Washington.

We also believe that day care funding from the federal government should be placed under a single agency with a consistent set of guidelines. This would permit state and local government agencies to adapt their day care programs to their local needs and facilities, avoiding both the duplication and the waste of funds that are badly needed at the local level.

We are well aware that making day care part of the public education system is not without its own dangers. It might be used as a dumping ground for unfit teachers, and it might get immersed in the bureaucracy and politics of local education agencies and schools. But it seems to us that while such dangers are real, the need for quality day care is also real and worth the risk. At the same time we believe that quality family care, proprietary care, and day care centers should be continued. Providing day care as a public education option should give parents an alternative form of care; it should not preempt other forms.

It is easy, in talking about the multiple problems and issues that stand in the way of delivering quality day care to children, to forget the children themselves. But it is well to keep them in mind. It is well to remember the thousands of children crowded in cellars and strapped stuporous to kitchen chairs. And we need to think, too, of the many Peters around the country who each day forage for their own lunch. If we keep these children in mind, perhaps we can find ways, in this rich and resourceful country, to provide quality day care appropriate to all these children who need it.

3
FROM GHETTO SCHOOL TO COLLEGE CAMPUS

Three discontinuities and three continuities encountered by
black students moving from ghetto school to college campus are
described in this chapter. Recognizing these continuities and
discontinuities can help college faculty to a better appreciation
of the dilemmas of a black student on a white campus.

The provision of a college education for disadvantaged black
students is a multifaceted problem which can be approached
from many different directions. As a psychologist, the side of
the problem which most interests me is its sociopsychological
aspect. The ghetto school is a different sociopsychological milieu
from the college campus, whereas the suburban school (particularly at the high school level) has already taken on many of the
modes, practices, and styles of the college domain.* So while
there is considerable continuity between suburban high school
and college campus, this is not the case for the ghetto high
school. Indeed, the continuities that do exist between the ghetto
school and the predominantly white college campus are largely
negative in their implications. Accordingly, it should be instruc-

---

*Until recently fraternities and sororities were common in suburban high
schools, but the decline of such groups reflects a comparable decline on college
campuses.
School Psychology, 1971, *9,* 241–45.

tive to consider some of the discontinuities and continuities between the ghetto school and the college campus as well as some of the implications these transitions have for the feelings and attitudes of black students.

DISCONTINUITIES

One of the fundamental discontinuities the black student encounters in the transition from ghetto school to college campus resides in the disparity between the attitudes of school and college teachers toward academic success and failure. School teachers are often made to feel, both during their training and thereafter, that if a child in their class fails academically then it is to a considerable extent the teacher's fault. The reverse is also true, however, and the teacher can take credit for his or her pupils' successes. This attitude is not destructive and may even be beneficial for teachers in a suburban school where by far the majority of children succeed academically. The teacher in the suburban school can tolerate a child who fails because he or she has had so many successes to bolster his or her ego.

When this attitude is carried into the ghetto school, however, the results are catastrophic. The teacher in the ghetto school is confronted with the fact that the majority of students are failing academically in the sense that they are one or two years behind the national norms in reading, spelling, and arithmetic. In the ghetto school, therefore, the teacher cannot afford, from the standpoint of self-esteem and sense of personal competence, to take the blame for pupil failure upon himself or herself. In self-defense the teacher blames the students and comes to regard them as "stupid" and "unteachable." This attitude is definitely not lost upon the students.

Among college teachers, an interesting reversal of this process occurs. The college teacher, usually unsullied by teacher training values, believes that if a student fails then it is the student who is responsible for his or her failure. This attitude assumes that the student is capable of doing the work or he or she wouldn't be there. Such an attitude is partially warranted since college, unlike public school, is selective. If a student fails, therefore, it is due to lack of application, poor study habits, or dislike

for the subject matter. With disadvantaged black students, however, the college teacher is not as likely to blame the student for
his or her failure. Instead, the instructor will blame the subject
matter, the student's lack of adequate preparation in high school,
or even the instructor's own ineptitude. In today's climate it is
appropriate to call white, but not black, students lazy.

The resulting discontinuity for the black student might be
summarized as follows. The school teacher is likely to blame
himself or herself if the child who fails is white but to blame the
youngster if he or she is black. To the contrary, the college
teacher is likely to lay the blame for failure on the white college
student but to blame materials, preparation, or himself or herself when a black student fails academically. For the black student, the attitude of the college teacher will either reinforce his
or her anger at the ghetto school teacher, or cause the student to
resent the college teacher for treating him or her according to
criteria different from the white student, or both.

A second discontinuity experienced by black students making
the transition from ghetto school to college campus derives from
the different ways academic success and failure are handled in
the two milieus. In ghetto schools, promotion is to a large extent
independent of academic achievement. Since the majority of
children are failing anyway, it is necessary to promote them to
make way for the new youngsters coming in. It is not unusual,
for example, to find ghetto high school students purportedly in
the tenth grade who are reading at the fourth grade level. In the
suburban school the same child would be in a special class or
remedial program.

These "social promotions" in ghetto schools do not prevent
the ghetto youngster from experiencing feelings of failure, they
merely reinforce his or her image of the school as ridden with
duplicity. Disadvantaged black children know that it is the
schools that have failed them and their social promotions are the
clearest evidence to them of this failure. Contrast this situation
with that in the suburban schools where the child who is doing
poorly is often held back so that he or she can master the earlier
work before being permitted to proceed any further. Only the
most retarded ghetto child is permitted the luxury of repeating a
grade.

When we look at how success and failure are handled at the college level, a very different scene emerges. College students who fail are required, like advantaged children, to repeat the course or to take remedial work. Academic success at the college level is a prerequisite to promotion and a degree as it was not in the ghetto school. This discrepancy between criteria for promotion in ghetto school and in the college can cause difficulty for the disadvantaged youth accustomed to the automatic promotion of the ghetto school. If, after twelve years of social promotions, he or she now confronts a college program where academic success is the only road to promotion, the student may well feel frustrated, cheated, and duped.

A final discontinuity encountered by the disadvantaged black student moving from the ghetto school to the college campus is of a somewhat different order. In ghetto schools black children are usually in the majority whereas in most colleges and universities they are in the minority. The ghetto school provides a feeling of community and strength in numbers: it is black culture which domintes the ghetto school. This is true for the language, the clothing, the mores, and the attitudes openly displayed toward white students and faculty. While the ghetto school may not accomplish a great deal educationally, it does provide the black student with a defined social situation where he or she is in the majority and where his or her customs prevail.

This is certainly not the case when the disadvantaged black student enters the college or the university where, unless the student enters a black school, he or she is clearly in the minority. What usually happens is that black students band together in self-defense and adopt certain group strategies that were seldom needed in the ghetto school. I would not be surprised if much of the black militanism, on campuses where there are large numbers of disadvantaged blacks, derives, in part at least, from the discontinuities mentioned above and primarily from black students' sense of being a minority.

CONTINUITIES

One of the things that the black student who moves to the white college discovers is that the white college teachers are as unprepared for him or her as were the white school teachers. Schools of education are only now beginning to train teachers for work with ghetto children and even this training is, in a good many cases, woefully inadequate. Most teachers of ghetto children have little understanding of and respect for the family structure, language habits, and mores of black children. Nor do they grasp the intensity of the black child's obsession with skin color. The teacher who hopes to teach without first coping with the cultural and attitudinal barriers between himself or herself and the students is beaten before he or she begins because the pupils want to have these issues of trust, truth, and mutual respect settled before they will cooperate in any constructive fashion.

At the college level, unfortunately, the same lack of preparation is likely to obtain. To be sure, the college teacher generally prides himself or herself on having liberal attitudes and feels enlightened and unprejudiced. He or she has read widely the books written by black authors, has friends and colleagues who are black, and may even live in an integrated neighborhood. Nonetheless, the white professor still bears the burden of his or her middle-class history and retains the traces of the black stereotypes so current until only a few years ago. If the college professor tries to treat black students in the same way that he or she treats white students he or she finds that the black students will refuse to be treated as if the teacher were colorblind. The black student wants his or her blackness recognized and respected. Hence the college teacher, like the ghetto school teacher, often finds himself or herself at a loss to know what stance to take with black students.

A second continuity experienced by black students entering predominantly white colleges is a persistent confusion between educational goals and social ends. This confusion is as common among college teachers as it is among instructors in the ghetto schools. Indeed it permeates the thinking of the white community generally. What the black student encounters in school as well as in college is the belief, on the part of whites, that the provision of good education for blacks will resolve the problem of racial prejudice in America. The fact that there are a good many well-educated blacks in America who are still subjected to restricted housing and job discrimination has not served to quell the idea that if blacks are provided with quality education our racial problems will be solved.

Unquestionably, education is very important in the effort of blacks to gain equality in this country. But a good education without equal job opportunities, without merit salary increments, and without equal status and equal opportunities for advancement may not be so "good" after all. Black youngsters know this and until they have concrete evidence that education will get them farther than the multitude of illegal or semilegal "hustles," they will, more likely than not, choose the hustle. The black student knows that education alone will not solve his or her problems and is more than a little frustrated that white teachers are so unaware of this fact.

The final continuity between the ghetto school and the white college is the relative absence of black teachers at all levels of schooling. It is true that there are increasing numbers of black teachers working in ghetto schools, but these teachers are almost all females. At the college level, the dearth of black teachers and the new demand for them has made black college teachers the most sought after faculty in the college community. Despite this rush to hire black teachers, however, the number of such on predominantly white campuses is ridiculously small.

The lack of black male teachers has particular consequences for black male students. White males who are taught by females in the grade schools nonetheless have fathers who provide a male role model at home. They have someone concrete whom they can imitate and model their behavior after. This is much less true in the ghetto family, where fathers are often absent from the home. When the white male enters the university he finds an abundance of white male teachers with whom he can identify in order to establish his professional identity. The situation is quite different from the black male. For black students, establishing a professional identity means in part that he must identify with an adult male who is white—a male towards whom he has strong antipathies. The black male in the predominantly white university thus has built in resistances to acquiring a professional identity that has nothing at all to do with his intelligence or talent.

A comparable but somewhat different problem exists for black females. Like black males, they find very few black female teachers with whom to identify. But this is true for women in general and not just for black females. For women, both black and white, the discontinuity between school and college is the shift from predominantly female teachers to predominantly male teachers. So the problems of black females in a predominantly white university are not quite as disparate from the problems of white females in a white university as are the black males from the white males. This may be one reason black females do somewhat better at white colleges and universities than black males do.

SUMMARY AND CONCLUSION

In summary, then, there are at least three discontinuities experienced by the black student moving from the ghetto school to the predominantly white college campus. These discontinuities reside in the considerations that: a) the ghetto school teacher ascribes academic failure to the pupil in the case of the black child but to himself or herself in the case of a white child. Just the reverse holds true for the college teacher who will lay the blame for school failure on the white student, but will place the blame on materials, preparation, or himself in the case of a failing black student; b) in ghetto schools, promotion is made on a social or age basis and is almost entirely independent of school performance whereas at the college level, promotion is entirely on an academic basis; and c) in the ghetto schools blacks are in the majority whereas they are a minority in the college and university.

The continuities experienced by the black student moving to a white college campus are threefold: a) the majority of college teachers, like the majority of ghetto school teachers are poorly prepared to teach black youth; b) both college teachers and school teachers confuse educational goals with social ends and believe that education in of itself will resolve the problem of racial prejudice in America; and c) the black male student finds that there are no more black male teachers at the college level than there were in the ghetto school.

Many colleges and universities about the country are currently engaged in efforts at providing liberal arts and professional school training for disadvantaged black students. While I do not want to minimize the many academic and financial problems posed by this undertaking, I have chosen to focus upon the sociopsychological problems encountered by the black student moving from the ghetto school to the predominantly white college campus. These problems, if overlooked, could be a source of constant dissatisfaction and friction if they are not acknowledged and attended to. Effective education presupposes good communication, which means the ability to take the other person's point of view. In this chapter I have tried to look at college programs for disadvantaged youth from the point of view of these students, which ought to be the first step in any attempt to provide higher education for disadvantaged young people.

4

ETHNICITY AND READING
THREE AVOIDABLE DANGERS

Efforts to eliminate racial stereotypes from children's literature
are hampered by the subtly opposed enticements of intuitive
psychology, reverse prejudice, and easy conscience. The best
way to combat these dangers is to be aware that they are, in
fact, operative.

In recent years the children's book field, like other media, has
striven to be in the forefront of the movement toward racial
equality in America. Efforts to attain racial equality in children's
literature have moved in two complementary directions. One of
these directions is towards eliminating from existing literature
materials which are degrading to a particular race or which
perpetuate derogatory stereotypes. The other movement is towards introducing black children, urban settings, and black
themes into the literature for young people.

While these movements are laudable in principle, they are not
always so in practice. The fact is that we have so little concrete
data as to what is degrading and what is egalitarian that decisions in these regards are often made on an individual, arbitrary
basis. To some people, for example, "Little Black Sambo" is a

---

*Modified version of an invited paper presented at the International Reading
Association convention, Atlantic City, April 19, 1971.

degrading story and at least one contemporary children's record album has a song entitled "Little Gray Sambo." To others, like myself, the story is not degrading because Sambo's failings and successes are those of all young children and are not part of a stereotype of his race. In such cases of honest disagreement, who is to decide what is egalitarian?

As a psychologist, I do not have any pat answers to this question, but I do know some of the typical dangers that occur whenever one group tries to help another which it feels it has abused and mistreated. The dangers are psychological and threaten the success of the intended reforms. Accordingly, I want to stress some of the dangers that should be avoided in attempts to make children's literature "relevant" to black youngsters. These dangers include: a) the danger of intuitive psychology; b) the danger of reverse prejudice; and c) the danger of easy nonscience.

THE DANGER OF INTUITIVE PSYCHOLOGY

Psychology, like education, has the disadvantage that everyone believes they know something about it without ever having studied the subject. While it is undoubtedly true that most people do know something about psychology, it is also true that they can make educational or psychological decisions on the basis of biased data and without reflection. From a more informed scientific point of view, however, these decisions can often be quite wrong and even harmful. Let me give you a few examples in tbe domain of the children's book field.

One of the most predominant trends in reading series for young people today is the introduction of black children and ghetto settings into the story material. The assumption is—and black parents are often vehement about this—that children will read about what is familiar to them and touches upon their experience. Often too, black parents will object to fantasy material because it lacks educational content and does not move the child forward in his school work.

While it is easy to understand the intuitive psychology behind the wish to provide black children with stories about ghetto settings, it is also easy to show that this intuitive psychology is in error. First of all, research suggests that the major causes of reading retardation among black children include: a) inadequate preparation in the preschool years, and b) a written dialect which is at variance with their spoken dialect. While having black as well as white characters makes good psychological and common sense, there is no evidence that the setting of the stories (in suburb or ghetto) has anything to do with aiding or hindering reading achievements in black children.

Furthermore, despite the "rightness" inherent in the intuitive idea of providing ghetto stories for ghetto children, this might do more harm than it would do good. One of the complaints about the "Dick and Jane" reading series for children has been that they are too commonplace and familiar. What intrigues children is the unfamiliar, not the familiar. A case in point is the "family" television show: "Courtship of Eddie's Father," "The Partridge Family," "Family Affair," where the peculiarity of such programs is that *one or the other parent is missing.* It is the unfamiliar events that result from this peculiarity that makes these shows intriguing to children. From this point of view, ghetto stories are likely to be more interesting to children from the suburbs than they are to children in urban settings.

There is still another bit of intuitive psychology embedded in the desire to present ghetto children with ghetto stories, and this is the distrust of fantasy. Ghetto parents in particular seem to feel that fantasy is detrimental to mental growth. Nothing could be farther from the truth: fantasy is an important mechanism of mental growth. An essential aspect of mental growth is learning to distinguish between reality and appearance, between how things look and how they really are. As children engage in fantasy, they learn to distinguish between what is pure mental construction and what is based upon underlying fact.

The child who, due to parental or societal pressure, is overly tied to reality is often bound by the appearances of things and by their immediateness. He or she cannot get to the levels of abstraction required for complex intellectual endeavors. Engagement in fantasy activity keeps the mind open and prevents it from being structured and closed too early. Children who mature too early in their knowledge of the ways of the world may not develop as far intellectually as youngsters who have

had a more prolonged childhood. Childhood fantasy is the starting point for creative thinking and scientific, mathematical, and
philosophical thinking all have a fantasy component. Contrary
to the assumptions of intuitive psychology, a reasonable amount
of fantasy activity is essential to full realization of intellectual
potential.

THE DANGER OF REVERSE PREJUDICE

Our new awareness of the plight of black Americans has made
us supersensitive to the differences between white and black
children in the kinds and amounts of intellectual stimulation,
parental instruction, and support which they receive. Awareness of these black-white differences has been accentuated by
the wealth of new research studies on ghetto children which
repeatedly emphasize the racial differences. Stories in the new
readers for children also stress racial differences insofar as they
usually depict black children in ghetto settings.

It is clear that this emphasis on racial differences is well-
intentioned and meant to make society aware of the black experience as well as to give value to this experience in the eyes of
young children. Unfortunately, it may be doing just the reverse.
What the social scientists have inadvertently done is create a
new stereotype of the black child who lives in a ghetto, who
comes from a broken home, and who has limited conceptual
abilities. In many ways, we have substituted a new stereotype of
the black which is hardly more complimentary than the old one.

The facts are, of course, quite otherwise. Not all blacks live in
the ghetto and among those that do there is the variation found
among all people. On the same block one can find a cleaning
woman who is sending her children to college, an alcoholic
whose children are in foster homes, a lawyer and his family with
children doing very well in school. The emphasis on black-white
differences badly misrepresents the hetereogenity among black
families and children.

Although such generalization and stereotyping are probably
inevitable in our attempts to redress the racial imbalance in
America, something can be done about it. One of the things that
could be done is to make the diversity of the black experience

apparent in the reading material for children. The depiction of black children in non-ghetto settings and in stories with non-ghetto themes will certainly not undo the reverse prejudice that has derived from the new black stereotype. It could help, however, to present a more realistic picture of the black experience to both black and white children.

I want to mention, finally, a more pernicious form of reverse prejudice, namely, *role reversal*. Let me give you an example from children's fiction which recently came to my attention. While in a pediatrician's office, I picked up a book entitled *The Five Little Bears*, which was about five black bears called "Eenie," "Meenie," "Meinee," "Moe," and "Nig." The black bears fell into some white paint and were mistaken for polar bears by a mother polar bear. When they pleaded that they were not her cubs, she gave them a trial by ice water, which they failed. They were then returned to their mother, who washed off the white paint and scolded them for their escapade. Finally, like all naughty children since Peter Rabbit, they were put to bed without any supper.

This story has messages at several different levels. By using the names Eenie, Meenie, Meinee, Moe, and Nig, the writer evokes a familiar and racially derogatory children's rhyme which makes it clear where the "Nig" came from. Then the author makes the "white" mother the "bad" mother, and the cubs learn how painful it is to be white (polar bears) and how much nicer it is to be black. The writer's intent is not entirely clear because he seems to be saying that black is better than white but also that blacks ought to be satisfied with their lot and ought not to try to be whites. Although the writer probably meant this as a racially enlightened story, it can be read quite otherwise. In trying to reverse black and white roles, the writer unwittingly revealed his real belief that blacks should "stay in their place."

THE DANGER OF EASY CONSCIENCE

The third danger in trying to make children's literature free of stereotypes and relevant to black experience is complacency. It is convenient to assume, once we have put black children in black settings in stories with black themes, that we have done our share toward equal rights for blacks. Certainly the children's book field was in the vanguard of efforts to eliminate degrading depictions and to change the negative stereotypes about blacks that have abounded in children's literature.

Complacency about these efforts is, however, not justified. As I mentioned earlier, the real factors involved in the reading retardation of black children probably derive from lack of preparation and from the fact that black children speak a different dialect from the language in printed stories. There is thus a discrepancy between the spoken and written language for black children which does not hold for white children. The poetry of Langdon Hughes appeals to black children for just this reason, namely, it is in a familiar dialect. Until we begin to deal with these real issues in the reading retardation of some black children, complacency about our efforts in making children's literature relevant to blacks is probably premature.

There is another area in which we may be too complacent as well. We may be too satisfied with the ability of white authors to write for black children. From my own limited reading of the new literature for black children, my impression is that writers such as Ezra Jack Keats (*Whistle for Willie, Hi Cat*) are the exception rather than the rule. In addition to changing the content of children's literature to eliminate stereotypes and to make it relevant to black children, we also need to bring blacks into all phases of the writing and publishing field. If we do that, the danger of complacency will be countered by the presence of individuals who will not permit token modifications to pass for real changes.

SUMMARY

In the present chapter I have tried to describe some of the dangers which arise whenever one group tries to help another which it formerly oppressed. These dangers—threats to the successful execution of social reform—occur in every domain including the children's book field. The dangers reside in our tendency to rely on intuitive psychology, our proclivity for reverse prejudice, and our eagerness for an easy conscience. While these are all very basic and very human tendencies, they can effectively sabotage well-intentioned efforts at remedying the racial injustices of the past.

The children's book field, like so many other institutions in American society, both black and white, is embarked on a humanitarian mission, the righting of wrongs done to blacks in society. Success depends, however, not only upon what we do for others but also upon what we do about ourselves. If we can overcome our tendency to make decisions on the basis of intuitive psychology, if we inhibit our readiness to reverse prejudice, and if we do not succumb to the desire for a quick, easy conscience, we might still win the battle for racial equality in general, and in the children's book field in particular.

5

CHOOSING TO BE GAY
THE ROOTS OF HOMOSEXUALITY

Despite much mythology and prejudice, the bulk of social science evidence suggests that homosexuality is a normal rather than a pathological deviation. Some of the mythology about homosexuality together with some of the extreme conceptions regarding it are presented along with the majority social science consensus. It is concluded that becoming a homosexual is a conscious, and often a courageous, choice, and that homosexuals should not be discriminated against because of their sexual preference.

As human beings, one of our less admirable traits is our tendency to attribute the worst possible motives to behavior which we don't understand. When, for example, another driver refuses to let us change lanes in traffic, we are quick to assume that he is a hostile, aggressive person bent on provoking us. So strong is the sense of outrage at this behavior that not a few drivers, when "put upon" in this way, pursue the culprit in search of revenge. The fact that the other driver might be rushing home for an emergency or is merely preoccupied and inattentive seldom occurs to us. It is not surprising, therefore, that homosexual behavior—which often appears incomprehensible to most heterosexuals—is often regarded as unnatural and as willfully degenerate.

These prejudicial attitudes towards homosexuality persist despite our increasingly enlightened orientation toward sexuality generally and despite the accessibility of information made possible by almost a century of social science research on the subject. Among social scientists, homosexuality is regarded as part of the human condition, having its origin in a constellation of constitutional factors and social experiences not unlike those which give rise to heterosexual behavior. Although social scientists disagree as to whether or not they regard the homosexual person as "sick," they all agree that such behavior is entirely natural and has to be dealt with as a social, and not as a moral or religious, problem.

The thinking of social scientists on the origins of homosexuality should be of more than casual interest to the laymen. It has been estimated that about four per cent of the adult male population in America is exclusively homosexual. If a comparable percentage holds true for female homosexuals, then about four percent of the adult population, or some ten million Americans, are gay. Since people who are gay have families (which would include an average of at least four people), homosexuality is likely to touch the lives of some fifty million Americans, almost a quarter of our entire population. The very real likelihood of homosexual offspring occurring even in an "average" family was brought home to Americans in a very graphic way by Lance Loud, one of the sons in the television epic, "An American Family." Homosexuality is clearly a social issue of major proportions.

Before presenting the range of social science views regarding the origins of homosexuality, it might be well to begin by dispelling some of the myths and misunderstandings regarding homosexuals and their behavior. The discussion will deal largely with male homosexuals, both because most of the literature deals with this group, and because society seems more tolerant and accepting of female homosexuality than of male homosexuality. This may relate, in part at least, to the fact that the "tomboy" is more acceptable than the "sissy," that the masculine female is less offensive to public sensitivities than the effeminate male.

MYTHS ABOUT HOMOSEXUALITY

One of the most widely held, yet erroneous, ideas about gay males is that they are all effeminate. In fact, however, the "screaming queen" with his tight pants, open shirt, eye make-up, and feminine gestures and vocal intonations is the exception rather than the rule. The vast majority of gay males cannot be distinguished from heterosexuals in either appearance or demeanor. (Most homosexuals, however, believe that they can tell whether or not a person is gay, but they believe that straight people cannot.) As far as the "screaming queen" is concerned, he is more likely to be asexual than homosexual, and his behavior is more narcissistic and exhibitionistic than it is seductive. Indeed, such queens are as repugnant to the majority of gay males as they are to men who are straight. Gay men are not attracted to females and particularly not to poor facsimilies of females. The belief that all gay males are effeminate and are attracted to effeminate men is a gross denial of the reality of male homosexuality, namely, that gay men are attracted to other men.

Another common myth about gay males is that they are out to corrupt and seduce boys and young men. In actuality, only a very small percentage of homosexuals are pederasts or child molesters. Such men are emotionally ill and the innocent should be protected from them. While such molestation is a traumatic experience for any young person, it does not usually result in a lifelong pattern of homosexual behavior. In general, seduction in childhood or adolescence is a contributing factor to a homosexual orientation in only a small percentage of the homosexual population. But the main point is that the vast majority of gay males desire only adult partners and are as appalled at the thought of child molestation as heterosexuals. The majority of gay males are no more pederasts than the majority of straight males are rapists. In fact, heterosexual males sexually abuse children proportionately more often than do male homosexuals.

Likewise, the belief that gay males are on the lookout to

seduce young males into their way of life is equally unfounded. To be sure, many gay males go "cruising," or looking for partners, but they seldom trouble a male who does not respond to a complex signal pattern of eye movements, gestures, and verbal phrases. Very few men are seduced who do not want to be, and the rape of a male is a rarity. On the other hand, many gay males are victimized by aggressive young men who beat them and rob them with impunity because they know that the homosexual cannot call the police. Some young men who pick up homosexuals in order to rob them become so frightened of their own latent homosexual feelings that they can actually kill the other man in a so-called *homosexual panic*.

Another common misunderstanding about gay males is that they are feminine in their mode of sexual expression just as lesbians are masculine in their mode of expression. Again this common misunderstanding does not accord well with the facts. The sexual modes of gay males are quite masculine, just as the sexual modes of gay women are feminine. Gay males, like males who are straight, often seek immediate gratification of sexual desire without long-term emotional involvement. Contacts are often made in gay bars or in other places known to be frequented by homosexuals, including certain public toilets or "tea rooms." (In England these places are known as "cottages" and the activity is known as "cottaging".) The pattern is not all that dissimilar from a heterosexual male who goes out to pick up a prostitute.

Lesbians, on the other hand, seldom go "cruising" and tend to establish lasting relationships with another individual where there is intense emotional involvement. Many of these relationships last for a good number of years. Gay males also set up more long-lived relationships with other males, but feel more free than gay females to have sex with someone other than their lover. Because the homosexual pair is not bound by way of legal contract or by responsibility for children, there is considerable freedom in breaking up long-lived relationships. But many pairs stay together long after their sexual activities have ebbed or terminated. In any case, the sexual pattern of gay males is basically masculine and polygamous, whereas the sexual pattern of gay females is basically feminine and monogamous. Whether these patterns are innate or acquired, it is clear that gay men and women differ as much as straight men and women insofar as their patterns of sexual relations are concerned.

A last common misunderstanding has to do with the manner in which gay males attain sexual gratification. There are four basic patterns: mutual masturbation, full-body masturbation, anal intercourse (sodomy or buggery), and fellatio. Mutual masturbation is frequent among young adolescent males, many of whom will become heterosexual later. The other forms of gratification become more common as the individual becomes convinced that he is a homosexual and finds more experienced partners who introduce him to the other methods. As in the case of heterosexuals, preferences for particular forms of gratification vary widely among different individuals. Some men prefer to be receivers and others to be givers and still others enjoy either role. Body build is no clue to preference: an effete male may always be the giver and a tough, muscular type the receiver. Sodomy, which has been the most prohibited and punished sexual act, is preferred by less than half of the males who are exclusively homosexual.

These facts about the nature of homosexual behavior have been collected by social scientists who are also concerned with how people become homosexual. While few people dispute the facts about homosexuality, there is considerable dispute about its origins. At one extreme are a small group of psychoanalysts who regard homosexuality as a neurotic symptom or defense which can be treated and cured in psychotherapy. At the other extreme is an equally small group of behavioral scientists who argue that homosexuality is but one of many possible normal expressions of human sexuality. Between these two extremes are the majority of psychiatrists and social scientists who do not see homosexuality as necessarily neurotic, but who do not see it as entirely normal either. Before presenting this middle position, it might be well to look at the extremes.

THEORIES OF HOMOSEXUALITY

Among psychoanalysts who argue that homosexuality is a disease, Edmund Bergler, in his book *Homosexuality, Disease or*

Way of Life, has been one of the most outspoken and vehement. Bergler is categorical in his contention that "homosexuality is aneurotic disease in which extremely severe and unavoidable self-damaging tendences engulf the whole personality." In Bergler's view, homosexuals are "psychic masochists" who in every case show the following personality traits:

1. Masochistic provocation and injustice collecting
2. Defensive malice
3. An overt flippancy which covers depression and guilt
4. Extreme narcissism and superciliousness
5. Refusal to acknowledge accepted standards in nonsexual matters on the assumption that the right to cut corners is due to homosexuals as compensation for their suffering.
6. General unreliability of a more or less psychopathic (irresponsible) nature.

Bergler concludes that "The most interesting feature of this sextet of traits is its universality. Regardless of the level of intelligence, culture background or education *all* [my italics] homosexuals possess it."

On the basis of his extensive clinical practice with homosexuals, Bergler felt that homosexuals were not only a menace to society, but to themselves as well. Homosexuals were a menace first because they were out to seduce young men and second because they married unsuspecting women as a front for their homosexual activities. In this connection, Bergler cites the case of a little-known actor who was married to a well-known actress. One day the actress found her husband in bed with another man, an experience which made her physically sick. The wife went to Bergler to ask him whether he would treat the husband, but the husband, according to Bergler, only wanted him to convince the wife that his behavior was quite normal.

Bergler's conclusions about homosexuality are based on considerable clinical experience and have to be taken seriously. What he says about homosexuals may well be true for those individuals who seek out psychiatric treatment, though the absence of any exceptions to the patterns he proposes is rare in clinical practice, where lack of universality is the rule. But even if Bergler is correct as far as his patients go, they can hardly be regarded as representative of all homosexuals any more than neurotic heterosexuals can be said to represent all heterosexuals. In clinical cases, homosexuality is part of a syndrome, not its cause. Likewise, Bergler's contention that homosexuals go about seducing young men is not supported by either clinical or statistical evidence. Bergler's argument about the homosexual as a menace to unsuspecting women is also questionable. Some homosexual men do marry women without informing them, in hopes perhaps of becoming straight. But many women who are told beforehand still want to marry the man, sometimes even more so. In any case, the statistics on divorce do not suggest marriage to a homosexual mate as a major factor in the rupture of many marriages.

A somewhat more objective argument for the same position, namely, that homosexuality is a neurotic illness, has been provided by Irving Bieber and his coworkers, in a book entitled *Homosexuality: A Psychoanalytic Study of Male Homosexuals*. Bieber and his coworkers compared 127 homosexuals with 100 heterosexual psychoanalystic patients in New York City. The patients were being seen by a large number of different analysts who reported their findings with the aid of questionnaires. Their general conclusion from the data was that homosexuality in the male always had its basis in "hidden but incapacitating fears of the opposite sex." This was a theory that has been advocated by the late Sandor Rado, a well-known analyst. A number of different patterns of family life were found to give rise to this fear which was found in a large number of cases. They argued that homosexuality as an adjustment to a pathological fear of the opposite sex could not be regarded as either healthy or normal.

The most frequent pattern found by Bieber and his colleagues was a combination of close-binding intimacy and seductiveness on the part of the mother and detachment and hostility on the part of the father. What happens in these circumstances is that the boy becomes overly attached to his mother, who is not only seductive but also restrictive with respect to his sexual interests and behavior. The result is that the child is placed in a "double bind" position wherein the mother both stimulates him sexually and punishes his sexual interests and advances. As a consequence of the hurt and frustration she causes him, the boy

learns to fear and hate his mother and to repress any sexual
feelings toward her and toward all the women for whom she
stands. Homosexual relationships become the only safe and
comfortable outlet for sexual gratification.

The problems with this investigation are in many ways the
same as the problems with Bergler's clinical descriptions. The
patients in the study can hardly be representative of the total
homosexual population and of the total normal population.
There were, for example, 40 Jewish men (about 33 per cent)
among the 127 homosexuals and 67 among the 100 controls.
Since there are more homosexuals in this country than there are
Jews, the sample could hardly be representative. Then too there
were many exceptions to the general findings. Nevertheless,
Bieber and his colleagues argue that the fear of women holds for
all homosexuals and they dismiss contrary findings from studies
of non-patient homosexuals as being wrong. Clearly, while
these clinical cases provide insights into the origins of the "sick"
homosexual, they tell us nothing about the vast majority of relatively "healthy" homosexuals.

At the other extreme are social scientists such as Kinsey and
his colleagues, who argue that homosexual behavior has to be
considered as normal and as healthy as heterosexual behavior.
According to Kinsey:

> Males do not represent two discrete populations,
> heterosexuals and homosexuals. The world is not divided
> into sheep and goats. Not all things are black and white. It
> is a fundamental fact of taxonomy that nature rarely deals
> with discrete categories. Only the human mind invents
> categories and tries to force facts into separate pigeon holes.
> The living world is a continuum in each and every one of its
> aspects. The sooner we learn this concerning human sexual
> behavior, the sooner we shall reach a sound understanding
> of the realities of sex.

On the basis of their survey data of some 5,000 males, Kinsey
and his coworkers arrived at a seven-point rating scale (0–6)
which ranked individuals from exclusive heterosexuality (rank
of 0) to exclusive homosexuality (rank of 6). At the midpoint of
the scale is the bisexual (rank of 3) who is equally attracted to
men and to women and who gains equal gratification from

either one. According to this scheme bisexuality would be the norm, or most frequent orientation, were it not for cultural mores and taboos. Exclusive heterosexuality, like exclusive homosexuality, would have to be attributed to cultural conditioning which leads to the repression of alternative sexual outlets.

Evidence to support the normality of homosexual behavior comes from a wide variety of different sources. Among animals, homosexual play is quite frequent between the young, but occurs occasionally among mature animals as well. The potentiality for homosexual behavior in mature animals was shown in a study wherein the longer the time period male rats were separated from females, the more they engaged in homosexual behavior and the less likely they were to return to heterosexual behavior once females were again available. Something similar happens to men in prisons and in other situations where males are secluded from women for long periods of time.

Cross-cultural data provide further evidence for the universality of the potential for homosexual as well as for heterosexual behavior. In a survey of 76 primitive tribes, it was found that in 49 (64 per cent), homosexual behavior of some sort was prevalent and was regarded as culturally acceptable. In North Africa, to illustrate, there is a tribe called the Siwans which expects all men to engage in sodomy and which expects men to have both heterosexual and homosexual affairs. Among the Aranda of Australia, young male bachelors live together in a homosexual alliance until one of them decides to take a female wife. History also provides evidence of many clutures, particularly that of Ancient Greece, wherein homosexuality was socially accepted or pardoned.

A rather different kind of evidence for the essential normality of homosexual behavior comes from studies which have compared the physiognomy, physiology, and psychology of homosexuals with those of heterosexuals. In general, these studies show that homosexuals do not differ in statistically significant ways from heterosexuals in such things as body build, hairiness, hormonal balance, or personality structure. Male homosexuals come from all social classes and are engaged in many different lines of work ranging from stevedore to hairdresser. (In New York State, however, a homosexual cannot legally be a hairdresser.) The notion that all homosexuals are engaged in feminine occupations is simply not in keeping with the facts. The presence of the homosexual propensity across such a wide spectrum of the population is taken as still another evidence of its universality and of its normality.

A rather interesting implication of the view that bisexuality is the real norm of sexuality is given by Wainwright Churchill in his book *Homosexual Behavior Among Males.* Churchill claims that much of the antipathy toward homosexuality in America derives from our repressed homosexual tendencies. The situation is not unlike that which occurs in a person who has successfully dieted for a number of months and then is confronted with a table containing all of his favorite sweets. He experiences an aversive anxiety which results from the fear that if he tastes even a morsel he will lose control and eat everything in sight. Better not to have any and to convince oneself that sweets are bad for the teeth and health. If this interpretation of our aversion to homosexuality is correct, then it would have to be regarded as a defense against losing control over homosexual inclinations, much as anxiety about eating certain foods is a defense against losing control over the inclination to consume them.

Churchill also suggests that this aversion to homosexuality is perpetuated because it is in accordance with the frontier image of manliness which is still prevalent in American society. The American male was, until recently, supposed to be hard, tough, and insensitive where women were concerned. With other men he was supposed to show his strength, courage, and manliness, but not his feelings. As a consequence, American men were generally inhibited in their relations both with women and with men since displays of feeling were regarded as unmanly. In other countries, such as those of Southern Europe, where homosexuality is much more accepted, men are more open in showing feelings toward one another and toward women. Such openness does not mean actual homosexual activity, but rather sensitivity to other people's feelings and an openness in expressing one's own feelings. Could it be that the Latin lover is renowned, in part at least, because he is comfortable in expressing his feelings toward men as well as women?

Unfortunately, the fact that homosexual behavior occurs in

animals, is accepted in many primitive societies, and has been the norm at various times in history does not gainsay the fact that homosexuality is still repugnant to the majority of heterosexuals in America today. This is a reality that must be faced. Cultural attitudes and tradition change slowly and are exceedingly long-lived. While bisexuality may be the biological norm and homosexuality a healthy variant in a perfect biological world, in reality bisexuality and exclusive homosexuality impose very real burdens on those who practice them in this country. Moreover, the norm of our society in child rearing is toward heterosexuality so that patterns which allow individuals to become bisexual and homosexual are contrary to the culture norms.

These are some of the considerations which have led the majority of social scientists to an intermediary position regarding the "health" of homosexuals in America today. In most cases the homosexual chooses, at a certain point in his or her life, to be a homosexual despite all the culture pressures to the contrary. Heterosexuals never have to make such a choice nor do they have to bear the consequences of such a decision. The exclusive homosexual is likely to have problems for no reason other than that he lives in a society where homosexual activity is prohibited by law and vilified by tradition. And yet, with their eyes open to the consequences, some individuals do choose to become homosexual in our society. What are the conditions which lead to homosexuality despite all the many and varied social pressures to the contrary?

Not surprisingly, it was Freud who gave us our basic insights into some of the origins of homosexuality in modern society. For his time, Freud was much more objective about homosexuals than are many of his current disciples. He argued that it was important to distinguish the sexual drive from the object to which it gets attached for satisfaction. Freud believed that the association between drive and object was neither innate nor acquired, but came about as a consequence of the interaction of constitutional factors and experience. Accordingly, for Freud, the choice of a heterosexual object needed to be explained every bit as much as the choice of a homosexual object. He wrote: "Psychoanalytic research very strongly opposes the attempt to separate homosexuals as a group of special nature. . . . it discovers that all men are capable of homosexual object selection and actually accomplish this in the unconscious. Indeed, attachments of libidinous feelings to persons of the same sex play no small role as factors in normal psychic life."

In Freud's view, a homosexual male's object choice usually comes about through his excessive love for his mother. When, in the course of development (age four or five), it is time for the boy to detach his love from his mother and to identify with his father (and thus resolve the oedipal conflict by attaining his mother vicariously through identification with the father), the identification with the father does not occur. Instead, the child identifies with the mother and takes himself (as beloved son) as the sexual object. In adulthood the homosexual seeks men who remind him of himself. According to Freud, male homosexuals are often sexually stimulated by women, but then they can identify with the woman and look for a male partner. In this way, the male homosexual repeats the pattern of attachment, detachment, and identification that was initated in relationship to his mother.

For Freud, however, homosexuality was not a neurosis but an adaptive alternative. He said that neurosis was the negative of inversion (homosexuality). The neurotic represses his sexual attachment to the parent of the opposite sex and it is this repression that causes the neurosis. But the homosexual does not repress his attachment to his mother, but rather *expresses* his identification with her in his homosexual activities. Freud explicitly said that homosexuals were not degenerate, that they often lead healthy productive lives, and he even urged that they be allowed to practice psychoanalysis as lay analysts. He seemed to regard many homosexuals as healthy individuals whose major problems stemmed from social disapproval.

It is generally recognized today that while the dynamic pattern described by Freud holds true in the case of some male homosexuals, it does not begin to cover them all. A more general explanation of homosexual behavior in America is given by Donald Webster Cory. Cory claims that the most pervasive factor in the origins of homosexuality is the lack of a well-balanced home in which "mother and father display affection for one another and for the child." Cory described a number of different family patterns that he regarded as conducive to homosexuality.

The problem with all such explanations of homosexual behavior is that there are many families in which the particular constellation occurs and yet in which none of the children turn out to be homosexual in orientation. On the contrary, some individuals develop a homosexual orientation even when they come from integrated homes where there is much love and affection between parents and between parents and children. We have to assume therefore that a group of factors, including child-rearing practices, natural inclinations, and social experiences of many different kinds brings some individuals to the realization that they are attracted to members of their own sex. At this point in their lives, the individuals have to choose which path they wish to follow. The choice is made for many different reasons, some of which may be more healthy than others. Far from being wantonly degenerate, it takes a kind of courage to choose to be a homosexual in our society. In a very real sense, therefore, the psychologically healthy homosexual is gay because, for whatever reasons, he or she chooses to be so.

CONCLUSION

If we consider the multiple ways in which an exclusive orientation to homosexuality can come about, it seems unlikely that it will either disappear or increase significantly in frequency. Homosexuality is definitely here to stay. The homosexual who has accepted his or her homosexuality is, in the great majority of cases, a constructive and productive member of society. Insofar as his or her sexual preference does no harm to others and is not imposed upon them, there would seem to be no justification for legal penalties against the practice of homosexual activities between consenting adults. This was the conclusion of the famous Wolfenden Report in England which led to the removal of some of the laws against homosexual activities there.

When we did not understand homosexuality and the conditions that brought it about, it was human to think of it as unnatural and degenerate. Now that we understand that homosexuality originates in the same matrix of factors as heterosexuality, it would also be human to accept homosexuality as part of mankind's condition and to allow those who are gay to live in peace and without fear, prejudice and threat of intimidation.

HOME AND FAMILY

6
COGNITIVE FRAMES AND FAMILY INTERACTIONS

Frames are the set of implicit rules, expectancies, and under-standings that regulate social behavior in repetitive situations. In such situations individuals exhibit demeanor and proffer deference in socially proscribed ways. The nature of frames, demeanor, and deference, how they are acquired by children and some of the difficulties that young people encounter along the way, is the focus of the present chapter.

In contemporary sociology the concept of a "frame" is used in several different senses. As employed by Basil Bernstein (1971), "frame" and "framing" have to do with the structuring of the environment. For example, the office of a clinician practicing behavior modification would be differently framed from that of a clinician who employs psychoanalysis. One might expect the office of the behavior modifier to be relatively plain and the office of the psychoanalyst to be relatively rich in terms of furni-ture, paintings, and plants. In this sense framing helps set the tone for the kind of interpersonal interaction that will take place in the particular environment. Although Bernstein's concept of framing is of relevance to clinical work, it is not the sense in which frame will be employed in the present paper.

V. C. Vaughn (ed.) *The Family: Can It be Saved?* Chicago: Yearbook Pub-lishers, 1976, 167–184.

Rather, the term frame will be employed as Erving Goffman (1974) uses it in his book, *Frame Analysis*. For Goffman, the frame is not a surface structure, as it is for Bernstein, but a deep structure. It is the set of rules, expectancies, and understandings that regulate human behavior in repetitive social situations which Goffman calls *social encounters*. For Goffman, much of human behavior is situationally determined, but this does not mean that it is casual or accidental. Rather Goffman's point is that even momentary social situations are highly structured and that these structures play a very important part in human behavior.

While Goffman's concept of frame is more general than Bernstein's, it remains relatively ahistorical. It is, to use a favorite phrase of Jean Piaget, "a structuralism without a genesis" (Piaget, 1967). In this chapter, I will try to add some genetic considerations to the concept of frame. Assuming that frames operate in the way Goffman says they do, how are they constructed or reconstructed by children in the course of their development? And more importantly, from a clinical point of view, what part does children's understanding of frames, or their lack of it, play in their everyday behavior, particularly in their family interactions? These are the questions for which the present chapter will attempt to supply some early, tentative answers.

THE NATURE OF FRAMES

In the everyday life of the child there are many repetitive social encounters, some with adults, some with children, and some with children and adults. Each of these encounters has its own set of rules, expectancies and understandings which serve to make the encounter successful. Each social encounter involves a social equilibrium that all members seek to maintain. Disruptions of the equilibrium are usually not catastrophic, but they are often socially uncomfortable. Frames, then, are basic units of social interactions, and the understanding of frames is an important part of every child's socialization.

Consider the adult-child frame of bedtime. When a parent suggests that it is time to go to bed, his action elicits characteristic frame behavior. Parents expect children to resist, but are prepared to permit some token resistance so long as they are eventually obeyed. Children, too, know that it is all right to protest, but only up to a certain point. Sometimes, of course, the frame rules may be broken. The parent may be in no mood for fun and games and demand immediate obedience. Or the child may go to bed without protest (and baffle his parents) or put up a violent, uncompromising fight.

Violations of frame rules are important because they make the implicit frame rules manifest and because they illustrate, as Goffman suggests, that each frame has its own emotional rhythm. When a frame rule is broken, so too is the emotional rhythm and some remedial work has to be done to complete the emotional cycle of the frame. For example, suppose a child goes to bed without protest. This spoils the rhythm for the parent who is prepared to deal with a little bit of rebellion. In its absence the parent is almost forced to provoke it and may say, "You mean you are not going to give me a hard time? I can't believe it." In effect, the going to bed frame provides the parent an opportunity for verbal banter; when the child's resistance does not provide the occasion for the banter, then his or her non-resistance becomes the occasion. Without the banter the ritual is spoiled for the parent and for the child.

CUES TO FRAMES

Children and adults can be put into frames by different sorts of cues. Sometimes a setting is sufficient to cue a frame. In a public library, for example, the setting cues a "keep quiet" frame that involves talking in whispers, walking quietly, and taking elaborate measures not to disturb others who are in the setting. If anyone should violate these frame rules, the looks of recrimination and the librarian's reprimands usually suffice to punish the offender and restore the frame's equilibrium.

Frames can also be cued by particular activities. The "going to bed" frame described earlier is but one of many activity frames. "Lunchtime at school" is an interesting frame because many of the rules about talking and moving around are more relaxed than in the classroom. Of course, the lunch room setting adds to the cuing of this frame behavior. In general, frame cues are usually multiple rather than singular and, as in the case of the "lunch room" frame, reinforce one another as signals for particular behavior patterns.

Some frames are cued by particular people. Just about everyone has a favorite person who exudes happiness and enjoyment of life. When such a person enters the room a new frame comes into play wherein the other participants can be freer and more open in their expressions and language. Such individuals often bring out the latent wit, good humor, and human concern of otherwise dour people. In the presence of such vital personalities, other individuals feel permitted to be more alive themselves. The same is true for children who recognize, in the presence of a favorite uncle or aunt, that they can behave in ways not usually permitted or condoned by their parents. The reverse is also true, however, as some puritan personalities signal a "best behavior" frame.

Frames can also be cued by emotional moods and attitudes. Children learn to read these cues very early in their careers as offspring. Take, for example, the "asking for things" frame. Children learn early that to initiate the "asking for things" frame when the parent is angry or upset may not be worth the gamble. On the other hand, when the parent is in a good mood, initiating an "asking" frame carries little risk. Even if the parent refuses the request, it is likely to be done with good humor. Of course a child may initiate an "asking" frame when the parent is in a bad humor, just to get the parent's goat. A child's understanding of frame cues thus has offensive as well as defensive possibilities.

DEMEANOR AND DIFFERENCE

When children or adults behave in frames, they alternate between two postures, that of *actor* and that of *audience.* As an actor in a frame, the child has to present himself in a particular way if he is to receive *deference* (recognition or approval from others). A child who shows the proper *demeanor* (who behaves in a manner appropriate to the frame) obtains confirmation by others of his social acceptability and thus of his humanness. Hence the motivation for learning the appropriate frame rules and for obeying them is social acceptance or validation as a bona fide member of the group.

If the child is on occasion an actor, he or she is also on occasion an audience. When a parent is putting together a model, changing a tire, or mowing the lawn, the child is often in the audience mode and can award approval or criticism. At such times the parent is the one who must maintain the appropriate demeanor if the child is to provide the complementary deference. If the parent slips up and makes a mistake on the model, or curses while changing the tire, children withdraw their deference and hoot with glee. When the parent is the actor and the child is the audience, the parent is every bit as vulnerable as the child in a similar position. The child, no less than the adult, must constantly alternate between the orientation of seeking social approval and validation and being the arbiter of social acceptance and confirmation.

Deference and demeanor are thus the motivational components of frame behavior. When child-child and parent-child interactions are viewed from this perspective, some forms of these interactions appear in a different light. Teasing, for example, is an instance of child-child interaction wherein the child being teased assumed he was adopting the appropriate demeanor. His anger at being teased is, in part at least, a reaction to not receiving the proper deference. The child doing the teasing has found a flaw in the other child's demeanor which makes the teasing possible. Because younger children are less adept at maintaining demeanors than older children, they are more susceptible to being teased. Put differently, the young child's lack of sophistication with respect to frame behavior makes him or her more vulnerable to teasing.

In adult-child relations the deference-demeanor distinction helps clarify why children are so often put down by adults. In most child-adult frames, the child is the actor who must show appropriate demeanor to attain adult deference. The adult, in contrast, although he or she may occasionally require the deference of children, does not value it very highly. Adult failure to show children common courtesies ("please," "thank you") reflects the fact that adults do not value the deference (social approval) of children and hence do not bother to maintain the same demeanor they would with other adults. Such treatment by adults has its repercussions, particularly in adolescence when young people get sufficient deference from peers that they can afford not to maintain the expected demeanor with adults.

Frames, deference, and demeanor are thus concepts which enable us to look at family interactions from a cognitive-social perspective. So far we have discussed this interaction in general, primarily sociological, terms. We now need to look at the developmental dimension. How do children and adolescents come to appreciate frames and the communication of deference and demeanor? Inasmuch as this is still a new field of investigation, I can only give some hypotheses, based on previous research, as to how it comes about. A more definitive answer will have to await systematic study. Let us look at the acquisition of frames in childhood first and then turn to frame behavior in adolescence.

CONCRETE OPERATIONS AND FRAME BEHAVIOR

The beginnings of childhood proper, roughly the ages of six or seven, is marked by the appearance of what Piaget calls "concrete operations." These operations allow the school-age child to engage in activities not possible during the early-childhood years. He or she can now solve "in the head" problems that before he or she had to solve by motoric trial and error. A young child, faced with a finger maze, will explore it in trial and error fashion until he or she finds the correct solution. But a grade school child can look at the image, explore it mentally, and discover the right path without putting a finger to the maze. This is what Piaget means when he says that children at the concrete operational level can perform "mental experiments."

At this stage too, children can learn rules and abide by them. Young children have difficulty with rules because they cannot move easily from the one to the many, from the single instance to the category and back again. Saying "please" and "thank you" is difficult for young children because each situation that calls for such a response is somewhat different and the child cannot appreciate the general rule that unites them. The school-age child can move from the particular to the general and hence can appreciate and apply rules such as "i before e except after c." Formal education of the sort provided in grade school is a matter of inculcation of rules.

Perhaps the most familiar accomplishments made possible by concrete operations are the various conservation concepts; of space, time, number, and so on (Piaget, 1970). With the aid of concrete operations the child is able to construct concepts of quantity that remain the same despite changes in their appearance. The concept of a conserved quantity, like that of a conserved object, is a construction, something to which the individual attributes permanence despite changes in the immediate perceptual world. When shown six pennies in a pile and then in a row and asked whether their number is the same, an elementary school child will say that "no matter how you arrange the six pennies they will always be six." He does not need to see all the arrangements to be sure that the conservation of number is independent of any perceptual configuration.

An important characteristic of conservation is that once it is attained, it is externalized and seen as a property of the real world rather than as a mental construction. To the child, and to the adult for that matter, conservation does not reside in the head but rather in the external material, in the six pennies of the preceding example. Externalization is a very adaptive process for the most part, except when it comes to the interactions between children and adults. In the physical realm adults are surprised to discover that children do not have conservation because they regard it as existing outside themselves. Because of externalization it is hard for adults to appreciate that children perceive the world differently from themselves.

I must apologize for recalling these familiar matters to your attention, but they are essential to the continuation of my argument. The construction of the social world, though more complex than the construction of the physical world, shares many processes in common with it. The construction of frames is a case in point. Frames are not *a priori* archetypes that the child brings with him or her at birth, but rather are mental constructions, like conservations, that intelligence must elaborate in the course of development. And, also like conservation, frames are externalized once they are constructed so that they appear to

reside in the social event and not in the heads of the participants.

In acquiring frames the child has to construct sets of rules that
are common to diverse social situations. A crucial step in this
construction is the understanding that a person can be both an
individual (his or her proper name) *and* the representative of a
class of people (men, Americans, Protestants, and so on). The
problem is analogous to understanding the concept of a unit, a
concept that is basic to the understanding of all quantity concepts. A number is like every other number in that it is a
number, but it is also different from every other number in its
order of enumeration. The number three is the only number that
comes after two and before four. And a person is like every
other person in being a person, but different in name, appearance, and personality from other persons.

Young children do not yet distinguish between the one and
the many, the person as a unique individual *and* as a member of
the class of people. The young child who calls several different
men "daddy" shows this confusion because "daddy" means
both a particular individual and a member of the class of adult
males. Young children use the same term in two different senses
without grasping the difference. But with the aid of concrete
operations the child can distinguish between the individual as a
person and as a representative of a class of persons. This discrimination is crucial to understanding and conceptualizing
frames. To understand a "gift" frame the child must grasp that
any adult can also be a "gift giver," and that when any adult
gives a gift, the rule of politeness or "thank you" holds true.

The understanding that an individual is both a unique person
and a member of one or more classes of people is also essential
to grasping the rules regarding deference and demeanor. To act
appropriately in a frame, the child must be able to see himself,
or herself, as well as others, as both one and many, as both a
unique person and a representative of a class of persons. When
he plays the role of an actor, the child's demeanor is that of
himself as an individual reflecting individual needs, training,
and background. But as an audience, he represents not only
himself, but at the very least a class of children.

In responding to the advances of a stranger, for example, the concrete operational child often thinks of himself in the "child" mode as representative of all children in response to an adult who is representative of all adults. When a stranger says, "Hey kid, I'll give you a dime to shut off the lights in my car," the child knows that he is being responded to as a member of a class rather than as a unique person. When the teacher says "Children," the child knows that he is being approached as a group member and not as an individual. Under such circumstances, the child will respond in kind as representative of the class rather than speaking for himself. It is in this mode that the child will say "Mr. Jones doesn't like kids," or "Miss Smith is a neat teacher." In these modes the child speaks for all children and not just for himself.

The understanding of frames, of the appropriate demeanors and deference, does not happen all at once. Which frames the child will learn depends to a considerable extent upon individual circumstances. Frames such as "playing" and "gift receiving" are probably universal and learned early; others, such as "dinner with grandparents," are probably more or less unique. In each case the child must learn the appropriate cues to the frame as well as the appropriate behaviors of demeanor and deference that are necessary to maintain both the frame and the social equanimity of the situation. In the next section we will look at some typical childhood behaviors from the perspective of frames.

ASSUMPTIVE REALITIES AND FRAME BEHAVIOR

Elsewhere (Ch. 17) I have suggested that a major cause of maladaptive behavior in childhood is the tendency to form "assumptive realities." Thanks to concrete operations the school-age child is able to form hypotheses about how things work and function. But he lacks the mental operations to test these hypotheses out in a systematic fashion. Moreover, the young person often is not aware that his proposed solution is a hypothesis at all. Instead he takes the hypothesis for reality and tries to adapt facts to fit the hypothesis rather than the reverse. Hypotheses that the child mistakes for reality are "assumptive realities."

The school-age child's tendency to operate according to assumptive realities often gets him into trouble in acquiring frames. First of all, some frames are frightening and upsetting. A child whose father is abusive and assaultive when drunk has difficulty acquiring a "drunken father frame" even when this would lead to protective, defensive behavior. Rather, the child may cling to the "good father frame" and explain away the father's behavior as a momentary aberration or illness.

Assumptive realities can get children into difficulties in other ways as well, particularly in shifting orientations from actor to audience. They often get carried away in playing games of various sorts: they won't take turns or will break the rules or use more than their alloted portion of time. The trouble is that they have trouble shifting from demeanor to deference. Seeing themselves as "winner" or "player," it becomes hard to shift and see themselves as audience. A good deal of fighting among young school-age children can be accounted for in terms of their difficulties in shifting from being the actor who demands deference to the audience who proffers it.

Swearing and talking back among elementary school children can be looked upon from the same perspective. In elementary school, children's swearing originates in peer frames as an accompaniment to activities. What happens is that children may use the wrong cues and swear even when adults are present. This can occur, for example, when adults are rough-housing with them. Since rough-housing is a cue to swearing among peers, it is used as a cue to swearing when adults are present. The child may also mistakenly assume that swearing is a significant aspect of adult demeanor and use it in the hope of attaining adult deference. The failure of adults to respond deferentially to swearing can be misinterpreted if the child adopts the assumptive reality that the adult admires swearing but does not wish to show it.

Talking back to adults is another example of inappropriate frame behavior. When a child tells an adult to "shut up" or "be quiet," he is adopting an inappropriate demeanor. This might be called "identifying with the aggressor," but it is still necessary to explain why it occurs when it occurs. Usually such talking back occurs when the child has been playing with other children to whom such statements are more appropriate. It may happen that the child is simply unable to shift from the peer-peer frame to the adult-child frame, from the child-child demeanor to the child-adult demeanor. Usually such behavior is stopped by putting the child into the appropriate frame. "You do not talk that way to your mother."

Clearly, fighting, swearing, and talking back in school-age children have a dynamic dimension. Fighting can be an attention-getter or an expression of sibling rivalry or of identification with the aggressor. Swearing can be regarded as a form of oral aggression and attention-getting, and talking back can be both identifying with the aggressor and a provocative asking for punishment. These few interpretations in no way exhaust the domain of dynamic factors in children's behavior. But the question remains as to why these behaviors are so characteristic of childhood proper. The same dynamics are operative in pre-school children and adolescents, and yet do not result in the same behaviors, or at least not to the same extent.

What I am suggesting here is not that the dynamic interpretations are wrong, but only that they are incomplete. Rather than ask why children fight, swear, and talk back, one might ask why adults usually do not. The answer, it seems to me, is that adults have learned frame behavior and operate according to the rules of deference and demeanor in most social situations. But children of school age have just acquired both concrete operations and the means for understanding social frames and comprehending demeanor and deference. It follows that they will manifest more social improprieties than more mature, fully socialized individuals. But their failure of socialization may be as much a matter of intellectual immaturity as it is of emotional disturbance and poor child rearing.

Fighting, swearing, and talking back are rather usual childhood behaviors that can be interpreted, in part at least, as expressions of frame lapses, or of intellectual immaturity. They may result from the child's difficulties in determining what social frame is in play, or in shifting orientation from being actor to being audience, or from adopting inflexible assumptive realities about deference and demeanor. What has to be stressed is that these behaviors in childhood are normative, and that, while they can be put in the service of protecting the ego, they are, in the majority of children, not necessarily defensive in origin.

FORMAL OPERATIONS AND FRAME BEHAVIOR

Around the age of eleven or twelve, most children begin to acquire a new set of mental abilities which Piaget (1950) speaks of as *formal operations*. These operations enable young adolescents to do many things that they could not do before. For example, formal operations enable them to understand metaphor and simile, to construct ideals and theories, and to think about thinking, their own and other people's. Moreover, formal operations enable adolescents to deal with many variables simultaneously, an ability that is required for abstract and experimental thinking.

Not surprisingly, the attainment of formal operations in adolescence also makes possible a whole new dimension of frame behavior not possible in childhood. That is to say, adolescents now become conscious of frames and frame rules and begin to deliberately manipulate them (Goffman calls this "strategic interactions"). In addition, adolescents' ability to construct ideals allows them to construct ideal frames. This often makes them supersensitive to frame violations, particularly on the part of their parents. In addition to these difficulties engendered by formal operations, there are other frame problems created by the adolescents' adult stature and the necessity of changing patterns of deference and demeanor acquired in childhood, as we will now review.

STRATEGIC INTERACTIONS

In strategic interactions, adolescents manipulate frame rules and demeanor and deference to satisfy their own ends. Consider the adolescent boy who comes to appreciate his English teacher's "embarrassment" frame. This teacher likes to choose young people who have not done the required reading in order to embarrass them before the class. This adolescent makes it a point to raise his hand on occasion and always to know the answer when he does. He thus establishes a strategic demeanor.

After these frame rules are established he can raise his hand and be assured the teacher will not call on him because the teacher is sure he knows the answer. This young man has learned the frame rules and how to exploit them. Used on occasion, this procedure of raising the hand can protect him when in fact he does *not* know the answer.

In family interactions, similar strategic games are played every day. The adolescent girl who wants to go to a dance that her parents might question arranges a date for a friend whom her parents respect because she knows they will say, "Well, if Ellen is going, I am sure it is all right." Young people who have chores to do, such as cleaning their rooms or doing the dishes, keep some homework in abeyance so that when parents ask them to do the chores, there is homework to be done and no time for chores. "You don't want me to fail, do you?" reflects the adolescent's keen awareness of parent frame priorities.

A somewhat different method of strategically employing frames involves what Goffman calls "the management of expressive control." Young people are particularly good at this in contrast to children, who have trouble keeping a straight face when they are deliberately telling a tall story. But adolescents can lie with great conviction and can put on an amazing performance. The writer recalls when, as a young clinician, he saw an adolescent delinquent for over a year. Although the young man occasionally described some questionable behavior, he never really told the truth about his almost constant delinquent activities which came to light only after a year in therapy. Skill at impression management can aid adolescents in undermining adult frame expectations.

Of course the young adolescent's awareness of frames can work to his detriment as well. In social situations, such as asking for a date or talking to someone in the lunchroom, the adolescent may say something not appropriate to the frame, then realize it and castigate himself harshly. Part of frame behavior is giving to others a certain impression (demeanor) of self, and young people as well as adults often torture themselves when their behavior inadvertently gives the impression opposite to the one that they wished to convey.

Examples of such spoiled frames are familiar enough. The

78

young man who trips while bringing refreshment to his date spoils the impression of masculine cool and control necessary to the "romantic" frame that was in play. The young lady who gets a very visible run in her hose when wearing a short skirt finds that her attempts at an appearance of being well dressed have been undermined by bad luck. The frames within which young people interact often involve giving certain impressions, and the frames are spoiled when the impressions are not effective.

In family interactions, the adolescent's sensitivity to frames is turned toward parents. Recognizing that surface appearance is an important part of frame behavior, the adolescent becomes hypercritical of parents: their dress, their manner of speech, and their eating, smoking, and drinking habits. Young people feel that what they regard as their parents' inappropriate frame behavior (particularly in interaction with their own friends) embarrasses them and lessens their standing in the esteem of their peers.

It is important to recognize that whether or not parents actually break frame rules is less important than the adolescent's sensitivity to these rules. This sensitivity exaggerates even minor infractions and reflects as much upon the young person's concern with frame behavior as it does upon the parents' actual violations of frame rules. The contention of the present chapter is that much of the day-to-day antagonism between parents and adolescents may have to do with disputes about appropriate frame behavior. This is not to deny that emotional conflicts are present as well, only that these conflicts can often be consciously expressed in conflicts over frame behavior.

Some of the adolescent's difficulty with frames stems from his or her adult stature and demeanor. It is a simple fact that some frames must be given up as children mature. Trick or treating on Halloween is a case in point. In the trick or treat frame, the child wears a costume, rings the bell, and politely says "trick or treat." Within moments the adult puts a sweet in the bag, the child says "thank you," and the frame is terminated. But the frame holds only for children and adults, not adolescents and adults. The gangling adolescent who puts on a sheet and goes ringing door bells may get gentle and not so gentle reprimands. Adolescents have to learn that as grownups they now have to enter the frame at the other end, as providers of deference rather than as exhibitors of demeanor.

Other frames undergo a subtle transformation as young people mature. The "going to bed" frame, for example, is progressively transformed into a "don't stay out late" frame. The emphasis is no longer on being in bed, but rather on being in the house, at a certain time. Again parents expect a little resistance, and young people often stay out just a little longer than the time limit. The ritual is spoiled if the parent becomes too adamant about the young person being home "on the dot," or by the young person who does not arrive until the early hours of the morning without a "saleable" story.

In general, therefore, during adolescence young people not only engage in frame behavior at a new level (strategic interactions), they are also required to change from demeanor to deference in some frames and to change the contents if not the forms of others. It seems reasonable to say that one way of looking at the perennial problems of adolescence is that they involve, in part at least, significant alterations in frame behavior.

SUMMARY

Frames are the implicit rules, expectancies, and understandings that operate in repetitive social situations. In such interactions some individuals have to exhibit a particular demeanor for which they are accorded deference by others. Much interpersonal interaction is governed by frames, and the socialization of children is largely a matter of acquiring frames. This acquisition process is, however, hampered by a variety of circumstances including the child's level of intellectual development. Much childish and adolescent "misbehavior" is probably a consequence, in part at least, of insufficient familiarity with frames and the difficulty of switching from exhibiting demeanor to conferring deference. An understanding of frame behavior complements the explanations of behavior offered by dynamic psychology.

7
EXPLOITATION AND THE GENERATIONAL CONFLICT

This chapter elaborates the thesis that exploitation (breaking of implicit contracts) by parents and adults is often the issue on which the conflict between young people and adults is centered. The first section of the paper presents a general scheme of development of parent-child relations in terms of a series of implicit contracts and explicit agreements and bargains. The next section describes work with middle class delinquents which suggests that developmental exploitation (breaches of the contract by demands for age inappropriate behaviors) and egocentric exploitation (breaches of the contract by demands for excessive amounts of age appropriate behavior or uncompensated behaviors) are related to two phenomenologically different forms of delinquent behavior. In the third section of the paper it is suggested that some forms of exploitation of youth are institutionalized and that changes in the nature of institutionalized exploitation can help to explain, in part at least, the character of youth revolt for any given generation of young people.

The generational conflict between parents and their adolescent offspring is a big problem and one which can be studied from the standpoint of many different disciplines including an-

Mental Hygiene, 1970, 54, 490–97.

thropology, sociology, psychiatry, and social psychology. This chapter, however, deals with the generational conflict from the standpoint of developmental psychology, that is to say, from the position which sees parent-child interaction as evolving in a sequence of stages that is related both to the age of the child and to the maturity of the parents. From this perspective, the generational conflict can be viewed as a stage in the process of self-differentiation whereby youth seeks to further emancipate itself from adult authority by attacking that authority directly.

A conflict, however, never takes place in the abstract and always occurs in the context of particular issues. I believe that a major source of issues for the generational conflict lies in the real or imagined violations of implicit contractual arrangements between parents and their children. When parents violate such a contract, their offspring usually interpret this breach as stemming from selfish motives on the part of the adults and hence experience violations as exploitation. It is this feeling of exploitation, or so it appears to me, which is one of the prime foci of the generational conflict, whether it manifests itself individually in parent-child quarrels and more dramatically in delinquent acting out, or collectively in such movements as student revolts.

To make this proposition concrete, I propose, in the first section of this paper to describe the development of parent-child contracts in general and the major clauses of those contracts in particular. Then, in the following sections, I want to try and show how violations of these contracts can be related to two different manifestations of the generational conflict, namely, middle-class delinquency and youth revolt. It is perhaps well to emphasize at this point that I am not arguing that the violation of contractual agreements is necessary and sufficient to explain the generational conflict. Far from it. What I am saying is that in Western society such violations have provided youth with at least some of the issues upon which to base their struggle for independence.

THE DEVELOPMENT OF PARENT-CHILD INTERACTIONS

One way in which the development of parent-child relations can be viewed is from the standpoint of the kinds of give-and-take arrangements that are explicitly or implicitly operative at all levels of development. At least three types of arrangements can be distinguished: the bargain, the agreement, and the contract.

The simplest and most temporary parent-child arrangement is the bargin. In the bargaining arrangement, the parent offers the child some reward or withholds some punishment in return for a particular behavior on the part of the child. To illustrate, when the parent offers the child a piece of candy if he will go to bed, this constitutes a bargain, a sort of one-shot arrangement. A child, at least a middle-class child, soon learns to initiate his own bargains at a fairly early age. A child-initiated bargain is illustrated by the following remark, "I'll get undressed and brush my teeth if I can stay up and watch the ball game." Bargains change in their content as the child grows older, but continue to be a viable means of socialization and interfamilial interaction.

A somewhat more complex, and more long-lasting, arrangement is the agreement. In the agreement arrangement, the parents and child agree to abide by certain rules over an indefinite period of time. Agreements with young children often involve the threat of punishment: "If you hit your little brother again you will have to go to your room and miss the cartoons," which can be translated as, "If you agree to leave your little brother alone we agree to let you watch the cartoons." Like bargains, agreements change in their content as the child grows older, but are present at all age stages of parent-child interactions. And whereas bargains appear to predominate at the preschool levels, thereafter, agreements appear to become increasingly more prominent.

The most complex and least explicit parent-child arrangement is the contract. A parent-child contract consists in the unspoken demands made by parents and child upon one another and which determine their mutual expectations. It is the sequence of parent-child contracts which most clearly reveals the developmental nature of parent-child relations. Because contracts are mostly implicit and are seldom verbalized directly, their existence often comes to the surface only in the breach. The mother who says, "Look how they treat me after I worked and slaved for them," reveals her belief in an implicit contract as does the remark of an adolescent, "No matter how much I do around the house, it is never enough."

The contracts written during the major periods of growth—infancy, preschool, childhood proper, and adolescence—all have their own particular characteristics. In addition, the contracts at each age level also appear to have at least three invariant clauses—compensatory demands between parents and child: the responsibility-freedom clause, the achievement-support clause, and the loyalty-commitment clause.

During each of the four major growth periods, the parents demand that the child accept particular responsibilities while the child contracts for complementary freedoms. Parents generally require very little in the way of responsibility of an infant, and the infant, in turn, asks for little in the way of freedom. During the preschool period, however, parents begin to demand that the child take responsibility for feeding and dressing himself, for bowel and bladder control, and to a certain degree for emotional behavior. Children on their side ask for some of the freedoms made possible by their new mobility and motor control. They demand free access to the various rooms of the house, for crossing the street, and for handling tools and mechanical devices. In childhood, the responsibilities required of children become even more diverse, and they are asked to look after their clothing, their rooms, and their younger siblings. Children in their turn, demand new freedoms in the way of staying away from home for longer periods and for going further away from home. Again in adolescence, the contract is once more rewritten as parents request that young people take responsibility in the areas of sex, money, and cars, and the teenager asks for new freedoms in the way of late hours, dress, and friendships.

A similar developmental course is taken with respect to achievement and support. Parents demand little of the infant in the way of achievement other than that he walk and talk at the usual ages. The infant demands some emotional support for these achievements, but such skills are largely self-reinforcing. During the preschool period, however, parents begin to make demands for achievement in the way of bowel and bladder control, linguistic prowess, and social behavior. The child asks that the parent praise his accomplishments and devote time to supervising and instructing him. As the child enters school, parental demands for achievement come to center upon three major areas—academic performance, athletic skill, and social popularity. In return children make complementary demands for material, intellectual, and emotional support for their activities. During adolescence, parents intensify their demands in these areas and young people correspondingly escalate their requests. Because of the prominent monetary demands of this age group, parents of adolescents are sometimes fooled into believing that their offspring are no longer interested in the more psychological forms of support. This is not the case: psychological support from parents is perhaps more necessary during adolescence than at any other time.

Finally, in the area of loyalty and commitment, a developmental progression is equally discernible. Parents usually demand little from the infant in the way of loyalty other than that he respond to them positively and with affection. Likewise, the infant appears only to request that the parents be committed to their caretaking function. As the child grows older the loyalty-commitment clause begins to shift its focus. During the preschool period parents demand that the child maintain his loyalty and affection for them in the face of his exposure to new adults such as nursery school teachers and babysitters. The child, in turn, asks that parents maintain their commitment to him as new children are born into the family and as he makes new and greater demands upon their time and energies. Once the child enters school, parents generally require that loyalties to his family supersede his loyalties to the teacher and peer group. On his part, the child demands that parents give evidence of their commitment to him primarily in terms of the amount of time and interest they devote to his endeavors. In adolescence, this loyalty-commitment clause takes on a still another coloration as parents ask loyalty to their beliefs and values while the young person demands that parents be committed to the beliefs and values which they espouse.

This all too brief sketch of the development of parent-child contracts may, nonetheless, suffice to illustrate both the age-related character of these contracts and the pervasiveness of the clauses regarding responsibility-freedom, achievement-support and loyalty–commitment. Obviously this is a normative schema which holds primarily for intact, middle-class families in

America. While I believe that parent-child contracts are written in families at all socioeconomic levels and in all cultures, the nature of the contracts and the invariant clauses they entail will necessarily vary in importance, if not in kind, for boys and girls and for different socioeconomic and cultural groups.

CONTRACTS AND DELINQUENCY

As I suggested earlier, our knowledge of parent-child contracts often comes from those cases in which the arrangements have gone awry rather than from the cases in which the contracts have been honored. As so often happens, the exceptions illuminate the rule. My own awareness of the importance of parent-child contracts come from my work with middle-class delinquents. Elsewhere (Ch. 15) I have discussed the role of contractual violations in the production of delinquent behavior. My aim here is not to recapitulate that discussion but rather to expand it and to differentiate between two different ways in which parents can exploit children and to describe the different patterns of delinquent behavior which seem to result.

When a parent ignores the contractual obligations imposed by the child's age and demands behaviors which are either above or below the child's actual level of maturity we can speak of *developmental exploitation*. Parents, for example, who over-protect their children have in effect not only demanded inappropriate behaviors but have also offered inappropriate freedoms, supports and commitments. On the other hand, parents who provide freedoms, support, and commitments which are too advanced for the child's level of responsibility, achievement, and loyalty have also failed to meet their contractual obligations and so engage in developmental exploitation. In such cases the parents are often too rigid or too anxious to flexibly adapt their behavior and expectations to the child's constantly changing powers and abilities. It is, therefore, the parents' inability to cope with their child's growth that lies behind their attempts to unduly impede or accelerate his development.

Exploitation, however, can also occur when the reciprocal demands of parent and child are appropriate to the child's age level. In such cases the exploitation results from a quantitative rather than qualitative violation of the contract and which might be called *egocentric exploitation*. We encounter egocentric exploitation when the responsibilities, achievements, and loyalties required of children are appropriate for their age level but are requested in excess of what is reasonable or are demanded when the parent fails to provide the complementary freedoms, supports, and commitments. Such exploitation is egocentric because in these cases the parent sees his or her own needs and problems as more important than those of the children.

In my work with middle-class delinquents I have observed what appears to be a reasonably close relationship between developmental and egocentric exploitation and two phenomenologically different varieties of delinquent behavior. Among middle-class adolescents who get into trouble with the law are those who are clearly emotionally disturbed and have internalized conflicts of long-standing. On a purely descriptive level, these youngsters usually engage in delinquent behavior alone or with someone appreciably older or younger than they are: The act itself is frequently symbolic and bizarre (shooting up a school, molesting young girls). Young people of this kind tend to be authority rather than peer oriented in their moral and social judgment and are, moreover, generally immature in their interests and choice of companions. In cases of this sort I have frequently found a history of developmental exploitation on the part of the parents wherein either the mother or father, and not infrequently both, treat the child as younger or older than his true level of maturity.

In contrast to such neurotic youngsters in whom unconscious feelings of exploitation sometimes find expression in illegal acts, there is a much larger group of young people in whom the feeling of exploitation is quite conscious and clearly tied to parental behavior. Phenomenologically speaking, such adolescents are quite easy to distinguish from the neurotic youths. First of all, they usually get into trouble as a member of a group and seldom do so while acting alone. Their delinquent actions are moreover, conventional in the sense that they steal cars, become truant, act out sexually, or run away from home. They are, in addition, peer rather than authority oriented: they will not, for example, tell on friends whom they see engage in delinquent actions, and they respect peer ethics and standards rather than abstract, adult value systems. Such young people generally have interests and friends appropriate to their age level. Again, in many of the cases of this sort which I have seen, the pattern of parental exploitation has been of the egocentric rather than of the growth variety. Parents of "socialized" adolescents are found either to be demanding behavior in excess of what is reasonable or, on the contrary, to be remiss in fulfilling their part of the parent-child contract.

EXPLOITATION AND THE GENERATIONAL CONFLICT

In the preceding section it was argued that parental exploitation on the part of individual parents could lead to delinquent or neurotic behavior. Exploitation is, however, not only a familial matter; it can be fostered by the moral, political, and socio-economic forces operative at any given time in history. As I suggested earlier, the conflict between adolescents and their parents is probably endemic to our society. But the particular issue which will be the focus of the conflict for most young people is often determined by the general climate of the times. All that one can say with certainty is that one or another of the parent-child contracts will be chosen as a basis of dispute.

This point is nicely illustrated by what has occurred in the last three decades. During the 1950s young people were usually em-ployed and not particularly concerned with social issues. Battles with parents continued to revolve, as they had before WW II, around issues of freedom and responsibility. Cars were expen-sive and not yet numerous, so there were battles about owning and using cars and about moving away from home. Parents were accused of not granting sufficient freedoms while children were regarded as not showing adequate responsibility.

During the sixties a number of events, including the civil rights movement, the Viet Nam War, and awareness of the need for environmental conservation, turned young people away from the issue of freedom and responsibility to the issue of loyalty and commitment. When young people became aware of what was being done to minorities, of the illogicality and im-morality of the Viet Nam War, and of the destruction of the

environment, they felt that adults were abrogating their responsibility to future generations, that they had violated the loyalty–
commitment contract. Hence, young people felt that they did
not need to show loyalty to parental values and beliefs. The
rebellion of the youth of the sixties, with its flouting of adult
values and codes of dress, behavior, and morality was, in part at
least, youth's reaction to what they believed to be adult society's
failure to be committed to their future. If adults were looking out
only for themselves ("don't trust anyone over thirty"), then
youth was not required to be loyal to adult proscriptions.

During the seventies, the focus of the generational conflict has
shifted to still another parent-child contract. With the end of the
Vietnam War and with environmental and conservation programs well underway, youth again has become interested in
getting an education and making a living. But what has happened is that the expanding economy has ceased to expand, at
least at its previous rate. Jobs are difficult to obtain even for
those with college degrees. Once again young people feel exploited, but this time with respect to the achievement-support
clause of the parent-child contract.

What young people said, and are saying, is that they were
made false promises. They were told if they went to school, if
they got good marks, and if they went to college, they would be
assured rewarding jobs and solid incomes. More and more
young people are discovering this is not the case and feel that
they have been cheated and not given the support they had
been promised for their achievements. Not surprisingly many of
these young people are no longer achieving in the domains valued by their parents. They may drive trucks, work in a bakery,
or just travel around for awhile. If parents and society are not
going to provide support in the way of jobs, then they are no
longer going to achieve in parentally and societally approved
directions.

SUMMARY

One way of looking at parent-child interactions is in terms of
momentary bargains, more long-lasting arrangements, and implicit contracts. Contracts, like bargains and agreements, are

give-and-take understandings that are of three kinds. At each stage of development parents require children to: demonstrate responsibility in return for freedom; achieve in return for support; and to be loyal in return for commitment. Although these contracts are broken by all parents and children on occasion, when they are broken consistently they can give rise to one or another form of delinquent behavior.

If parents habitually demand behaviors that are either below or beyond the child's level of competence, we can speak of "developmental exploitation." Such exploitation can result in children who engage in neurotic delinquency (that may involve bizarre behavior). Parents who habitually fail to meet their end of the parent-child contract or who demand that their children give more than what might be reasonably expected can be said to engage in "egocentric exploitation." Young people who have been exploited in this way over a long period of time may engage in "socialized" delinquency wherein several young people are involved.

Contracts operate at the societal as well as at the familial level. At any given time in history youth will revolt against adult authority in order to define itself. But the content of the rebellion will depend upon social historical circumstances that bring one or another contract into prominence. In the fifties youth felt that it was not given the freedoms warranted by its show of responsibility. Then in the sixties youth felt that it had not been shown the commitment to its future justified by its loyalty. In the present decade youth are arguing that they are not being provided the support (namely jobs) that were promised them in return for their academic achievements. Although it is impossible to predict which contract the next generation of young people will find to contest, one can predict that one or another contractual violation will be involved.

8

UNDERSTANDING THE YOUNG ADOLESCENT

Many behaviors that young adolescents engage in are annoying and troublesome to adults who often attribute these behaviors to bad motives. This chapter attempts to explain some familiar adolescent behaviors in terms of the intellectual constructions from which they derive. Understanding these mental constructions enables us to appreciate that many disturbing adolescent behaviors are the product of intellectual immaturity rather than mental depravity.

In a way, this title is somewhat misleading. I once had a professor who asserted that if you *really* understood something you could build it. Unfortunately I am not prepared to provide you with a "do it yourself build a young adolescent kit." What I would like to do is to introduce several ideas that may make some types of annoying and/or perplexing teenage behavior more meaningful and, hopefully, less troublesome.

Before I do that, however, it is necessary to set the stage for these ideas. Not surprisingly, any insights I may have about adolescents are, in large part, borrowed from my mentor, Jean Piaget. However, these insights also have to do with the affective as well as with the cognitive domain. Piaget's work and

Adolescence, 1978, XIII, 127–134.

theory have so often been discussed in connection with thinking, that their implications for feelings have been overlooked. The ideas I want to present have an affective component with respect to both adults and young people.

To understand the kind of affective significance I have in mind, an example of the impact of some of Freud's ideas may be helpful. At the time that Freud introduced his theory of infantile sexuality, puritan notions regarding sex still held sway. Infantile sexuality was regarded as evil and as evidence of original sin. Parents were encouraged to take extreme measures to combat such pleasure-seeking activities as masturbation and thumbsucking. If a child masturbated, the parent was instructed to sew the sleeves of the child's pajamas outside of the bed clothes. And if the child was a thumbsucker, parents were to sew the sleeves of the child's pajamas beneath the bed clothes.

Of course there were always those parents unlucky enough to have a child who both masturbated and sucked his thumb. But those who wrote for parents around the turn of the century were undaunted by such a problem. Showing the ingenuity for which America is famous, they encouraged the parents to sew up the ends of the pajama sleeves so that the pleasure-seeking fingers could never attain their goal! Thanks to Freud, such measures are no longer taken. Today we recognize that these behaviors are normal to most young children who very quickly give them up on their own.

What is apparent in this example is that if we don't understand someone else's behavior, we are likely to attribute the worst possible motives to it. Before we understood that thumbsucking and masturbation were normal developmental characteristics, we assumed them to be the result of evil intentions. The same holds true for many behaviors that young adolescents engage in. Because we don't understand them, we attribute their behavior to bad motives. When we are confronted with such behaviors, we believe they are done purposively to frustrate or infuriate us.

It is at this point that Piaget's work has affective, as well as cognitive, significance. By providing insights into the troubling behaviors of adolescents, Piaget permits us to deal with such behavior more calmly and rationally than we might do otherwise. It enables us to overcome our all too human tendency to attribute the worst of all motives to behavior that we don't understand. Accordingly, I want now to describe some troubling behaviors of young adolescents in the context of the intellectual processes that bring them about.

PSEUDOSTUPIDITY

We are all familiar with Edgar Allen Poe's story of the purloined letter. In that story Poe demonstrates that the obvious is overlooked when we anticipate something to be hidden. We all have a tendency at times to respond to situations at a more complex level than is warranted by the situation. Recall the child who was filling out an application and asked his father, "What does 'sex' mean?" After some embarrassed hesitation, the father went into a detailed explanation of the birds and the bees. At the end the child said, "That was very nice but I still don't know what 'sex' means. Do I put a check by the 'M' or the 'F'?"

While the tendency to interpret situations more complexly than is warranted happens to all of us at times, it is much more common to young adolescents. The obvious often seems to elude them. In trying to find a sock or a shoe or a book, they ignore the obvious places and look into the esoteric ones. Simple decisions as to what dress or slacks to wear are overcomplicated by the inclusion of extraneous concerns such as why and by whom the clothes were bought in the first place. In school, young people often approach subjects at a much too complex level and fail, not because the tasks are too difficult, but because they are too simple.

Such behavior on the part of young adolescents is what I call *pseudostupidity*. It derives from the newly attained thinking capacities made possible by what Piaget calls formal operations. Formal operations, which appear at about the age of eleven or twelve in most young people, bring about a copernican change in young people's thinking. They become capable of holding many variables in mind at the same time, of conceiving ideals and contrary-to-fact propositions, and of comprehending metaphor and simile.

But in the young adolescent, these newly-attained formal operations are not fully under control. The capacity to conceive many different alternatives is not immediately coupled with the ability to assign priorities and to decide which choices are most appropriate. Consequently, young adolescents often appear stupid because they are, in fact, too bright.

They seek complex, devious motives in the behavior of their siblings and parents for the most innocent occurrences. And even the simplest interpersonal exchanges can be complicated by the young adolescent's overeager intellectualization. I recall telling my son Paul, when he was thirteen, that he had some pizza sauce on his cheek. I pointed to the left side of my face to indicate it was on the left side of his, but he insisted on taking my point of view and kept wiping the right side of his face until I reached over and wiped it off for him. He not only took my point of view, but assumed that I had not taken his. Again such *contretemps* derive from the young adolescent's newfound cognitive abilities and not from an early adolescent regression to cretinism.

THE IMAGINARY AUDIENCE

Recently I was having dinner alone at the O'Hare Airport. During the course of the meal I happened to drop my knife which made a horrible clang as it hit the floor. I was sure, at the moment, that everyone else in the restaurant heard the racket and was looking at me thinking, "What a klutz!" In fact, of course, few people heard it and even those who did, did not care. But at the moment I was surrounded by an audience of my own making, an *imaginary audience.*

Everyone has experienced similar moments. But what happens only occasionally in adults is characteristic of the young adolescent because of the formal operations which make it possible for young people to think about other people's thinking. This newfound ability to think about other people's thinking, however, is coupled with an inability to distinguish between what is of interest to others and what is of interest to the self. Since the young adolescent is preoccupied with his or her own self—all the physical and physiological changes going on—he or she assumes that everyone has the same concern. Young people believe that everyone in their vicinity is as preoccupied with their behavior and appearance as they are themselves—they surround themselves with an imaginary audience.

The imaginary audience helps to account for the super-self-consciousness of the young adolescent. When you believe that everyone is watching and evaluating you, you become very self-conscious. In the lunch room, on the bus going home, standing in front of the class, the young adolescent feels that he or she is at the center of everyone's attention. It is a different sort of self-consciousness than that experienced by children. The child is self-conscious about appearances, about clothes which are too big or the wrong style. But the young adolescent is more concerned about personal qualities, traits, physical features, and abilities which are unique to himself. Fantasies of singing before an audience, of making a touchdown before a cheering crowd, of playing a concerto in a concert hall are common imaginary audience fantasies in which the individual is the center of everyone's attention.

Groups of adolescents are amusing in this regard, for when they come together, each young person is an actor to himself and a spectator to everyone else. Sometimes groups of adolescents contrive to create an audience by loud and provocative behavior. Because they fail to appreciate what is of interest to themselves and what is of interest to others, they cannot understand adult annoyance at their behavior.

In general, imaginary audience behavior tends to decline with age, as young people come to recognize that each individual person has his or her own preoccupations. To be sure, all of us occasionally have imaginary audience reactions, but these are usually short-lived, as was my experience in the airport. Imaginary audience behavior in adults is a relic of early adolescence which all of us carry with us and to which we revert on occasion. But we need to recognize that it is pervasive in young adolescents and that it accounts both for their self-consciousness and for their often boorish public behavior.

Before closing this discussion of imaginary audience behavior it might be well to mention one of its more pathological and disturbing forms, namely, vandalism. In destroying property the vandal imagines the audience's reactions—how the teachers and principal will look and feel when they see windows and furniture broken. Vandalism, which seems so irrational, so incomprehensible, and so senseless, becomes less so when we recognize that it is done with audience reaction in mind. The vandal is angry and wants to insure that his audience will be angry too. In committing vandalism, the young person has in mind how the audience will react, and it is the reaction of the imagined audience which motivates the distructive behavior.

THE PERSONAL FABLE

There are other actions which young people engage in which are also perplexing. These actions, however, often appear self-distructive rather than injurious to others. The young girl who gets pregnant or the teenager who experiments with drugs causes us to shake our heads in amazement. They know better, we say; they know the facts of life—how women get pregnant and what the dangers are of playing with addictive drugs. Why, we wonder, are they so intent on harming themselves?

I am sure that the Freudians have a number of answers to this question. But we cognitive types have an answer too, an answer which may complement, rather than contradict, Freudian dynamic interpretation. Consider the young person who believes that he or she is always center stage, at the focus of everyone's attention. It is quite natural under these circumstances to feel that you are someone special and above the usual order of things. Other people will grow old and die but not you; other people will get pregnant but not you; other people will be endangered by drugs but not you. This belief that the individual is special and not subject to the natural laws which pertain to others is what I call the *personal fable*. It is a story that we tell ourselves about ourselves but which isn't true.

The personal fable does have adaptive value. It begins in childhood when youngsters fantasize that they are the favored child, and remnants of it are retained in adulthood where our sense of specialty softens the blows of aging and of career and marital stagnation. But while for the child and the adult the personal fable is in the background, for the young adolescent it is front and center. The self is an all-important preoccupation of the young person who has just attained formal operations, and personal fable attitudes appear in many different forms.

One way the personal fable manifests itself is the failure of the young person to distinguish that which is unique to the self from that which is common to mankind. Indeed, young adolescents makes a characteristic mistake. They assume that what is common to everyone is unique to themselves. And conversely, they assume that what is unique to themselves is common to everyone. These personal fable confusions result in behaviors which are as familiar as they are annoying to parents and teachers.

One example of this personal fable confusion is provided by the daughter who says to her mother, "Mother, you just don't know how it feels to be in love," or a son who says to his father, "You just don't understand how much I need that metal detector." The young person typically believes that his or her feelings or needs are unique, special, and beyond the realm of understanding by others, particularly adults. The confusion here is between feelings (of love and affection) and needs (for material things) which are common to everyone and those feelings and needs which are unique to the self.

The reverse confusion is also familiar. This occurs when the young adolescent feels that his or her personal preoccupation and concern is shared by everyone. A young man may feel that his nose is too long, that everyone knows his nose is too long, and that everyone, naturally, thinks he is as ugly as he thinks he is. Arguing with him about the fact that his nose is not too long and that he is, in fact, good-looking has little impact. His belief in his ugliness is part of his reality and there is little point in arguing with another person's reality.

In such circumstances, it seems to me, the only helpful thing that we can do is accept the young person's reality while also encouraging him to check his version of reality against that of others. When working with delinquent adolescents, for example, I quickly discovered that arguing with them about their parents did no good at all. On the contrary, when I agreed with them and said, "Yes, your parents do sound pretty rotten. Wonder how you got stuck with those bummers," they often came to their parents' defense. My guess is that if you agreed with a nice-looking young man that his nose *was* too long and that everyone did think he was ugly, you would get an interesting reaction.

The personal fable accounts, in part at least, for a variety of perplexing and troubling behaviors exhibited by the young teenager. It helps account for what appears to be self-distructive behavior but in fact results from a belief that the young person is special and shielded from harm. "It can happen to others, not to me." And the personal fable also accounts for the young adolescent's self-deprecating and self-aggrandizing behavior. In general, personal fable behavior begins to diminish as young people begin to develop friendships in which intimacies are shared. Once young people begin to share their personal feelings and thoughts, they discover that they are less unique and special than they thought and the sense of loneliness they have in being special and apart from everyone else also diminishes.

APPARENT HYPOCRISY

In general, hypocrisy has to do with a discrepancy between one's words and one's deeds. Young adolescents are often quite hypocritical in this sense. A young man of my acquaintance, for example, often carries on at great length, and with considerable eloquence, about his brothers going into his room and taking his things. And he berates his father for not taking stronger measures against the culprits. This same young man feels no compunction, however, about waltzing into his father's study and using the typewriter and calculator located there—not to mention playing rock music on his father's stereo set (reserved for classical records). It would not be surprising for the father to feel that the son was a hypocrite—and I did!

But I also realized that this *apparent hypocrisy* is but another by-product of formal operations that have not been fully elaborated. When an adult shows hypocritical behavior, we assume that he or she has the capacity to relate theory to practice and to see the intimate connection between the two. But in early adolescence, the capacity to formulate general principles of behavior is not immediately linked up with specific examples.

The young adolescent is in much the same position as the

preschool child who fails to say "please" or "thank you," despite having been told many times to do so. The rules regulating "please" and "thank you" are general and the child lacks the ability to see the commonality between diverse "please" and "thank you" situations. In the same way, the adolescent is able to conceptualize fairly abstract rules of behavior but lacks the experience to see their relevance to concrete behavior.

To be sure, the personal fable is at work here too. The young person often believes that rules which hold for everyone else fail to hold for him or her. Not surprisingly, adults regard such behavior as self-serving and are upset by it. Again, however, it has to be remembered that such behavior results from intellectual immaturity rather than from defects in moral character.

The apparent hypocrisy of the young adolescent can be observed at the group, as well as at the individual, level. I recall driving out to the airport one Sunday morning when young people were marching in a "Walk for Water." Sponsors agreed to pay a young person a certain amount of money for every mile they walked. The money was to go for testing the water of Lake Ontario and for pollution control. As I drove along the route of the march, I was impressed by how many young people were marching and how very well behaved they all were. I was pleased and began to feel that young people today are not as valueless and materialistic as they have sometimes been described.

It would have been better for my peace of mind and for my assessment of young people had I not returned the next day. As I rode along the route I had taken the day before, I was appalled at the litter: McDonald wrappers and soda and beer cans almost obscured the grass and sidewalks. As I watched the teams of city workers cleaning up the mess, I couldn't help but wonder whether the cost of cleaning up didn't amount to more than was collected. Under the circumstances it would have been easy to tag the young people as hypocrites. Weren't they defacing the environment in the name of walking to protect it?

This adult evaluation is not entirely fair to young people. For the early adolescent, expressing an ideal is tantamount to working for and even attaining it. Young people believe that if they can conceive and express high moral principles, then they have in effect attained them and nothing more in a concrete way needs to be done. Indeed, the pragmatic approach of adults—who believe that ideals have to be worked for and that they cannot be attained at once—is regarded as hypocritical by young people. "Don't trust anyone over thirty" means don't trust anyone who recognizes the practical difficulties involved in realizing ideals in everyday life.

Here, I believe, is a fundamental cause of the "generation gap." The idealism of the adolescent clashes with the pragmatism of the adult. If we recognize, however, that adolescent idealism is healthy and that pragmaticism is too, we can value adolescent idealism without getting upset at their failure to follow through. As young people begin to engage in meaningful work they come to appreciate the need to expend effort toward attaining ideals, and in so doing, they enter the adult estate. But a certain amount of idealism is healthy in adulthood too. We need to help young people become more pragmatic without, at the same time, making them cynical about ideals and moral principles.

SUMMARY

I have tried to show that many early adolescent behaviors that adults attribute to bad motives derive instead from intellectual immaturity as described by Piaget. The pseudostupidity of young people actually reflects a lack of control over newly-attained mental powers. Adolescent self-consciousness, boorishness, and vandalism result from constructing an imaginary audience that monitors their every move and thought. The imaginary audience is a mental construction made possible by the operation of adolescent intelligence. Complementing the imaginary audience is another mental construction, the personal fable, which also gives rise to troublesome behaviors. Young adolescents sometimes behave as if their feelings or thoughts were unique when they are common to every one, and they sometimes assume that their own personal evaluation of themselves is automatically shared by everyone. Finally, adolescent hypocrisy is only apparent and is most often a failure to distinguish between the expression of an ideal and its pragmatic realization.

Piaget, then, has helped us to shift a whole new set of behaviors from the realm of the "bad" to the realm of "behavior typical for this age group." However, I am *not* saying that because these behaviors are "normal" we should ignore or neglect them. What I am suggesting is that if we understand why adolescents sometimes act dumb or boorish or insensitive or hypocritical, we can deal with it calmly and without a sense of moral outrage. If we recognize that these behaviors reflect intellectual immaturity, we can ourselves be more rational in our reactions to young people.

So Piaget's work does have affective significance, but of a very special kind. By helping us to understand the behavior of young adolescents, it enables us to respond rationally rather than emotionally. Freud hoped that his psychology would change us so that "Where id was, there shall ego be." Piaget's psychology helps us to change so that "Where moral indignation was, there shall rational understanding be."

9
THE EARLY YEARS
THE VITAL YEARS

How shall we view early-childhood education and the early years of life—as critical for all later growth and development or as trivial and easily reversible? This chapter describes a more moderate position and suggests that the early years are vital, important in their own right, and need to be valued in and for themselves rather than for what they do or do not portend for the future.

For the past fifteen years, early-childhood education in America has been the subject of considerable controversy and debate. In the early sixties, early-education programs were touted as panaceas for most of the nation's ills, from educational under-achievement to racial prejudice. Today, however, opinion has moved to the other extreme and early-childhood programs at their best are being described as "doing children no harm." Where once the early training programs were regarded as "critical" for children's future growth, some contemporary opinion regards them as "trivial" with respect to later life.

Both these exaggerated positions about the value of early-childhood education are clearly wrong. So too are the correlated opinions about the significance of the early years of life for later

The Journal of the Canadian Association for Young Children, 1977, 3, 14–23.

growth and development. Early-childhood education programs were never meant to produce geniuses, nor are they merely prefunctory. The aim of quality early-childhood education is, and always was, the facilitation and enhancement of the child's growth. Likewise, as far as children are concerned, the early years are neither critical nor trivial; they are simply *vital* in the sense of being a period of active growth and development.

It seems worthwhile, then, in view of these wide swings of professional and public opinion, to reassert the values of early childhood—the vital years. In doing this, however, I want to reverse perspective and to look at early childhood in terms of its contribution to adult thought and feeling, since I believe that these years are as vital to adults as they are to children. Perhaps if we focus upon what we have to learn from children, instead of what we do or do not have to teach them, we can begin to get some recognition from outside the field of the true value of the early-childhood years.

THE VALUE OF DIFFERENCES

One of the most important lessons young children teach is that differences can be valued as well as evaluated. Young children think differently than we do and see the world in other ways than do older children and adults. And children try to make sense out of the world in the best way that they can. A child who says "underbrella" is trying to make sense of his experience in the rain. Such a concept is not wrong, it is just different. Likewise, a child who calls socks and stockings "stocks" has created a concept that encompasses both his father's socks and his mother's stockings.

These examples are commonplace but illustrate how the child's world differs from our own. It differs in other ways as well. Young children believe that events that happen together also cause one another. A teddy bear that a child clings to in a moment of fear and which is associated with a pleasant feeling comes to be regarded as "causing" the child to feel safe. Similarily, the child who asks, "If I eat spaghetti, will I become Italian?" is expressing a very special view of causality. It would be a mistake, however, to call these ideas wrong and try to correct them. They express the child's view of the world at the time and need to be valued as such rather than seen as "errors" that have to be eradicated.

Children also differ from adults in their capacity to process information and stimulation. When my sons were small I once took them to a three-ring circus. During the performance I again and again tried to draw their attention to one or another of the rings where all sorts of exciting activities were going on. In one ring a man was riding a unicycle. In another, a lady in a pink dress was riding standing up on a pony. In another, a juggler had a cane and three silver balls balanced on his nose. But my efforts had no effect. What captured my boys' attention were the men in the aisles who were selling hot dogs, peanuts, and cotton candy. Going home I was sure the whole trip had been a failure. Indeed, I began to doubt my own childhood memories of the circus which I had recalled as a tremendously new and fascinating experience.

Some weeks later, however, the children quite spontaneously began to talk about the circus at the dinner table. To my amazement, they had noticed the man on the unicycle, the lady in the pink dress, and the juggler with the cane. But it took them longer than it did me to process the information. We all have limitations in these regards. After about three paper sessions at a psychological convention I am ready for a fresh brain because the one I have is simply too full to take in any more information. Again, the child's slow pace in processing information is something to appreciate; it is not something to be overcome.

I am not saying that these differences, which are to be valued in their own right, must never be challenged or changed. Most of the ideas children hold about the world that are different from adult conceptions are eventually transformed as the child interacts with the physical world and with other young people. But it is one thing to try to change something that you value and quite another to try to change something for which you have no regard. It is an important lesson that we can learn from children but which also has much broader implications. Consider a policy which tries to change an Indian tribe's eating practices which happen to be nutritionally unsound. A program based on respect for the tribe's cultural investment in age-old eating habits is much more likely to be effective than one that ignores this investment. In the same way, an early-education program which respects the young child's unique view of the world is much more likely to be successful than one which ignores it. Children, no less than adults, are more willing to change if their views are understood and respected than if they are not.

Because young children are far removed from adults in their modes of thinking, they have much to teach us in the domain of valuing differences. If we can look at young children's ideas as interesting and different and not necessarily right or wrong, or bad or good, we have learned something of great value with implications far beyond the early-childhood classroom.

THE VALUE OF GROWTH

Another phenomenon we can learn to value by working with young children is growth and development. Too often, I am afraid, growth and development are seen as simple increases in amount. It is assumed that the child's mind matures as his body does, in quantity not in quality. But this is a false analogy: children's thinking goes through a truly remarkable transformation between the ages of four and six. Attention to these transformations leads to enormous awe at the miracle of human development.

One way of looking at the developmental changes that occur during early childhood is to think of this period as one of *structure formation*. The structures being formed are those which Piaget calls "concrete operations" that take their final form about the age of six or seven. Concrete operations enable school-age children to perform many mental feats they could not perform as young children. They can follow rules imposed from without, reason in syllogistic ways, and understand space, time, and causality in quantitative terms.

These structures are formed during the preschool years in part as a matter of growth, but also as part of the child's own activity. It is in this regard that the miracle of growth becomes apparent. When structures are in the process of formation, there is an intrinsic motivation to enhance this formative process. In effect, during this period children seek out all sorts of stimuli and activities to nourish their growing abilities. Because concrete operations feed on quantity relations, young children seem obsessed with counting, with size, and with "who has more."

Montessori clearly recognized the young child's need for stimuli to nourish his growing mental abilities. And she intuited that these were "sensitive periods" for certain kinds of learning. But she erred in attributing too much to the value of stimuli and too little to the ingenuity of children. Young children need stimuli to nourish their mental abilities, but they can transform almost any and all materials to this end. Indeed, the very effort of bending materials to their own needs provides important nourishment for mental growth. The way in which young children transform pots and pans, boxes, clothespins, and much more into play materials is vivid testament to the motivational force of structures in the process of formation.

One can observe the same growth forces at work in the evolution of children's language. Without formal instruction of any sort, children not only learn to speak and to comprehend, but also to master an elaborate syntax and generative grammar. These abilities, it must be stressed, do not simply unfold: they reflect the child's active involvement with the environment. The child's language skills, like his or her mental abilities, reflect both growth processes and the characteristics of the environment.

One aspect of growth is particularly important to emphasize, namely, individual differences. Children vary tremendously in their rates of growth. Some children seem to have growth hiccups: they change in fits and spurts. Other children change gradually. Rates of growth also vary tremendously. Some children who are behind suddenly catch up quickly, while other children who seem to be ahead suddenly get stalled. Although individual differences are present throughout the life cycle, they are particularly marked during periods of structure formation. That is why it is so dismaying to me to hear of kindergarten programs in which young children are already in lockstep programs. It makes as little sense to begin all children in reading programs at age five as it does to retire all adults at age sixty-five.

Once children attain concrete operations, the intrinsic

motivational forces that directed children to interact with all sorts of materials are dissipated. This means that children are no longer intrinsically motivated to interact with materials and to learn new skills. At the school-age level, children enter a *structure utilization* period when the motivation to use mental abilities is social or derives from the satisfaction of a skill well learned. The concept of the school-aged child intrinsically motivated to learn to read and to do math is a myth that lays heavily on the conscience of teachers. In grade school, children learn to read and do math because the adults to whom they are attached encourage and reward such behavior. Academic achievement is socially, not intrinsically, motivated.

Observing young children then, can teach us great respect for the processes of growth. This does not mean, however, that we should stand by and do nothing. Rather it forces us to ask ourselves just what sort of intervention is appropriate for this phase in the growth cycle. Clearly it is a time for providing children with an environment rich in materials to observe and to manipulate. And it is important to provide children with guidance in the handling and manipulation of some materials. Children do need help in how to hold a gerbil or a kitten. On the other hand, it is not a time to get children to utilize their still incompletely formed mental structures in the attainment of academic skills. In effect such skill training (particularly formal reading instruction) amounts to a kind of pruning during the growth season. Much better to let the child grow a little free and to trim him or her back a bit during the dormant period of middle childhood.

Close observation of children during the early-childhood years can teach us to respect and to admire the processes of growth. Hopefully, too, such observation will make us courteous and thoughtful about our own interventions. But a respect for growth, gleaned from observation of young children, should not stop there. It should extend to people at all stages in life. In a recent study, college students who were treated as elderly began to act senile. If we respect the capacity of people to grow at all age levels, we will continually ask the question: Will this intervention help or hinder this person's growth toward a fuller and richer life? It is a question we have to ask, not only with respect to the children we teach, but also with respect to our own children, our friends, and not least of all, ourselves.

VALUE OF INFORMAL EDUCATION

It is a very human tendency to think in terms of either/or, of absolutes, of blacks and whites. This seems particularly true in the case of education. Somehow many people tend to think of education as a unitary entity, a body of information and practices all of one piece. From this standpoint, there is only one kind of education: the inculcation of skills and information to the young by means of specified practices of which the major one is repetitive drill. This concept of educational homogeneity has probably done early-childhood education more harm than any other single concept.

It is, of course, not true. The idea that there are many different forms of education is one of the most important insights we can glean from the observation of young children. The children described so dramatically by Maria Montessori were engaged in *informal* education, an education in which the materials were self-didactic. Recall Montessori's description of the little girl so involved in her work that she could not be disturbed even by children circling her work table and clapping. Such activity is informal not so much because it is self-didactic as much as because it is *structure forming*.

In effect we have to distinguish activities which nourish the child's emerging cognitive structures from those which require their exercise. An analogy may help here. When a bodily structure such as the heart or lungs, is in the process of formation, the processes in play are quite different from those which operate once the structure is fully formed. The beating of the heart is of a very different order from the processes which led to the heart's construction. In the same way, in education, we have to distinguish between activities related to structure formation and those which are related to structure utilization.

In this discussion I propose to call those activities utilized for the purpose of structure formation *informal education*, whereas those activities that require the utilization of mental activities I propose to call *formal education*. Clearly, the distinctions are not always easy to make. But during a period of rapid mental growth, the emphais has to be upon providing an environment rich in materials capable of nourishing the child's structures in the process of formation. When mental growth is less rapid, it is important to provide children with materials with which to exercise their newly attained mental abilities.

It should be apparent from the foregoing discussion that both informal and formal education are important to the full development of the child. Perhaps it is also apparent that the ratio of informal to formal education has to be different at different levels of development. Informal education, or activities geared to the formation of mental structures, needs to be emphasized during the early-childhood years. Formal education, geared to the utilization of mental structures, needs to be given precedance in the elementary-school years. Likewise, this approach suggests an emphasis upon informal education for early adolescents and upon formal education for young people in middle and late adolescence. *Both* formal and informal education need to be present at all age levels but with developmentally oriented variations in emphasis.

How does one distinguish between formal and informal educational activities? Although this is not always easy to do, there are a few criteria that can help one discriminate. First, those activities that are generated or initiated by the child are likely to be structure-forming activities. Activities suggested or initiated by the teacher are likely to be structure-utilization activities. Secondly, activities at which children persist for long periods without external reward are likely to be structure forming. Those which are undertaken and maintained for external rewards are most likely structure-utilization activities.

What I want to emphasize here is that informal education has to take precedence over formal education in the early-childhood years. I wish I knew some way to shout this from the rooftops so that everyone would hear. The idea that formal education well suited to young children is so widespread in this country that I wonder if we can ever turn the situation around. It stems, or so it seems to be, from the monolithic conception of education as being all of a piece: All education is formal education, and if we are to teach young children, they must be taught in a formal way.

And yet, if we look at young children we see that they learn much more from their self-regulated activities than from teacher-regulated activities. To be sure, the early-childhood educator may introduce an activity such as finger painting, or block building, but the children regulate the activity. In contrast, young children retain little from a program in which they are required to learn by rote or by drill. Such an approach deprives young children of the active manipulation of materials that is so crucial to the formation of their mental structures. Formal education at the preschool level is, to me, a very sad mistake. It assumes that there is only one kind of education and deprives young children of the manipulative experiences best suited to their developmental needs.

VALUES OF BEING HUMAN

At the end of a lecture which I gave to the parents of a suburban school system, I received an interesting question. I was advocating a child-centered approach to discipline and urging parents to try to see things from their childrens' point of view. I was asked if I thought there was such a thing as a "naughty" child. I am afraid I didn't answer the question very well at the time and said something to the effect that I believed children should be reprimanded if they disobeyed rules that have been clearly and explicitly laid down.

If I could answer that question now, having had some time for reflection, I would say that children are human and that they make mistakes for any number of reasons, just as adults do. And I believe that if those mistakes are injurious to others, then children should be reprimanded. To call children "naughty" or "bad" or "hostile" suggests that somehow the child is outside the pale—inhuman and basically evil.

In effect we are all human. And as far as I have been able to determine, no children have committed crimes anywhere of the magnitude or cruelty as those committed by adults. Somehow it is much easier for me to accept the minor mistakes of children as human error than it is the major mistakes of adults. I have to wonder whether our treatment of children as evildoers, rather than as humans who make mistakes, doesn't contribute more to the creation of adult "monsters" than does an understanding heart.

In this regard we have another important lesson to be learned from children. I have seen children fighting so hard that they would have killed each other had they been able to. And I have seen one child bite through another's leather jacket hard enough to break the skin of the wearer's arm. And yet, but a few short hours later the same children are playing peaceably with one another. The hatred and acrimony of the earlier dispute was forgotten. Children do not bear a grudge.

To be sure, children are not practicing forgiveness in the adult sense. But in another sense they are. Children do not bear a grudge because they do not attribute abiding character traits to others. Because they cannot intellectually construct the concept of an "evil" person who is always that way, they accept other children and adults on the basis of current behavior, not on the basis of past aberrations. In a very real sense, children are situationalists, who relate a person's behavior to the immediate situation rather than to abiding personality traits.

Children, in their situationalism, are probably extreme and might do better if occasionally they ascribed more abiding traits to others. But the capacity of young children to forgive, particularly their parents, is a charming and an endearing trait. Adults, in contrast, probably go to the opposite extreme and attribute almost all of an individual's behavior to abiding character tendencies. Accidental statements and actions are immediately ascribed to abiding attitudes and motives.

Perhaps what we can learn from children is to take a more moderate stand. Sometimes behavior upsetting to ourselves can be the result of inattention or carelessness rather than bad motives. Young children do not always knock over their milk "on purpose," and hostile remarks made in conversation can sometimes be inadvertent. Observation of young children can thus help us to recognize that we are all human, that we all make mistakes, and that at least some of these mistakes are unintentional. Young children in their failure to attribute long-

lived bad traits to individuals provide a model of humanness
that could be a very positive example to adults.

SUMMARY

I began this chapter with the observation that public opinion
regarding early childhood and early-childhood education has
swung from viewing this age period as critical to seeing it as
trivial. Both positions are incorrect and fail to do justice to the
early childhood period. Underlying both extreme positions is a
lack of understanding about the nature of young children and
the kinds of educational programs best suited to them. I have
tried here to stress some aspects of early childhood and of
early-childhood education that have relevance for adults and for
education at all age levels. We have much to learn from young
children, and it would be a great loss if we blind ourselves to the
insights this age period can provide.

Somehow we must learn to communicate the value of early
childhood to the public. It is not an easy task, particularly for
early-childhood educators. The reason, paradoxically, stems
from the very same source as our openness to learning from
young children. We in early childhood tend to see children as
active learners who can make choices and take responsibility for
their own learning. Consequently we tend to take a more quiet,
observing, facilitating role with all people. However, while such
a role is beneficial when dealing with children, it may not be
when we are dealing with administrators and legislators.

Indeed, consider the stance of those who view children as
passive, as capable of learning anything at any time if it is only
taught in an appropriate and an honest way. Such people tend
to be active not only in their interactions with children, where
they dominate the educational scene, but also with administrators and with legislators where their views, opinions, and
interests often prevail. Recently, for example, child development legislation in the U.S. was not passed because of an
avalanche of letters to congressmen from a biased, but active
minority.

I believe that it is time that we in early-childhood education
became more active in our dealings with administrators and

legislators. We have to recognize that our facilitative stance with respect to children is ineffective in administrative and political arenas. We must begin to be more active educationally and politically while retaining a certain passivity with respect to children. It is time that those who know and appreciate the values of early childhood and early-childhood education made themselves heard.

As I have tried to indicate here, young children teach us the value of differences, of growth, of informal education, and of humanness. What we need to communicate to the general public is that early childhood is vital not only to children, but to adults as well. The early years are one of our few remaining sources of moral insight. In a very real sense, young children are an endangered species today, and it is only through our efforts that this rich repository of human values has a hope of survival.

THE SCHOOL

10
TEACHER-CHILD CONTRACTS

Contracts emerge in the context of parent-child and teacher-child interactions and are unique to those interactions. For advantaged children there are many continuities between home and school, in particular the fact that advantaged teachers, like advantaged parents, show a reward orientation toward contracts. Disadvantaged children, however, often learn to keep contracts to avoid punishment. This paper discusses some parent-child and teacher-child contracts and how these operate to produce classroom harmony and disharmony.

Every historical period has a particular emphasis or focus that gives it a unique quality and character. In many ways we are perhaps too close to our own era to see it clearly and with perspective. Nonetheless, I would like to venture the opinion that one theme of our era in history is the concern with creativity, with new and emergent phenomena and the processes that have brought them about. We are, I believe, moving rapidly

Commencement address delivered at Bank Street College of Education, June 5, 1970. *School Review*, 1971, 79, 575–589.

away from the reductionist theories which dominated physical, biological, and social science in the nineteenth and early twentieth century, and which have been progressively challenged by the derivations of Einstein's theory of relativity.

Within psychology, the movement away from the reductionism of more complex to more simple phenomena was hampered by the dominance of learning theory in academia and of psychoanalysis in the clinic. Although these two approaches to human behavior were and are often violently opposed to one another, they are alike in holding to the belief that complex human behavior can be best understood either by reducing it to its more elementary components (learning theory) or to its historical and instinctual determinants (psychoanalysis). It is my belief that psychoanalysis and learning theory could co-exist, despite their differences, because of their common belief that human behavior can not be taken at face value but rather has to be seen as something else, something more simple, before it can be understood.

There are many evidences, however, that a new *epigenetic* approach to human behavior is becoming increasingly prominent in modern psychology. The work of Jean Piaget, to illustrate, has emphasized the emergence of new mental structures at successive age levels that cannot be derived from or reduced to the preceding structures in any simple way. Likewise, the work of Erik Erikson has emphasized the emergent strengths and traits that occur at each stage of the life cycle and which again are not reducible to instincts or past history alone. The growing "human potentials" movement is still another illustration of the trends away from reductionism and toward an appreciation of creation and of emergent phenomena in human behavior.

The following discussion of teacher-child contracts stems from this new mode of thinking within psychology. It assumes that interpersonal relations are themselves creations or constructions which cannot be reduced to the personalities, or personal qualities, of those who participate in them. Just as crowd or mob behavior cannot be understood solely in terms of the personalities of the members of the crowd, so the interaction between even two people cannot be understood solely in terms of their individual personalities. To understand their behavior we need also to know what emerges in the process of interaction. This chapter is concerned with one such emergent phenomenon.

INTERPERSONAL CONTRACTS

Let us begin with the assumption that every human interaction presupposes some form of contractual relationship. Take, for example, the most casual encounter between acquaintances. After greetings have been exchanged and polite conversation begins, certain contractual obligations come into play. Each participant agrees to listen to the other and to respond with appropriate signs of interest and concern. That such contracts do exist is immediately obvious when the contract is broken. If participant A is inattentive—looks at the girls passing by, calls participant B by the wrong name, and gives evidence of not having listened to a word that was said—participant B will become angry. He becomes angry because participant A broke the implicit contract between any two people who hold a conversation.

I could give many more examples, but perhaps this one will suffice to suggest the generality of interpersonal contracts. There are certain advantages to looking at human interactions in terms of contracts. One of the most important of these advantages is that it keeps from looking at interpersonal problems in terms of personality. Any man could have been sufficiently preoccupied at some point in his life to violate the conversational contract in the manner of participant A in the example. To attribute A's difficulty with the participant B to A's personality would thus miss the crux of the problem which as to do primarily with a breach of contract and its consequences.

The same, it seems to me, holds true in education. Too often the academic failure of students is attributed to personal qualities such as low intelligence or "laziness" when in fact the problem lies in the relationship between pupil and teacher or child and parents. Likewise the failure of many teachers in the inner city is often attributed, directly or indirectly, to the evilness of their personalities. In fact, however, the culprit is more often a real or imagined breach in the implicit contractual arrangements between teacher and child. So long as we search for "the personality" of the school dropout or of the unsuccessful teacher, we will be seeking something as ephemeral as a will-o-the-wisp. A more productive approach, in my view,† is to look at both school failure and success from the standpoint of the extent to which teachers and children fail to meet their unspoken contractual obligations.

As a general rule, a contract consists of mutual expectations on the part of the contracting parties. In the case of children, these expectations arise in the context of the child's earliest interpersonal relations with his parents and are then generalized and modified as the child's social world expands and he begins to interact with other children and adults. Most economically advantaged children, by the time they enter school, have come to operate on the basis of three more or less general contractual arrangements. These parent-child contracts dictate the initial contractual expectations children have with respect to their teachers.

PARENT-CHILD CONTRACTS

First of all, the economically advantaged child has come to expect that he will be given new freedoms to the extent to which he is willing to accept new responsibilities. The basis for these expectations is laid early in childhood when parents allow the child to do such things as pour his own drinks and handle his own food if he demonstrates he will not spill the drink or throw the food on the floor. As the child grows older, the freedoms and responsibilities change as the child's capacities and skills mature. A preschool child may be allowed to cross the street if he demonstrates that he looks both ways and does not cross until it is safe. In adolescence the same contract holds with different content. The adolescent boy may be allowed to use the car to the extent that he shows skill and care in driving. The young person thus comes to expect that he will be granted freedom to the extent that he demonstrates a reciprocal willingness to assume responsibility.

A second expectation held by the economically advantaged

---

†Contract (or "exchange") theory is widely applied in economics and sociology, but to my knowledge has not yet been employed in the discussion of educational issues.

child is that his achievements will be rewarded with emotional, intellectual and material support. Again, the contents of the achievements and supports change as the child matures, but the nature of the contract remains the same. The young child expects to be rewarded for going to the toilet by himself, for putting on his own clothes, for learning the alphabet, and for being able to count to ten. He is rewarded with hugs and kisses, with verbal approval, and with toys and sweets. At a more advanced age, the child's achievements in school, in extracurricular activities, and in sports are again supported in multiple ways. The child who does well in school is rewarded materially, verbally, and affectively by his parents. Likewise the child's extracurricular activities, such as participating in drama or playing a musical instrument, are supported by the parents' financial investment in coaching and lessons and by parental attendance at plays and recitals. At all age levels, the economically advantaged child comes to expect that his achievements will be rewarded by support from his parents.

Still a third expectation the economically advantaged child brings to school has to do with loyalty and commitment. Generally a child is loyal to his parents, in part at least, because the parents are the basic providers. As the child grows older and more independent, he begins to assess parental commitment in terms of the time parents spend with him. The child tends to apportion his loyalty to parental values and activities according to the extent to which he regards parents as committed to him. This particular contract, and this is true somewhat for the others as well, has something of a sleeper clause. The child who feels he has not received sufficient freedom, support, or commitment may not express his dissatisfaction until adolescence. In part at least, the intensity of the adolescent rebellion may be proportional to the number of real or imagined wrongs that the young person experienced at the hands of parents during childhood.

However that may be, even the kindergarten child from an economically advantaged home comes to school with expectations that he will be given freedom in return for taking responsibility, that he will be given support for his achievements, and that the teacher will be committed to his education to the extent that he is loyal to the values and activities she represents. Let us look now at the expectancies held by the teacher as she enters the classroom.

In a majority of cases, the teacher herself comes from an economically advantaged family and is therefore aware of the contractual expectancies of her pupils and is ready to reciprocate. The relative ease of teaching in suburban schools derives from the fact that teachers and children come into the classroom with reciprocal and matching contractual understandings. The teacher perpetuates the contracts of the parents when, for example, she allows a child the freedom to go to the library on his own when he demonstrates that he will not abuse this privilege. Likewise she rewards academic success with verbal praise and high grades. Finally, she reciprocates the loyalty shown her by her pupils, usually in the form of demonstrations of respect and obedience, with her commitment of much time and energy.

TEACHER-CHILD CONTRACTS

Over and above these contractual expectancies, which both teachers and children carry over from their experiences at home, are additional contracts unique to the school situation. The individual classroom, where the child is among a large group of his peers with a single adult present, perpetuates expectancies originating in the home while engendering three new contractual expectancies emerging out of the uniqueness of the classroom situation.

The first and perhaps most important teacher-child contract has to do with *fairness* and *cooperation*. Children, individually and as a group, expect that teachers will not show favoritism among their charges. They expect that special privileges and desired chores and grades will be distributed to all children on the basis of equality and merit rather than on the basis of personal attributes. In return for teacher fairness, children are willing to grant her the sina qua non for sanity in the classroom, namely, cooperation. (Obviously this contract holds in families, too, but age differences confound the expectancies since they make inequality of treatment—such as different bed times—fair because of inequality of age.)

A second contract that comes into play in the classroom has to do with *competence and respect*. Children think of the teacher as a professional or an expert, like a doctor or dentist, who knows her job. When a teacher comes to class prepared, when she shows she knows how to handle the group and children feel they are learning and growing, they extend their teacher that lovely attitude, respect. On the other hand, if the teacher does not come prepared, either in terms of educational materials or the ability to handle her pupils, she loses the children's respect because of her incompetence.

A final contract, which is a little harder to observe and quantify, involves the teacher's *warmth* on the one hand and children's *affection* on the other. The warm teacher is one who likes and enjoys children. Such a teacher makes the classroom a happy place by her laughter, by her willingness to play as well as to work, and by her tolerance of childish frailties. A warm teacher is not necessarily an overly permissive teacher, and can set limits with firmness but without harshness. Such teachers readily win the affection of their children.

These then are three of the contractual arrangements that emerge in the classroom interactions between teachers and children. The teacher who is fair in her treatment of children wins their cooperation and their cooperation strengthens her willingness to be fair. Likewise the teacher who is prepared, who demonstrates that she is competent to teach, wins the respect of her children and this respect strengthens her sense of being prepared and in control. Finally, the teacher who displays warmth toward her charges wins affection in return. Obviously, to the extent that the teacher is unfair, incompetent, or cold, children will be uncooperative, disrespectful, and hostile. However, it is also true that uncooperative, disrespectful, and hostile children can force a teacher to be unfair, incompetent, and cold. In other words, children as well as teachers can initiate the breach of contract. Let us now look at some familiar classroom offenses from the standpoint of the contract outlined above.

CONTRACTUAL LAPSES BETWEEN ADVANTAGED CHILDREN AND TEACHERS

Consider, for example, the undisciplined child. Such a child often takes liberties such as leaving his seat or the room without taking corresponding responsibility. That is to say, he not only leaves his seat but also bothers other children. Clearly the undisciplined child has violated the freedom-responsibility contract. What often happens then is that the teacher in effect rewrites the contract, which now becomes a freedoms-punishment arrangement. The child is told—and now the teacher verbalizes the new contract because the implicit verbal contract was not conformed to—that if he takes unearned freedoms he will be punished.

An alternative way of handling the situation is to verbalize the freedom-responsibility contract and to offer the undisciplined child desirable freedoms for taking responsibility. Here contract theory touches upon behavior modification procedures. Behavior modification involves rewarding desired behaviors and ignoring undesired ones, just what is urged on the basis of contract theory. In addition, however, contract theory suggests that what is being modified is not simply behavior but rather the expectations as to what that behavior will bring. Contract theory also dictates what *kinds* of rewards should be used to reaffirm the interpersonal contracts that underlie successful human interactions at home, at school, and elsewhere.

Children are, however, not the only ones in the classroom who break contracts; teachers can violate them as well. Consider the uncommitted teacher who is chronically unprepared and unwilling to do more than the absolute minimum amount of work for her children. This lack of commitment is immediately sensed by the children who correspondingly feel that they owe her no loyalty and that her poor teaching warrants no respect. As a result the children, among doing other things, talk and complain about her to their parents and to other teachers. Such a teacher can often be helped by a sympathetic supervisor or principal who sees the problem in contractual terms. Often the teacher in question is unaware of the relationship between her behavior and the pupil reaction. When the matter is discussed in terms of contracts rather than in terms of her character, the teacher is less threatened and more willing to change than if her personality were brought into question.

Many more examples of classroom difficulties could be discussed from the standpoint of contract theory, but the above examples may help to suggest how it can be applied in practical situations wherein teachers and children come with the same general contractual expectations. Before we turn to the situation where there is a marked discrepancy between the expectations of the teacher and the majority of her pupils, a few general comments about teacher-child contracts are in order to avoid misunderstanding.

First of all, of necessity both teachers and children all break their contracts on one occasion or another. By and large this does no permanent damage and the work of the classroom is only temporarily disrupted. When, however, the child or the teacher continually violates the contractual agreements, severe ruptures are bound to occur in the relationships in question. Children who are perpetually disruptive and teachers who are chronically unprepared force a rewriting of the teacher-child contract. In other words, it is only long-standing violations of the contractual obligations between teacher and child that severely disrupt the educational process.

A second aspect of contractual lapses is that ruptures in one contract can be remedied by close adherence to obligations under a different contract. For example, the undisciplined child who is also very loyal and a high achiever will be given more consideration than a child who is both a nuisance and a poor performer in school. Likewise children will tolerate a humorless, overly strict teacher if she is committed to her teaching activities and is assiduously fair with her students. Violations of one aspect of a teacher-child contract can, then, be softened by better-than-average fulfillment of obligations in other domains.

CONTRACTUAL LAPSES BETWEEN DISADVANTAGED CHILDREN AND TEACHERS

So far we have spoken of economically advantaged teachers and children and we need now consider the situation wherein the economically advantaged teacher is confronted with a room full of economically disadvantaged children. Such confrontations are dangerous for two different but related reasons. One reason is that teacher and children come into the classroom with quite different contractual expectations. The second, and more signif-

icant, reason is that both teacher and children are usually unaware that their expectancies are not in agreement with one
another. Under these circumstances, what often happens is that
both teacher and children feel that the contract has been violated. But the blame is not laid to a mutual misunderstanding,
but rather to the prejudice of the teacher (by the children) and to
the stupidity and poor upbringing of the children (by the
teacher). It is my sincere belief that much of the difficulty in
urban schools lies in the contractual violations unwittingly perpetuated by teachers and children in the ghetto school.

By and large, the economically disadvantaged child has also
had experience with responsibility, achievement, and loyalty
contracts. His expectations in these regards are likely to be different from those of a child from an economically more advantaged home. While it is dangerous to generalize, and there are
many exceptions, it is probably fair to say that on the average
children from economically distressed homes are more likely
than children from affluent families to have experienced negative rather than positive contractual arrangements. That is to
say, economically limited parents are more likely than affluent
parents to threaten punishment for lack of responsibility,
achievement, and loyalty. In such families, mothers often work
and fathers may be absent or holding two or more jobs.
Achievement, responsibility, and loyalty on the part of children
are seen as necessities for survival and for moving out of economic distress. It is because the econoically pressured parent
views achievement, responsibility, and loyalty as essential to the
survival of his children that he punishes them if the children fail
to perform appropriately.

When children with a punishment-avoidance orientation toward interpersonal contracts come into a room with a teacher
who has a reward-gaining orientation toward contracts, difficulties are bound to ensue. What often happens is that the children
want to clarify the contract and to discover the nature of the
punishments they will receive for any lack of achievement, responsibility, loyalty, or cooperation. They may, as a consequence, defy the teacher and refuse to work or to cooperate in
any other way. If the teacher does not understand this behavior
as an attempt to clarify the contractual arrangement, she will

interpret it as a flagrant example of uncooperativeness, disrespect, and hostility. Under these circumstances she feels no obligation to fulfill her part of the bargain (to be fair, warm, and prepared) and sees her role as one of merely meting out punishment.

What happens then is that the children are reinforced in their belief that the major reason for achievement, responsibility, loyalty, and cooperation is the avoidance of punishment. School then becomes a game wherein the children try to be as unachieving, irresponsible, disloyal, and uncooperative as possible without incurring punishment. The teacher, for her part, gives up her intention to teach and becomes, in many ways, the same kind of adult the children have already experienced, namely one who urges them to achieve and to be responsible and cooperative, not for positive rewards but rather to avoid punishment. The avoidance of punishment is, of course, the least effective of all educational motivations.

How can this vicious cycle be broken? It can be broken, it seems to me, if the teacher is cognizant of the expectations her children bring to class. In the case of economically disadvantaged children, the teacher's first task is to teach them the terms of the contractual relationship. She needs to emphasize the positive rewards of achievement, responsibility, and cooperation. Instead of punishing children for their misbehavior, she must reward their positive achievements. Again, the aim is not simply to modify behavior but to modify the child's understanding of the contractual arrangements.

Let me give you a concrete example. Several years ago I taught second grade children for one full semester. Most of the children were black and from the ghetto. In the beginning, the children did a great deal of testing to see what kind of punishment I would mete out. While I indicated that I did not approve of misbehavior, I took an accepting, somewhat joking attitude toward it. Moreover, I tried to introduce positive rewards for cooperation and achievement.

During reading, for example, everyone was given some special function. Two children, a boy and a girl, were "chooser's" who chose the children who were to read next. Another child was the "keeper of the place" and helped the other children who had lost their place in the story. Another child was "keeper of the page" and wrote the page we were reading on the board. A rather big, husky young man was chosen as the "shusher" to keep the whispering children from disrupting the reading. A good reader was chosen as the "helper" who helped children who were having difficulty reading particular words. Other children were chosen as "keepers of the books" and distributed and collected the books. Still other children were chosen to erase the board and to straighten the desks. Not only were the children kept busy, but they were learning that rewards, in the sense of special recognition, could be the result of achievement and cooperation.

While I do not suggest that my practice be adopted as a model, I do think the general principle is valid. The teacher's first task is to clarify the contractual expectations between herself and her children. If there is a discrepancy, then what she needs to do is to try to teach the children, or the child, what the nature of the contract is. And since positive rewards are much more effective than negative ones, teacher-child contracts based on rewards rather than punishments for achievement, responsibility, loyalty, and cooperation are likely to be more effective in furthering the educational process.

CONCLUSION

To be sure, the clarification of teacher-child contracts will not resolve all educational ills, many of which derive from other sources. What contract theory can do is give the teacher another perspective on her relationships with her pupils and a new way to handle interpersonal difficulties. The advantage of the contractual model for looking at the teacher-child relationship is that it gets away from the idea of "blaming" anyone for the difficulty and hence away from arousing defensive and educationally non-productive attitudes and behaviors.

It should be said that this way of looking at classroom interaction is a schema derived from my own experience in working with children and teachers. It would, however, be relatively easy to test out in an experimental way. For example, the schema suggests that teachers who were rated highest in competence, fairness, and warmth by their pupils or by independent observers in the classroom would have the most cooperative, respectful, and affectionate pupils. Likewise, one would predict that an extremely competent teacher who was also unfair would be rated less highly in respect than an equally competent teacher who was also fair. These are but some of the predictions which the contract approach to teacher-child contracts suggests. Whether or not this particular schema wins research support, however, I do believe that we need a theory which will look at teacher-child interactions as a new phenomenon which is not entirely reducible to the personalities and backgrounds of the participants.

SUMMARY

Teacher-child interactions are epigenetic in the sense that they emerge only in the presence of teachers and children. These interactions are governed by reciprocal rules and expectancies that are here called contracts. Contracts operate at home as well as at school and make the transition from home to school easy if teachers and children share the same contractual understanding, but can make it difficult if they do not.

At home, advantaged children learn that responsibility is the price of freedom, that achievement is the price of support, and that loyalty is the price of commitment. In effect, they learn that there are positive rewards for behaving in a socialized way. At school the interaction between teachers and children brings about new contractual understandings. Children learn to exchange cooperation for teacher fairness, to exchange respect for teacher competence, and to exchange affection for teacher warmth. Many classroom difficulties can be interpreted as breaches or lapses in these contracts.

Disadvantaged children often learn the same contracts as advantaged children but in a negative way. That is, children learn that if they don't achieve, if they are not responsible, and if they don't show loyalty, they will be punished. At school they expect a similar contractual arrangement. Conflicts between disadvantaged children and advantaged teachers occur because the children are seeking to avoid punishment while the teacher is seeking to proffer rewards.

It is concluded that looking at teacher-children interactions from a contract perspective can help us understand and remediate classroom difficulties without "blaming" either teachers or children.

11
HUMANIZING THE CURRICULUM

Three contemporary educational approaches for reconciling each child's need for self-realization with his or her need for social adaptation are described and evaluated in this chapter.

Educational programs, of whatever kind, must meet two basic yet contradictory human needs. One is the need for *individuality*, the striving of each person to be unique and to realize his or her full powers and potentials. The other need is for human *sociality:* to relate to other people and to subordinate one's personal inclinations for the benefit of others. In the broad sense, any educational program meeting one or both of these basic human needs could be said to be "humanistic." But in a narrower sense, humanistic education might be limited to those programs providing equal opportunity for the realization of human individuality *and* human sociality. In this chapter, I will discuss humanizing the curriculum in the broad sense and will outline three contemporary approaches to curriculum reform. These approaches can be distinguished by their desire to *add to, subtract from,* or *transform* existing curricula.

Childhood Education, 1977, 53, 179–182.

ADDING TO THE CURRICULUM

When an existing curriculum is regarded as not allowing sufficient opportunity for human individuality, new curricula may be added to the old. In recent years, for example, a variety of so-called *affective* curricula have been proposed and have been added to the school program at different levels. Innovations, such as classroom meetings, value clarification, and moral discussions, have been implemented to help individual children understand themselves and others better. Many of these activities are indeed useful to teachers and to children. They provide an additional set of tools and procedures to be used in educational practice and thus enrich the teachers' armamentarium.

But the affective curricula can present problems as well. They can, and often do, perpetuate the same errors that are imbedded in the traditional school curricula. That is to say, some aspects of the school curricula are too difficult for the cognitive level of the children to whom they are directed. Social studies offer a case in point. As commonly pursued, teaching first-grade children about the "cultures" of the world may be a futile exercise. How can one expect very young children, who cannot fully comprehend the ethnic differences in their own community, to understand the world of Australian aborigines?

Many of the affective curricula used in the schools repeat the error of demanding tasks beyond children's level of cognitive ability. Most children of elementary school age, for example, are not really able to rank their feelings from "1 to 5"; nor are they always able to reflect upon their own thinking in ways that permit assigning clear priorities to what they want most or least. My eleven-year-old son, for example, has changed his mind five times about what he wants for his upcoming birthday. Children's priorities are shifting and transient rather than abiding or lasting. Is it worthwhile for children to go through the procedure of assigning priorities that are momentary at best?

Moreover, if the affective curricula are simply added to the school curricula, they can become a burden to teachers. Teachers already have so much of the school curricula to "cover," and so little time to cover it, that the imposition of additional curricula can hinder rather than help them. And some affective curricula can backfire. A child whose parent has just died, or whose parents have just been divorced, may be deeply embarrassed or hurt by being required to reveal publicly what are legitimately personal feelings. Affective curricula that involve procedures geared to the child's level of understanding and meshed with the school curriculum can be beneficial. But if these methods and procedures are simply foisted upon the teacher as additional educational "objectives," the result may be just the opposite of what was intended.

In my opinion, the whole concept of affective education is based on a false premise. Affective education may lead to the inference that cognitive and affective processes are distinct and have to be addressed separately. But good teaching is always affective *and* cognitive, and the successful teacher is always "half ham and half egghead." Teachers' enthusiasm for the subject matter and their respect and good feeling for children provide all the affective education a child needs in the school setting.

SUBTRACTING FROM THE CURRICULUM

A somewhat different approach to curriculum reform is taken when current educational practices are regarded as not sufficiently geared to socialization—to the acquisition of tool skills required for the successful adaptation of the individual to society. The *back to basics* movement reflects this approach. It argues that too much attention in education has been paid to individuality and too little to sociality. Accordingly, those who advocate back to basics often want to substract those aspects of the educational program that speak to human individuality, namely, the arts. Presumably, the less time spent on the arts, the more time available to spend on the fundamentals.

The back to basics movement is based on another false premise but of a different order than that which gave rise to affective education. It is that if children today are doing more poorly in academic subjects than they were a decade ago, then this fact *must* be due to our having been too soft and too permissive. The widely reported drop in SAT scores over the last fifteen years has most often been interpreted in this way. Critics have argued that the drop was caused by schools' not requiring children to read and write enough and by young people's wasting time by watching television.

The belief that decline in performance must be a result of sloth is, of course, deeply imbedded in our Puritan heritage. But in this case it happens to be wrong. Just about fifteen years ago, the "new" curricula, stimulated by Sputnik, hit the schools. These curricula, created by university professors, were up-to-date—with the "new math" and "psycholinguistic" reading programs, not to mention a plethora of science programs. These curricula were much more hard-nosed than the child-centered "progressive" materials that preceded them. Far from being "soft" on children, the new curricula were more difficult than many others in recent American educational history. The drop in SAT scores then may reflect the fact that the new curricula were too *hard* rather than too easy.

Some evidence favors this last statement. For example, although SAT scores in math and reading went down, scores in creativity and analytic skills went up—just what one would expect if the new curricula were too difficult. In dealing with curricula beyond their comprehension, children have to be both analytical (to figure out what is going on) and creative (to find their own ways to deal with the curriculum demands). In addition, some of the curricula materials now coming out which reflect the back to basics philosophy are easier and more child-centered than much of the curricula of the sixties!

The back to basics movement, then, while it starts from a false premise, has had some positive effects. Under the guise of "getting tougher" on children, the new curricula have in fact often gotten easier. And this change is all to the good. Some recent data from the National Assessment of Academic Achievement indicates that reading scores for 9-year-olds have gone up over the last four years, but that this finding does not hold for 13- or 17-year-olds. My interpretation is that these 9-year-old children are products of the new curricula, which are child-centered and concrete.

What is more negative in the back to basics movement in elementary education is the de-emphasis of the arts. If the aim of the back to basics movement is to enhance socialization, then de-emphasizing the arts is a sad mistake. The arts are social as well as individual. In a very real sense the arts are a basic means of social communication, the way individuals can share a sense of beauty. By de-emphasizing the arts, the back to basics movement deprives children of a prime means of reconciling the conflicting demands of human sociality and human individuality.

TRANSFORMING THE CURRICULUM

When the curriculum is regarded as not paying sufficient heed to the integration of human individuality and sociality, a different approach to curriculum reform is taken. Those who see the curriculum in this way want neither to add to nor to substract from it but rather to *transform* it in such a way that the needs for individuality and sociality can be brought into harmony. To my mind, this approach to education is best exemplified by the *informal* or *open* education movement. In many ways the open-education movement is a modern version of Dewey's "project" method, in which social adaptation and pupil interest were both taken into account in choosing curriculum materials.

The open-education approach to curriculum is too well-known to be reviewed in detail here. Such programs allow for pupil choice and allow children to take responsibility for their own learning. The emphasis is upon teacher-made rather than commercial materials, and the teaching is heavily experience-based. The school day is loosely organized into large blocks of time rather than into closely-clocked intervals. Great emphasis is accorded the arts as an integral part of education, particularly in providing means of expression. In all these ways, open education tries to transform the curriculum so that the needs for individuality and sociality reinforce and complement, rather than conflict with, one another.

But the open-education approach to curriculum is not without its own problems. Good informal instruction is hard work, and the teacher has constantly to fight against the temptation to institutionalize innovation. And nothing is more deadly to children than an overdone idea. The opposite danger must be faced as well. I have seen children engaged in truly innovative science or math activities that were both interesting and fun. But these activities were not integrated with the rest of the school program, and neither I nor the children could see where they were leading. In the same way, I have seen children so conditioned to asking questions that they no longer bothered to wait for the answers. Done well, open education can be a model of truly humanistic education; done poorly, it can be a disaster.

SUMMARY

In this chapter I have briefly outlined three contemporary approaches to humanizing the curriculum, to reconciling each person's need for individuality and sociality. Each of the approaches—affective education, back to basics, and open education—speaks to an important need or needs. Each approach has limitations as well as virtues. We find, then, no one single answer to humanizing the curriculum. How we approach the task will depend upon our world view and our priorities with regard to human individuality and sociality. And children can adapt to and profit from each of these approaches, so long as each is taken with the children in mind. In the broadest sense, humanizing the curriculum means putting child need and child ability into the curriculum equation.

12
OBSERVING CLASSROOM FRAMES

One way of looking at classroom interactions is from the standpoint of the rules, expectancies, and understandings that occur in repetitive social situations and which are called frames. This chapter reviews a number of different facets of frame behavior including spoiled frames, frame clashes, frame switches, curriculum frames, and how to go about changing frame behavior.

Recently I visited a kindergarten classroom in which a student teacher was reading to a small group of boys. About halfway through the story the boys began to fidget, poke one another, and look about the room. They had lost interest in the story. But the student persisted because, from his (adult) standpoint, it was important to finish the story. The behavior of the boys finally registered on him, however, and he had the good sense to stop reading and allow the boys to move into the play area where they usually went at that time in the morning.

In this situation one might say that the student was not very aware of children's attending behavior and needed to acquire skills in this area of observation. But there is another way of looking at such interactions which provides useful insights about classroom behaviors. Reading a book to children is a repetitive classroom situation which encompasses a set of implicit

Instructor, 1977, LXXXVI, 78–90.

rules, expectancies, and understandings. The rules are that the teacher will pick an interesting book, that the children will listen quietly, and that the activity will be terminated when either the time is up or the teacher or the children have had enough for the day. Such repetitive social situations, with their own implicit rules, expectancies, and understandings, have been called *frames*. From a frame perspective one might describe the foregoing episode as one in which the student was indoctrinated into the rules of the "reading a book to children frame."

SPOILED FRAMES

One of the values of observing classroom frames is that such frames have emotional rhythms which, if broken, bring about reactive behavior that can be anticipated. Consider a familiar situation. In a "question and answer" frame, a child gives an incorrect answer to the teacher's question. The teacher, as all of us do occasionally, slips and dismisses the answer with "No, that's not it at all; please pay attention." Later in the day, the child whose answer was so abruptly dismissed "accidently" knocks over the teacher's coffee cup. Knocking over the coffee cup completes the broken emotional frame.

When teachers are asking questions and children are attempting to answer them, a set of rules, expectancies, and understandings are in play. The rules are that the children will hold up their hands if they think they know the answer and that the teacher will be fair in calling upon different children. In addition, it is also expected that the teacher will be gentle to those children who do not know the right answer. The emotional rhythm is that children are expecting a reward and so have a happy expectation. If they give the right answer or if the teacher says they were close or made a good try, the expectancy is satisfied and the rhythm is completed. But if it is not and the child is put down, a different frame is instituted, that of anger and revenge. It may not even be conscious, but the emotional pattern operates until the cycle is complete and the anger is appeased.

Clearly, many different frames operate in the classroom. There are situational frames—such as hall, library, playground, lunchroom, principal's office. There are also person frames, such as those engendered by the "visitor" or by the "substitute" or by the "new child in class." And there are activity frames, such as group discussion, reading, science, and math. In each case the frames have their own rules, expectancies, understandings, and emotional cycle or rhythm. Often, the best clues to the dynamics of a frame occurs when a frame rule is broken or an expectancy is violated or an understanding is ignored. When this happens, there is often new behavior that is designed to re-establish the frame. Consider the following examples of "spoiled" frames and the restitutive actions.

A familiar frame that is often spoiled centers around choosing children to perform special duties, such as erasing the board or distributing snacks. The basic frame rule in this activity is that the teacher will be fair and that the children will abide by his or her decision. If, inadvertently, the teacher chooses a particular child twice in a row, or more often than the others, there is an immediate outcry. A frame rule has been broken and children will not be satisfied until some restitutive action—such as choosing a different child—has been taken.

Sometimes, of course, it is children who spoil the frame. During a reading or math activity, a particular child may get up and wander about the room making noise and distracting the others. Some of the other children may complain to the teacher or to the disrupting child. Group pressure may suffice to settle the child down, or the teacher may have to intervene and reassert the frame rules. Some children, usually those with emotional problems, may not subordinate themselves to the frame rules. Obeying the rules insures group acceptance; breaking them insures group rejection, and some children seem to invite such rejection. One sure way to be rejected is to break frame rules.

In general, when frame rules, expectancies, or understandings are broken, some reparation activity occurs that is designed to restore the frame. There are a variety of reasons why frames are spoiled. I have illustrated two reasons— oversight on the part of the teacher and boredom or emotional problems on the part of the child. But frame rules can also be spoiled for many other reasons including forgetting and deliberate malice.

FRAME CLASHES

When a child comes from a cultural background different from the teacher and the majority of children, he or she may not know the rules of the majority frames, just as the teacher and other children may not understand the child's frame. In such instances we have what might be called *frame clashes*. I saw an example of such a frame clash in a New Mexico school where there were a number of Navaho children. Navaho children are taught not to look into adults' eyes when they are talking to them. But the Anglo frame for talking is that you *do* look the other person in the eye when you speak. What I witnessed was the teacher insisting that a Navaho child look her in the eyes when she spoke to him. The bewildered child did not know what to do.

I believe that many of the difficulties middle-class teachers have with minority children derive from such frame clashes where the participants do not understand one another's frames. Black children, for example, use their bodies as well as language to communicate. Much of the touching, jostling, and nudging black children engage in is not hostile or intrusive but rather an intricate form of nonverbal communication. White people frame their communications largely with words and facial expressions. It is easy, therefore, for white teachers to misinterpret black children's behavior, and for black children to misinterpret a white teacher's communication (from their standpoint, lack of body language signals emotional stiffness and uptightness).

Even children from the same socioeconomic background and ethnic group may experience frame clashes if they come to school from another state or even from a different part of the city. Every classroom quickly establishes a number of frames that are unique to it and to which a new child is not privy. To take a simple example, a new child might get up when the bell rings at the end of the day. But the teacher may have set up a frame such that children do not leave until he or she says that they may.

FRAME SWITCHES

A somewhat different frame difficulty arises when the child is unable to switch from one frame to another. I witnessed such an instance in a kindergarten class, where the teacher was talking to a boy named George who was modelling in clay. She turned to the class and said "Children, put your things away and line up at the door; it is time to go outside." But George continued to work on his clay as if he had not heard. The teacher said "George, didn't you hear what I said?" To which he replied, "Yes, but I'm not children."

In effect, the teacher was requiring a frame switch which was beyond the child's level of cognitive ability. To be able to think of himself as a unique person, George, and as a non-unique member of a class of people, children, the child requires the mental abilities that Piaget calls concrete operations, which most children do not fully acquire until the age of six or seven. It should be said, however, that even a five-year-old can think of himself as a unique person, or as a member of a group. What he cannot do is think of himself as both at the same time. The problem in this instance is that the transition from being called "George" to being called "children" was too abrupt for the child to handle.

This example illustrates the phenomenon of frame *switching*. Many different frame switches occur throughout a school day. There are, for example, situation switches as children move from one room to another or to the cafeteria or to the playground. Likewise there are activity switches, as children move from reading to math or from group to individual activities. There are also people frame switches, where someone else comes in to take over the class or the children move to another room where a different teacher presides.

Teachers develop different tactics for facilitating frame switches, but the general rule is to prepare children for a frame switch well in advance. And, the younger the children, the more preparation time they require to make a frame switch. One kindergarten teacher, who was formerly an airline stewardess, prepared her children for going home by saying "We are going to land in ten minutes. I want papers, crayons, and books stowed for landing."

Whatever technique the teacher uses, he or she is well-advised to prepare children to make a frame switch, whether the switch is of situation, activity, or person. It is easy to tell the difference between an experienced and an inexperienced teacher by observing how they handle frame switches. The inexperienced teacher does not prepare the children in advance to make a frame switch. An experienced teacher, in contrast, puts much thought and effort into helping children make transitions. The difference shows in the ease with which children move from one activity to another during the day.

CURRICULUM FRAMES

So far we have talked about interpersonal frames, those governing children in different situations, activities, and with different people. But frames can also operate with respect to a child's interaction with curriculum materials. Some of these *curriculum frames* can be transient while others are more abiding. An example of a transient curriculum frame is the child who has been doing well in a subject, but who one day seems to draw a blank and cannot understand what is going on. The next day he or she may do well again. Abiding curriculum frames occur, say, when a child routinely expects to do poorly in math.

Transient curriculum frames often result from false assumptions about what is going on. For example, suppose a child is learning "to carry" in math. But in the workbook there are some problems which do not require the child to carry. The child, however, assumes that numbers should be carried on all the problems (a "carry" frame) and proceeds to carry where no carrying is called for. In examining the child's paper the teacher may have some trouble understanding the nature of the child's error. In this situation we again have a frame-switch problem. The workbook introduces a "carrying" frame and then, without sufficient notice, switches to a "no carrying needed" frame. Without sufficient warning or notice, children may make errors, not because they do not understand the task, but rather because they do not understand the frame that is in play. In learning activities, as in interpersonal activities, children need to be made aware of frame switches.

When we turn to abiding curriculum frames, we encounter a serious problem with negative frames. Most children have positive abiding frames, anticipate that they will succeed, and are not set back by momentary failure. Some children, however, have negative abiding frames and are sure that they will never learn the subject matter in question. The sad thing is that each failure reinforces the frame while successes do not have a counterbalancing effect. This occurs because the child interprets the success as a failure in order to complete the emotional rhythm of the frame.

Clearly there are many children who encounter difficulty in learning because of slowness, some physical defect, or emotional disturbance. While negative frames may not be the *cause* of the difficulty for these children, they certainly compound the difficulty. For other children, negative curriculum frames may be the central factor in their school failure. In dealing with children who have abiding learning difficulties, we always have to deal with abiding curriculum frames as well.

CHANGING FRAMES

This brings us to the last frame issue we will discuss here, namely, how one goes about changing frames. To my mind, frames are the basic units of socialization, and children become social beings to the extent that they learn societal frames. Once frames are established, they are difficult to change because, in order to reestablish the emotional equilibrum of the frame, contrary data is interpreted to fit the frame and does not serve to change or to alter it.

My own feeling is that trying to change frames head on is not very useful or successful. Telling a child he "can do it" when he believes that he can't does not help him very much. A better procedure, it seems to me, is to teach the child a new frame that will compete with or contradict the other one. Success frames can be added by giving the child materials he or she can succeed with. Such children also need to build up new interpersonal frames wherein they can feel good about themselves as people.

A child has a chance of overcoming some of his or her negative curriculum frames if he or she re-enters the classroom arena with new positive achievement and interpersonal frames.

SUMMARY

I have suggested that much classroom behavior can be observed as frames, as repetitive social situations that entail their own rules, expectancies, understandings, and emotional rhythms. Frames are useful because they help us to understand behavior that otherwise might not make sense. There are person, situation, and activity frames. When frame rules are broken, children engage in behavior designed to reestablish the frame. Frames may be spoiled inadvertently, intentionally, through ignorance, and through lack of mental ability. Frame switching is often a problem with children and they usually benefit from preparation. Changing frames is difficult and it is usually easier to build in new competing frames than it is to change old ones.

13
PIAGET AND MONTESSORI IN THE CLASSROOM

Classroom practice, of whatever variety, presupposes a particular conception of the child. In this chapter, four components of Piaget's and Montessori's conception of the child are described together with examples of the sort of educational practice that follows from them.

Recently I had the opportunity to visit and to observe in two different Montessori classrooms. One was not at all like the other. In one room, several boys were making a train with the blocks usually used for the pink tower.* The teacher observed this but did not intervene since the boys were clearly involved in what they were doing. Something similar occurred in the other classroom, but in this instance the teacher did get involved. She showed the boys how to build a tower with the blocks and said that unless they were prepared to build a tower they should not take out the blocks.

I begin with this example because it illustrates the close connection between our conceptions of the child and of learning

---

Invited address, American Montessori Association meeting, Philadelphia, 1977.

*The blocks are size-graded and are usually used to build a tower with the largest block on the bottom and successively smaller ones on top. The blocks are pink and the "pink tower" is used to teach size relationships.

and classroom practice. From a theoretical point of view, one could find ample justification for both teacher behaviors. If one assumes that a child can learn from his or her own self-directed activity, then it makes sense to allow children to manipulate materials in their own way. On the other hand, if one assumes that certain types of activity are more beneficial than others, then it makes sense to encourage children to engage in those activities. In short, every classroom practice presupposes a particular conception about children and about how children learn. Any discussion of classroom applications of Piaget must then be presented in the context of his conceptions of the child and of learning. In this chapter I will present four aspects of Piaget's conception of the child, and will relate these to aspects of Montessori's theory and practice.

THE CHILD AS CAPABLE
OF SELF-REGULATION

Piaget, like Montessori, believes that the child has the potential for self-regulated activity, for using materials in such a way as to nourish his or her intellectual growth. Usually such activity has direction, organization, and self-correction in relation to the materials. But it is important to realize that self-regulational activity is a *potential* form of activity and not necessarily a spontaneous one. Whether or not a child can engage in self-regulated activity will depend upon his or her past history and upon the environmental circumstances.

The analogy is to the "norm of reaction" of biology. Some species of insects, for example, have a genetic potential for eye color from red to black. Which eye color is actually realized will depend upon the particular environment in which the insect develops. Something similar occurs in man. A child with a potential for asthma, for example, may show no symptoms if he or she is born and grows up in Arizona. Symptoms may appear, however, if that person moves to the East coast.

In the same way, the child has a range of potential behaviors only some of which are self-regulational. Children can, for example, engage in behavior which is self-distructive or other-destructive. A child who builds pink towers long after he or she has the basic concepts, may be engaging in defensive avoidance actions. And a child who uses the blocks as missiles to hurl at his neighbors is also not engaging in self-regulational behavior. In short, for Piaget as for Montessori, self-regulational activity is but one of many possible activities children can engage in.

To my mind, Montessori's genius was best shown in her understanding that certain environments—prepared environments—were necessary to relase and encourage self-regulational behavior. The materials she discovered and invented for encouraging self-regulated behavior are excellent models for all educational materials. But the environment itself may not be sufficient to encourage self-regulational behavior in all children. Some children come to us from environments which either discouraged self-regulation or which permitted children too much freedom. Such children may not be able to profit from the new environment as long as they continue to expect it to be like the one from which they came.

We come back now to my initial example of the two teachers, in which I assumed that the children in both classrooms were capable of self-regulation in the setting and therefore that teacher response was a function of differential conceptions of the child. But it could be that the same teacher behaved in both ways with different children. That is to say, some children may need more help in attaining self-regulation than others.

If we have a conception of children as *potentially* self-regulational, this permits a range of teacher interventions geared to the child's behavior. A different way of saying this is that self-regulation is in part learned behavior. Some children come to us who have much experience with self-regulation and are ready to take responsibility for their own learning. Others need help in these regards and, at least initially, require considerable teacher direction.

I learned this lesson the hard way. When we first started the Mt. Hope School,† I wanted the children to immediately begin setting their own work schedules. They could not. They came from settings where decisions were made for them and they were not ready to take responsibility for their own learning. We now start the year very tightly indeed. The children even have to ask to go to the toilet or for a drink of water. Gradually we

---

†A lab school at the University of Rochester.

ease up as the children begin to internalize the rules and the controls. By the end of the year they are working very much on their own.

I think it is no disparagement to Montessori to say that she may have overemphasized the "nature" of the child and under-emphasized the significance of social conditioning. In effect, modern biology and genetics teach us that there is not one but many child "natures." Which one appears will depend upon the environment in which the child is reared. What Montessori rec-ognized as the "nature" of the child was, in fact, perhaps the most fortunate and healthy expression of the child's norm of reaction.

A child's behavior, then, is not a fixed expression of the genome but can change with new environmental circumstances. This has both positive and negative implications. It means that children can learn self-regulation, but it also means that they can unlearn it. There are limits in these regards, but much reversa-bility is possible. I hope, after this discussion, that you will not think I'm an environmentalist. I continue to believe in the im-portance of the child's genetic endowment. But I also recognize that what aspects of that endowment are realized depend a great deal upon the particular environment in which the child is reared.

Please understand that I am not saying that young children's time in school should be spent exclusively on self-regulational activities. There are many things that children need to learn in other ways. Words, but not the concepts that they represent, are learned by imitation, and this is valuable. And rules for social interaction must also be learned by other than self-regulated activities. In short, there are several different modes of learning available to the young child and all of them are useful and im-portant. I do believe, however, that in young children, self-regulated activities should be emphasized to a greater extent than other learning modes.

THE CHILD AS A COGNITIVE ALIEN

A second component of the Piagetian conception of the child is that he or she is a *cognitive alien*. Young children do not think in the same way that adults do and this is not wrong of bad, it is simply different or alien. Let me illustrate. Recently one of the guinea pigs at the Mt. Hope school died. The children were quite upset and the teacher helped them deal with this by having a funeral and burying it in a shady part of the lawn. Many of the children (seven to nine years of age) wrote notes to the animal hoping that it would not be lonely and that it would hurry back. They lacked the adult concept of death. Their concept of death, as a temporary state, is foreign to us, just as our idea of death as a permanent termination is foreign to them.

The recognition that the child is a cognitive alien carries with it the implication that the child also speaks a foreign language. Certainly children use English words and grammar, but they also create their own words (like calling an attache case "Daddy's work purse," or a moustache a "mouth brow") and use words in ways different from adults. In this regard the child is also a linguistic alien. Like the person from a foreign land, children make mistakes with language and interpret it differently than we do as adults.

From a practical classroom point of view the concept of the child as a cognitive and linguistic alien has important implications. Basically, it means that *we cannot take anything for granted insofar as the child's knowledge or understanding is concerned.* In my experience this is the single most difficult rule for teachers to acquire and, once acquired, to abide by. Failure to follow this rule is, perhaps, the most important cause of ineffective teaching practice.

These strong statements warrant some amplification and elaboration. In no way do I mean that we underestimate or undervalue the child's very real intellectual abilities or knowledge. Nor do I mean that we have to talk down to children or be condescending to them. Quite the contrary. What I do mean is that we relate to children as we would to intelligent individuals from another country. We have to work hard to find out what they know, how they understand things, in order to establish a basis of communication and to learn where to begin instruction.

I should say, parenthetically, that the tendency to take for granted what the learner knows is not limited to early-childhood and primary school teachers. I have sat in on many college courses where the professors were teaching economics or statistics or something else, and where I was sure they were assuming too much about the knowledge and understanding of their students. The failure of the teacher to assess the level of understanding before proceeeding with instruction amounts to a kind of *instructional egocentrism,* the impulse to teach material without ascertaining whether the student is ready or prepared to learn that material.

The idea of finding out where children are before intervening is as much Montessori as it is Piaget. What impresses me most when I read Montessori, perhaps because it reflects my own bias, is how she always puts the child first and method second. Our natural tendency, however, seems to be to reverse those priorities. Again and again we put the need for new methods ahead of careful observation of the child. *The price of effective teaching is constant observation.* If we can learn to put children first and method second, then we can't take children's knowledge and understanding for granted.

THE CHILD AS A LOGICAL THINKER

If the first task of the teacher is to observe children, then how does one go about this in ways that are useful for instruction? It is in this domain that another component of Piaget's conception of the child, namely, the child as a *logical thinker,* can be of service. Basically, in observing young children we can take our cues from Montessori and our theory from Piaget. That is to say, Montessori observed children as they interacted with the materials she made available, and she gave accurate and detailed descriptions of the sequences children followed in using materials. For example, she observed that children wrote before they read and that they read posters and signs before they read books. She used these observations as clues to instructional sequences.

While Piaget's conception of children's thinking cannot add to the observations that Montessori made nor to those made by the contemporary teacher, his conception can provide a fuller understanding of the behavior observed. It is no disparagement of Montessori to say that, to use a linguistic analogy, she observed *surface structure*, the observable sequence of behaviors, whereas Piaget has sought for the *deep structures*, the underlying logical abilities which determine and regulate the child's surface behavior.

Let me give just a couple of examples of how deep structure interacts with surface structure to illustrate what a Piagetian analysis might add to a Montessorian observation. Consider the child who is working on a form-sorting task, but arranges the different forms into a circle rather than into separate piles, one for each type of form. How shall we interpret that behavior? Montessori might conclude, correctly, that such arrangements precede correct sorting. Piaget would add that correct sorting presupposes mental operations which allow the child to see that one and the same form can be both an individual form and a member of a class of forms. The child who builds a "graphic collection" rather than a series of piles of different forms reflects his or her confusion about the one and the many—the circle made of smaller forms is both a circle and a collection of forms.

What the deep-structure understanding of classroom observations permits, and what the surface-structure observations do not, is *generalization*. If we know that a child cannot sort according to form, then we know that he or she has a general problem with the one and with the many that is likely to appear in a variety of different ways that can be anticipated. For example, if this child was asked to say whether there were more boys or more children in the room, we could predict that he would say that "there are more boys than girls." The deep structure problem here is exactly the same as in sorting according to form. In both instances the child has to see that one thing can belong to more than one class. In sorting according to form, the child has to see that a "red square" is both red and square. In classifying, the child has to grasp that a person can be classed as a child or as a boy or girl.

One more example: Suppose a child successfully constructs a pink tower with all the blocks in a correct size arrangement. What does this tell us about his or her understanding of size relations? On the surface it tells us that he or she grasps *ordinal number*, the sort of numbers assigned to cakes at a bake sale or to photographs at an exhibition. The numbers suggest rank orders, but say nothing about the distance between ranks. The photograph ranked first is not twice as good as the photograph ranked second. Rankings tell us nothing about the extent of difference between the items ranked.

Suppose, however, that we want to know whether the child also has a conception of *interval number,* of numbers used to designate not only ranks but also equal differences between ranks. This is important because the concept of interval number is a necessary prerequisite to all mathematical computation—addition and subtraction involve a concept of interval number. To test for interval number, we need to have some additional materials, namely, a set of blocks intermediate in size to those of the pink tower. That is to say, when this second set of blocks is added, the tower will be twice as high because each new block fits between two of the older ones.

After a child has completed the first pink tower we give him the second set and ask that these new blocks be added to make a higher tower. Many children who succeed with the initial pink tower will not be able to add the additional blocks. To add additional blocks to an existing tower requires that they recognize that one and the same block is both smaller than the one below it and bigger than the one above it. Children who cannot add the blocks lack an interval concept of number and probably should not be involved in computational activities. A child who correctly adds the new blocks shows that he or she has an interval concept of number and hence is ready for numerical computation.

In these examples I have tried to show how Montessori's emphasis upon observing the child interacting with materials can be coupled with a Piagetian analysis of the deep structure of the behavior. The value of the deep-structure analysis is that it permits generalization beyond the immediate task and suggests the presence or absence of abilities required to interact with a variety of different materials. Accordingly, Piaget's conception of the child as a logical thinker adds a new dimension to the kinds of observations of children that Montessori taught us to make.

One other point needs to be made in connection with the deep-structure analysis of behavior. As I have suggested in the case of number, one concept can be understood at many dif-

ferent levels. Unfortunately, our language does not always provide designations for these levels of conceptualization. The term
"reading" is a good example. Being able to recognize a few
words by sight requires quite different abilities than does reading with decoding and comprehension. And yet often both activities are called "reading" with no attempt to distinguish the
different processes which underly these apparently similar surface behaviors.

As in the case of the pink tower, the ability to "read" a few
words can reflect quite different underlying skills and capacities.
In looking at behavior from a Piagetian perspective, therefore, it
is always necessary to ask about the structures that lie beneath
the behavior. And it also means that we be cautious with language and that we qualify our descriptions by saying that the
child has "ordinal" number or a "sight" vocabulary rather than
that he "knows his numbers and can read." Many controversies
in education are empty because the contenders on either side are
using the same words for different skills or different words for
the same skill.

THE CHILD AS EMOTIONAL COUNTRYMAN

The fourth component of the Piagetian conception of the child
has to do with the affective domain. If the child is a cognitive
alien, he or she is also an *emotional countryman*. Put differently,
children are least like us in their thoughts and most like us in
their feelings. Unfortunately we often turn that premise on its
head, both with adult aliens and with children. Tales of the
"ugly American" abroad are legendary. People behave abroad
as they never would at home. One reason is that Americans
abroad assume that foreigners don't have the same sort of feelings and needs that people have here. On the cognitive plane,
however, they assume that everyone does, or should, know
English and should immediately understand their questions and
demands.

Something similar happens when adults deal with children.
They often expect children to understand all that they say, but
not to share the same feelings. I recall once taking my son to a
pediatrician for a shot. The doctor came in, and without saying a

word, looked at the chart and began to swab Paul's arm prepa-
ratory to an injection. I intervened and told him that he could
not give the boy a shot without talking to him and explaining
what it was he was doing. He then took the trouble to talk to
Paul and to explain why he was giving the shot and that it
would only hurt for a minute. I am sure that if he were giving a
shot to an adult he would have said more than he did to my then
six-year-old son.

In education, this tendency to view children's feelings as different from our own appears in a rather peculiar way. It appears
as a separation between thinking and feeling or between cognitive and affective education. We currently have a number of
"affective curricula," such as value clarification and reality
therapy.

Whatever the original intentions of the proponents of these
programs, in fact they are often understood as something which
is appended to existing curricula. The implication is that when
children are working at reading or at math or at social studies
they are engaged in cognitive activities, but when they are engaged in, say, value clarification they are involved in affective
activities. For children, then, we assume that there is a sharp
separation between thinking activities and feeling activities.

But we make no such separation for ourselves. How many
times have we told ourselves or others, "I'm too emotionally
involved to be objective about this situation," which is to say our
thinking is colored by our emotions. The close relation between
feeling and thought is presented to us anywhere we want to
look. We feel good if we solve a problem or finish a job and feel
badly when we do not. What moves us on to do boring work is
often the anticipation of the pleasure to be produced by the end
result of the work, whether it be money or a product.

There is no need to belabor the point. From a Piagetian
perspective, thinking and feeling are simply different facets of
the same ongoing behavior. The child who is busy reading or
writing in the classroom is not an encapsulated thinking
machine. Far from it. Children work at school mainly for social
rewards, at least initially. But in any case, thinking is always
motivated by and hence always tied to feelings. We need to be

careful then not to infer, because people speak of affective education, that thinking and feeling are separate processes.

If we turn now to the implications of this view for classroom instruction, we can see the basic error of so-called affective education programs. Too often, as I have said, affective education is seen as adding a *new* and *different* mode of interaction. But if thinking always involves feelings, then all teacher-pupil interactions involve feelings, and our aim should be to change *existing* interactions in a positive direction.

In my opinion, therefore, we really do not need special affective education programs. What we do need are pre-service and in-service teacher training programs designed to give teachers a better understanding of child development. Affective education programs were devised because, apparently, there were unhappy or unresolved feelings in the classroom. But don't such feelings arise, in part at least, from the teacher's conception of the child? If a teacher sees children as like him or her in thinking but not in feeling, how will that teacher treat children?

Well, if the children do not learn what they are supposed to learn, the teacher will assume that they are not motivated or that they are dumb or that they are learning disabled. The responsibility for learning is laid at the brain of the child because the teacher assumes that the child understands what it is he has to do and is refusing, for one or another reason, to do it. This attitude is communicated to children and they react with frustration and anger. At the heart of the affective interaction between teacher and child, then, is the teacher's conception of the child.

That is why I believe that affective education as a separate entity is unnecessary. Consider the teacher who assumes that children are like him or her in feelings but not in thoughts, and who believes that children are self-regulational. Such a teacher will not take for granted what a child knows and will make efforts to understand where the child is and what materials are appropriate. The teacher who operates in this way communicates feelings of warmth, of caring, and of respect for the young person. And young people respond with similar feelings. In my view, such a teacher-child relationship is the most worthwhile affective education of all.

To be sure, there are useful techniques and procedures teachers can learn to use in certain conflict situations. But these techniques and procedures will always be transformed by the teacher's conception of the child. The best way to train teachers to be more effective with children is not by giving them more procedures and techniques but, rather, by giving them new insights as to how children think and feel. It is the teacher's conception of the child which, in the end, determines the nature of the teacher-child affective interaction. That is why, to my mind, acquiring the Piagetian conception of the child is as important for teachers as acquiring specific methods and techniques.

SUMMARY

I have suggested that classroom practice is always dictated by the conception of the child held by the teacher. It was necessary, therefore, to couple a comparison of Montessorian and Piagetian-based classroom practices with a description of the Piagetian conception of the child. From this standpoint the child is viewed, first, as *potentially self-regulational*—capable of learning in a directed, organized, and self-correcting way. But self-regulated behavior is but one of the many possible expressions of child "nature," and the extent to which a child engages in it is, in part at least, a matter of environmental input.

From a Piagetian standpoint the child is also a *cognitive alien*, a person who thinks differently than we do and who uses language in a different way. This view of children makes it imperative that we take nothing for granted as to what children know and understand and that we take the time to find out where children are before we commence instruction. Finding out where children are can be helped by a third component of the Piagetian conception of the child, namely, the child as a *logical thinker*. Piaget's description of the logical structures presupposed by different tasks adds a new dimension to classroom observation and allows generalization and prediction from one type of behavior to another.

Finally, Piaget suggests that children are *emotional countrymen* in the sense that they share the same needs and feelings that we do. Because feelings are but the other side of cognitions, we do not need affective curricula which are added on to existing curricula. Rather what is needed, if there are problems, are *changes* in the way teachers interact with children. If teachers learn to see children as potentially self-regulational, as requiring effort to be understood, as being logical thinkers, and as possessing adultlike feelings and needs, then the teacher will convey an attitude of respect toward the children. This attitude of respect will be reciprocated by the children who will learn to respect others as well as themselves. This is the best affective education of all.

In conclusion, then, the way in which we work with young people is always colored by our implicit assumptions about the nature of children. I am not advocating that everyone adopt the Piagetian position in this regard since diversity is beneficial to growth. I am saying that if someone decides he wants to apply Piagetian principles in the classroom, he must first understand and accept the conception of the child from which those principles derive.

14

WE CAN TEACH READING BETTER

Sometimes it is difficult for us, as adults, to fully appreciate the difficulties children encounter in acquiring skills that we have already mastered. This is particularly true in the case of reading. Some of the logical and motivational problems young people encounter in beginning and advanced reading are discussed in this chapter.

Can we do a better job of teaching children to read? Yes, I believe we can if we take into consideration how their minds develop. To illustrate this point, I'd first like to discuss beginning reading and the child's concept of letters and then move on to how children who are more advanced readers use their accumulated storehouse of knowledge to give meaning to the printed word.

BEGINNING READING

A basic error in much beginning-reading instruction centers about the concept of the letter, which is, in many ways, the basic unit of reading. To the adult, the letter appears as a discrete object which is a conventional representation of one or more sounds. But the letter as adults see it is not the letter known to the beginning reader.

Today's Education, 1975, *64*, 34–38.

As Piaget points out, children and adults see the world in different ways. The well-known "conservation" experiments are a case in point. Most adults are amazed to discover that young children believe that changing the shape of a piece of clay will change the *amount*.

This amazement suggests that most adults assume that children see the world in much the same way they do. They make this assumption because they are unable to recall or reconstruct the course of their own cognitive growth. This phenomenon, the loss of awareness of their own part in the construction of reality, is what Piaget means by *externalization*.

In general, externalization serves a useful adaptive purpose and allows the individual to operate more effectively in the environment. *Externalization* only becomes a problem when we try to teach the young; that is, when we try to present material that we have already mastered. In that case, we as adults, who have conceptualized and externalized many facets of the world, have trouble appreciating the difficulties children encounter in their attempts at making sense out of their world.

From the child's point of view, the concept of the letter poses many of the same problems as concepts of number, space, and time. before the age of six or seven, most children lack a true unit or number concept because they cannot coordinate two dimensions or relationships simultaneously. Such coordinations are basic to the construction of a unit concept because a unit is, by definition, both like every other unit and different from it in its order of enumeration.

In many ways, children's problems in understanding the concept of a letter are even more difficult than those they encounter in constructing the concept of a number. Like numbers, letters have an ordinal property, which is their position in the alphabet. And letters also have a cardinal property, which is their name (A, B, C, etc.) and which each letter shares with all other letters of the same name (all B's are B).

Letters are even more complicated than numbers because, in addition to their ordinal and cardinal properties, they also have phonic contextual properties. One letter can stand for one or more sounds and one sound can be represented by different letters. This is analogous to grasping that a child can be both a child and a boy at the same time. To understand phonics, a child must be able to perform logical operations on letters and sounds to understand all their possible combinations.

Many different kinds of evidence support this logical analysis of the difficulties in early reading. Written languages that are more regularly phonetic than English are apparently much easier to learn to read than is English. In these alphabets (such as Japanese), the logical difficulties are removed because one and the same element always has one and the same sound regardless of its position or phonetic context.

In addition to this cultural evidence, various collaborators and I have published a body of research which also points to the logical difficulties inherent in beginning reading. We have shown that reading achievement and logical ability are highly correlated; that average readers are superior in logical ability to slow readers of comparable overall intelligence; and that training children in logical skills has a significant positive effect upon some aspects of reading achievement.

All these findings are consistent with the view that the letter is a complex logical construction that requires the ability to reason, which Piaget attributes to the appearance of *concrete operations* for its full elaboration. To test this hypothesis in still another way, a collaborator and I have begun, in the last few years, to look at the cognitive competencies of children who read early; that is, children who read before they enter kindergarten. One of our hypotheses was that if reading involves concrete operations, which are usually attained at age six to seven, then early readers should show these abilities at an early age. In addition to assessing children's cognitive abilities, we were also interested in the personal-social characteristics of these children and in the educational-emotional climate that prevails in their homes.

We have now completed two studies of early readers, one with sixteen early readers and another with thirty-eight. In both studies, the early readers were matched with a control group of non-early-reading children on such things as age, sex, IQ, and socioeconomic status. All the children were given a large battery of achievement and intelligence tests as well as personality and creativity tests. In addition, their parents were interviewed. In both studies, we found that early-reading children were superior to non-early-reading children on Piagetian measures of conservation. They were also better on certain psycholinguistic measures, such as sound blending.

It is important to emphasize, however, that cognitive construction of a letter is only one of the requirements for successful early reading. Our parent interview data suggest that a rich background of early experience with spoken and written language provided by homes where books and magazines are plentiful and where parents frequently read to the children is also important for successful reading. In addition, social motivation to please significant adults appears to be a necessary, if not a sufficient, factor in giving zest to the dull and unrewarding process of learning to read.

In talking about cognitive development and early reading, it is therefore important to avoid the two extremes that are sometimes advocated when cognitive "readiness" is discussed. One extreme is the effort to train children of preschool age in cognitive abilities they have not yet attained. I have seen no evidence that such early intervention has any lasting effectiveness. But the alternative extreme, allowing children to learn in their own time and in their own way, is also unwarranted. Children need instruction in learning to read, but only after they have demonstrated the requisite cognitive abilities.

In summary, there appear to me to be at least four requirements for successful beginning reading: a language-rich environment, attachment to adults who model and reward reading behavior, attainment of concrete operations, and an instructional program. All other things being equal, namely, that the children in question are of at least average intellectual ability and are free of serious emotional or physical handicaps, the presence of these four characteristics should ensure that most children will learn to read with reasonable ease and considerable enjoyment.

ADVANCED READING

Let us now turn to advanced reading and the construction of meaning. It has already been suggested that the intellectual processes involved in beginning reading are analogous to those involved in concept formation. A child who is learning to read has to coordinate similarities and differences and construct concepts of letters which are both like every other letter in that they represent sounds but different in the specific sounds they stand for.

Concept formation also involves inferential processes, and these can be observed in beginning reading as well. Many errors in beginning reading, such as reading *where* for *when*, are inferential errors rather than discrimination errors. The child is inferring the whole from observing the part (the *wh*). Such inferential errors are high-level cognitive errors inasmuch as the child is doing what more advanced and accomplished readers do. These processes should be encouraged by temporarily sacrificing accuracy for fluency. Experience indicates that once children are fluent readers, they can always correct for accuracy, but an overconcern with accuracy can retard fluent reading.

When concept formation and inferential aspects of reading have become automatized and children can recognize printed words with ease and rapidity, they enter the phase of rapid silent reading. In silent reading, the major cognitive task is no longer concept formation and inference but rather interpretation, the construction of meaning. In constructing meanings, children have to relate representations—in this case, printed words—with their own concepts and ideas. Success in interpretation, or comprehension, depends upon a different set of characteristics than learning to read, and these are described below.

VISUAL INDEPENDENCE

Rapid silent reading and comprehension require, at the very outset, that the visual-verbal system become independent of the sensory motor system. Rapid reading involves fewer motor fixations and wider visual segments of scanning, and this in turn means less motor involvement and more conceptual inferential activity. In effect, in rapid silent reading, the brain does more work and the eyes do less. We have some recent evidence that supports the importance of visual independence in advanced reading.

In one study we found that while tactile discrimination of sandpaper letters was positively related to reading achievement among beginning readers, it was negatively correlated with reading achievement among advanced readers. Apparently, motoric identification and discrimination of letters, as advocated by Fernald and Montessori, is beneficial in the beginning phases of learning to read, but the coordination of visual and motor processes has to be given up if more rapid reading is to develop.

Put more concretely, it is helpful for beginning readers to use their fingers as markers to direct attention and exploration of printed matter. But once they become advanced readers, using a finger as a marker would impede reading. Rapid reading requires a certain independence from the tactile motor system.

Some recent data on perceptual exploration and memory demonstrate this growth of visual independence in another way. Children at different age levels (from age four through age eight) were shown large cards upon which were pasted sixteen pictures of familiar objects. On one card, the pictures were pasted in an upright position whereas on another, the same pictures were pasted at 180 degrees from their normal position.

At each age level, half the children viewed the cards with the pictures upright, while the other half viewed the cards with the pictures at 180 degrees to the upright. Each child had two tasks: to name each of the figures on the cards and then to recall as many of the figures as possible once the cards were turned over.

Among young children (age four to five), there was a significant difference in recall scores in favor of the figures rotated 180 degrees. This difference, however, diminishes as children grow older and disappears at about the age of eight or nine. A similar pattern appears to hold true for children with limited hearing, who use finger spelling and vocalization in communication. These data suggest that in young children the motoric system is still tied to the visual system. In identifying the 180-degree figures, these children may implicitly try to "right" the figures, which produces increased motoric involvement.

Our hypothesis is that the increased motoric involvement and attendant heightened attention account for the superior memory for upside-down figures in young children. Among older children, in whom identification can occur without implicit motoric "righting," this attentional advantage for upside-down figures is no longer present.

There is thus some direct as well as indirect evidence that rapid, silent reading involves the attainment of considerable visual independence from the tactile motor system. Apparently this occurs even among children with limited hearing who use finger spelling as well as vocalization to communicate. Indeed, among older deaf children, the rapidity with which they finger spell and read finger spelling is very much like rapid reading. Visual independence amounts to a kind of automatization of the visual aspect of reading in which the visual scanning process is relatively independent of tactile motor input.

MEANING CONSTRUCTION

A second prerequisite to advanced silent reading is facility in meaning construction. From a cognitive development point of view, reading comprehension is not a passive process of decoding written symbols. On the contrary, it must be regarded as a constructive activity analogous to creative writing.

The point is that meaning is not inherent in written or spoken words, but rather that the words are given meaning by readers or listeners who interpret them within their own storehouse of knowledge. Silent readers give meaning to the words they read by relating these to the conceptual system they have constructed in the course of their development. The richness of meaning they derive from their reading will depend both upon the quality of the material they are reading and the breadth and depth of their conceptual understanding. Satisfaction in reading often derives, in part at least, from the degree of fit between the material being read and the conceptual level of the reader.

A recent doctoral dissertation supports this position. The author chose thirty-three books that had won Newbery awards for excellence. She then determined how frequently each had been checked out over the preceding three-year period in a number of libraries. On the basis of these data, she selected the five most frequently chosen books and the five least frequently chosen books from her original list. She then analyzed the books from the standpoint of their congruence with the conceptual systems of the age group for which they were written. She found that the five most frequently chosen books were congruent with the cognitive level of the children for whom they were written, while this was not true for the five least chosen books. Apparently, other things being equal, children prefer stories which have meaning within their own cognitive organization.

Comprehension, or the construction of meanings, is also helped by the children's own efforts at giving meaning to (i.e., representing) their own experiences. The more opportunity children have to experience the effort and satisfaction of representing their own thoughts verbally and otherwise, the better prepared they will be for interpreting the representations of others.

In contemporary education, children do not do enough creative and expository writing. But I believe that the more children write, the more they will get from their reading. Writing and reading are reciprocal processes of meaning construction which mutually reinforce one another.

RECEPTIVE DISCIPLINE

A third prerequisite to effective silent reading seems at first to be a contradiction to what has just been said about the reader being an active participant in the process. This prerequisite is that the reader have a receptive attitude, a willingness to respond to the representations of others. Good readers, like good listeners, have to be simultaneously passive (receptive to the representations of others) and active (interpreting those representations within their own conceptual framework).

Many young people are poor readers for the same reason that they are poor listeners: they are more interested in representing their own thoughts and ideas than they are in interpreting the thoughts and ideas of others. They lack what might be called receptive discipline.

Young people demonstrate receptive discipline when they attend fully to the representations of others and resist following their own free associations and tangents. Many so-called slow readers have problems with receptive discipline and not with rapid reading.

Receptive discipline is not innate and can be facilitated and taught. Text material that is of interest to readers and at their level of competence facilitates a receptive attitude. Another way to encourage receptive discipline is to have goals for nonrecreational reading. When young people (or adults for that matter) know that they will have to present what they have read to a group, they are likely to be more attentive than if this were not so.

These are but a few examples of techniques that might be employed to encourage receptive discipline. Whatever techniques are used to instill it, receptive discipline seems to be an important ingredient for successful reading comprehension.

SUMMARY

Some of the difficulties young people encounter in acquiring beginning and advanced reading skills are discussed in this chapter. At the beginning reading level, children must construct the concept of a letter that, in English, requires the logical abilities that most children do not attain until the ages of six or seven. In addition to the requisite logical abilities, learning to read also presupposes a language-rich environment, parents who reward and model reading behavior, and a program of instruction.

Once young people move into rapid silent reading, new cognitive problems must be mastered. First, the visual system must become divorced from the motor system in reading, and visual decoding must become rapid and automatic. Once this happens, children can focus fully upon comprehension which involves the construction of meaning, the relation between representations and concepts. Finally, particularly in early adolescence, young people must acquire "receptive discipline," the ability to take in what they are reading before they answer, criticize, or reject the material.

At all levels of development, therefore, reading is a complex skill that requires many different cognitive abilities.

THE CLINIC

15
MIDDLE-CLASS DELINQUENCY

Middle-class delinquency, as it is conceptualized here, is a result of parental exploitation. The chapter describes some forms of parental exploitation together with some usual forms of middle-cass delinquency. A concluding discussion suggests that middle-class delinquency is much more anti-familial than it is antisocial and that this must be taken account of in any efforts at treatment or remediation.

The research literature on juvenile delinquency is already vast and continues to grow at an increasing pace (Quay, 1965). By and large, however, this research tends to deal with lower-class children living in slum areas of large cities. Much less is known about the young people from suburban, middle-class homes who also get into trouble with the law.

Some writers (Giffin, Johnson, and Litin, 1954; Johnson and Burke, 1955) have suggested that delinquent youngsters from "respectable homes" are acting out the parents' repressed anti-social impulses and are subtly encouraged by the parents in this regard. Although this explanation probably holds true in a certain number of cases, my own experience (as consulting psychologist to a suburban juvenile court) suggests that the vicari-

Mental Hygiene, 1967, *51*, 80–84.

THE CLINIC

ous satisfaction of antisocial needs is but one of many forms of parental exploitation that can lead to delinquent behavior on the part of children. In what follows I shall elaborate on some of the forms of parental exploitation and some of the possible adolescent reactions to such exploitation.

Before proceeding, however, it is necessary to distinguish among three quite distinct groups of middle-class delinquents. There are, first of all, those adolescents whose delinquency is a direct manifestation of a long-standing emotional disturbance and for whom the remedy is usually psychiatric rather than probationary. Secondly, there are those young people who come before the court almost by accident—quite often for pulling some prank that turned out to be more serious than they had anticipated—and who are seldom, if ever, adjudicated for a second time. By far the largest group, however, are those adolescents who get into trouble more or less regularly and who have a series of past charges filed against them. Although these young people do not appear to have serious internalized conflicts, they are usually in quite open conflict with their parents.

It is with the etiology of delinquent behavior in this third group of young people that the present paper is primarily concerned.

THE CONTRACT

The concept of parental exploitation makes sense only if there is an implicit contract between parents and their offspring. In middle-class families such a contract does exist. For their part, the parents agree to provide for the physical and emotional well-being of their children, who, in return, agree to abide by the norms of middle-class society. Although minor infractions of this contract on the part of both parents and children are to be found in most middle-class families, they tend to be temporary. For the most part, the contract is honored on both sides.

This appears not to be true in the families of the delinquent children under discussion. If one inquires deeply enough into the family relationships of these children, one finds that the contract has been broken by one or both parents *over a prolonged period of time*. More particularly, that part of the contract is broken which ensures that the parent will take responsibility for the emotional well-being of his child. What one finds in these cases is that the parent not only puts his own needs before those of the child, but, more significantly, attempts to use the child as an instrument in the satisfaction of those needs. It is because the parent violates the contract with his child while demanding that the child hold to his end of the bargain that such violations are legitimately called "parental exploitation."

FORMS OF PARENTAL EXPLOITATION

Although particular instances of parental exploitation are almost infinite in their variety, they can nonetheless be grouped under a few reasonably comprehensive headings. We have already noted that the *vicarious satisfaction of parental needs* is one frequent form of exploitation.

This form of exploitation is illustrated by a case in which a sexually frustrated mother encouraged her daughter to act out sexually. When the daughter returned from a date, the mother would demand a kiss-by-kiss description of the affair and end by calling the girl a tramp. When I saw the girl, who was being adjudicated for sexual vagrancy, she told me, "I have the name so I might as well play the role." When she left my office, her mother, who had been waiting outside, teasingly asked her how far she had gotten with the "cute psychologist."

A somewhat different form of parental exploitation might be called *ego bolstering*. In this category fall those parents who demand academic or athletic achievement far beyond what the young person is able, or has the capacity, to produce. This form of exploitation has an element of vicarious satisfaction in it, but the dominant affect seems to be the need to bolster flagging parental self-esteem. Although it is normal to want to take pride in one's child's achievements, it becomes pathologic when the parents' own needs to bask in reflected glory take precedence over the emotional welfare of the child.

A somewhat different variety of this form of exploitation is illustrated by the father who encouraged his 17-year-old son to drink, frequent prostitutes, and generally "raise hell." This particular father was awakened late one night by the police who had caught his son in a raid on a so-called massage parlor. The father's reaction was, "Why aren't you guys out catching crooks?" This same father would boast to his co-workers that his son was "all boy" and a "chip off the old block."

Still another form of parental exploitation occurs when parents use their youngsters as *slave labor*. In one instance, a father who owned a motel demanded that his son do all the lawn work and help to clean up the rooms and make the beds. In addition, he insisted that the boy take the lids off all the cans in the trash barrels and then flatten the cans so that the volume of trash, and hence the cost of disposal, would be lessened. The boy barely had time to do his homework, much less to visit with his friends. Mothers who get their teenage daughters to do more of the housework and the baby-sitting than is reasonable or equitable provide another example of slave labor exploitation.

A fourth form of parental exploitation is frequently encountered in broken homes in which the mother, who usually retains custody of the children, is relatively young and attractive. In one case a mother took a lover, much younger than herself, into her home over the protestations of her teenage daughter, who had to cope with the curiosity of friends and the indignation of neighbors. Another young divorcee had a baby out of wedlock whom she kept in the home without any explanation to her teenage children. Still another mother, who had lost her husband under tragic circumstances, took to drinking away her afternoons with a younger man to whom she gave large sums of money. She could not understand why her teenage son ran off to Mexico.

In all such cases, the mothers demand not only that their children accept the situation, but that they condone it. By demanding that their children accept and condone their behavior, these mothers hope to use their children to *assuage their own consciences*.

One of the saddest forms of parental exploitation involves parents who are very much in the public eye, particularly school principals, clergymen (of whatever faith), and judges. If a parent in one of these professions sees his child's behavior primarily in terms of what it means to his career, he may demand a degree of conformity to middle-class mores that is quite unreasonable from the young person's point of view. When young people of this kind get into trouble, it is not because the parents are too strict, but rather because the parents are using their children to *proclaim their own moral rectitude.* As in all cases of parental exploitation, the dominant affect in such children is not so much the feeling of being restricted as it is the feeling of being *used.*

REACTIONS TO PARENTAL EXPLOITATION

When a worker is exploited, he has at least four courses of action open to him. He can either quit, go out on strike, sabotage the plant, or passively submit to the exploitation.

Parallel types of reaction are found in middle-class delinquents. Some young people literally quit the scene. They may quit school and become truant, quit the home and become runaways, or quit the family psychologically and become incorrigible. Other adolescents go on strike. They continue to go to school, but refuse to perform; they stay in the home, but refuse to do their fair share of the chores; they stay out late, and they go with a group of whom the parents don't approve. In short, they defy parental authority generally. More serious reactions are observed in young people who wish to sabotage their parents. These kids get pregnant, steal cars, vandalize schools, get drunk, sniff glue, or take drugs. Such reactions cost the parents plent in worry, time, money, and bad publicity. The saddest reaction of all is that of the youngsters who passively submit to parental exploitation in the hope of winning or regaining parental love.

Despite the variety of these reactions, they all have one feature in common: parental exploitation is essentially private and is seldom recognized by anyone outside the home. Whereas the worker often has a union to voice his grievances and stand up for his rights, there are no unions for children. Consequently, the delinquent behavior of adolescents who are being exploited by their parents often serves as a kind of cry for help. Put differently, delinquent behavior often has as one of its components the desire to make the exploitation public, to let the world know what is happening behind the drawn drapes and closed doors. The sad thing about such cries for help is that they are as injurious to the young person as they are to the parents.

TREATMENT

To say that middle-class delinquency is difficult to treat psychotherapeutically is a gross understatement. The major reason for this is that, *although the pathology exists in the parents, the symptoms appear in the children.* Since it is the children who are in trouble, the parents find it hard, except on a superficial basis, to accept their responsibility in the matter. Blind to their own violation of the parent-child contract, they insist that the young person live up to his side of the bargin. For his part, the young person feels that he has been used and abused and generally will not take responsibility for his actions.

With both parents and children blaming each other for the difficulty, there is little motivation for change on either side. Usually, however, the children are more tractable than the parents on this score. In many cases all that one can do is either remove the young person from the home or help him to understand and deal with the exploitation in a more effective and less self-injurious way.

SUMMARY AND IMPLICATIONS

I have argued that middle-class delinquency is essentially a reaction to parental exploitation and have tried to enumerate some of the forms of exploitation as well as some of the reactions to it. Such a position clearly places the burden of blame for middle-class delinquency upon the parents. To some extent this is perhaps unjust, since children may encourage exploitation on their own behalf and may well exploit their parents in return. In many cases the exploitation is as likely to be circular as it is to be unidirectional. And, in addition, parents are, to some extent, the mediators of their own upbringing and of the larger society.

It should be said, too, that I don't offer the notion of parental exploitation as a complete explanation of middle-class delinquency. It is probably true that many of these young people have ego and superego defects of long standing. It is also true that we don't know why one form of exploitation will lead to a particular kind of delinquency and not another. In some cases, the connections seem direct and clear-cut, whereas in others they remain obscure. Unknown, too, is how prolonged the exploitation must be and how much of it is needed to incite an adolescent to delinquent acting-out. Such threshold values are probably a joint function of the child's personality and the quality of parental exploitation.

In short, a detailed understanding of any particular case of middle-class delinquency will have to involve a psychodynamic evaluation of the personalities of both parent and child. On the other hand, (or so it seems to me), a psychodynamic evaluation of the parent-child interaction, although providing an explanation in a particular case, may well miss the common theme that seems to run through all cases of middle-class delinquency, namely, parental exploitation. Taken together, however, the concept of parental exploitation and psychodynamic evaluations may well provide a general, as well as a specific, explanation for middle-class delinquency.

The value of such a general explanation of delinquency as parental exploitation is shown in the way it helps to make plausible why certain familial conditions are regularly associated with delinquent behavior. Broken homes, for example, have routinely contributed more than their fair share of the delinquent population (Burt, 1929; Glueck and Glueck, 1950; Monahan, 1957; Nye, 1958). It seems reasonable to assume that in broken homes one is more likely to find unmet parental needs than would be the case in intact families. Under these conditions, the temptation to put one's own needs ahead of those of the child and to use the child as an instrument in the satisfaction of those needs would probably be greatly enhanced. In short, the concept of parental exploitation might allow one to predict, or at least hypothesize, the kinds of family constellations that would be most likely to produce delinquent behavior.

Before closing, I want to take up one more point that has been raised by those who attribute middle-class delinquency to the antisocial impulses of parents that are vicariously satisfied through the child. It has already been noted that the vicarious satisfaction of parental needs is indeed one form of parental exploitation. Where I disagree with this position is in the implication that middle-class delinquency is antisocial, regardless of whether or not this is true of the parental need. If antisocial means the intent to harm or injure society in general, then I do not believe middle-class delinquency is antisocial. I do believe it is *antifamilial*. Looked at from the point of view of the adolescent and not necessarily from the point of view of society, delinquent behavior may be the most psychologically adaptive action a young person can take in the face of parental exploitation. Delinquent behavior not only calls attention to his plight, but also may remove him from the home on temporary or permanent basis.

Although I have limited the application of the concept of exploitation to the question of middle-class delinquency, it is possible that all delinquency is, at least in part, a reaction to exploitation and that society, as well as parents, can be culpable in this regard.

REFERENCES

Burt, C. *The Young Delinquent.* New York: Appleton, 1929.

Giffin, M. E., Johnson, A. M., & Litin, E. M. *Am. J. of Orthopsychiatry,* 1954, *24,* 668.

Glueck, S., & Glueck, E. T. *Unraveling Juvenile Delinquency.* New York: Commonwealth Fund, 1950.

Johnson, A. M., & Burke, E. C. *Proceedings of the Staff Meetings of the Mayo Clinic,* 1955, *30,* 557.

Monahan, T. P. *Social Forces,* 1957, 35, 250.

Nye, F. I. *Family Relationships and Delinquent Behavior.* New York, Wiley, 1958.

Quay, H. C. (Ed.) *Juvenile Delinquency.* Princeton, N.J.: Van Nostrand, 1965.

16

BORDERLINE RETARDATION IN LOW- AND MIDDLE-INCOME ADOLESCENTS

Young people perform poorly on mental tests for a variety of reasons. This chapter depicts some of the patterns of poor test performance in adolescents, provides a critical summary of some of the theories offered to account for the poor test scores attained by low income youth, and offers some alternative explanations, clinically and developmentally based, for this phenomenon.

Of all the levels of mental retardation, the diagnoses of "borderline" retardation (IQs roughly in the sixties and low seventies) are the most difficult to make and to interpret. This is particularly true for young people from minority subcultures whose values, language, and orientations are not adequately represented on mental tests. In the case of these young people and of many middle-income youth as well, the issue of borderline intelligence merges with the broader issues of the validity of mental testing and ethnic differences in intellectual ability.

Before proceeding it is important to say that I will be writing here primarily as a clinician and not as an experimental investigator. For over ten years I have been working with delinquent

R. M. Allan, A. D. Cortazzo, and R. P. Toister (eds.) *Theories of Cognitive Development.* Coral Gables: University of Miami Press, 1973, 57–86.

youth, many of whom fall into the borderline category. Accordingly, the discussion will build upon whatever knowledge I have been able to glean from my experience with adolescents who test at the borderline level. In the first section I will describe some varieties of borderline retardation found among middle- and low-income adolescents. In the next section I will review and evaluate some of the "deprivation theories" which have been offered to explain borderline retardation among low-income youth. The final section will introduce some developmental constructs that provide alternative explanations for test retardation among low-income youth.

VARIETIES OF BORDERLINE RETARDATES

In clinical practice one meets a wide variety of different young people who fall within the borderline IQ category. Such young people can, however, be placed within a few more or less distinctive categories. Easiest to diagnose are the *prima facie* retardates whose language and behavior give an impression of retardation which is then confirmed by the test results. Such retardates are found among both low- and middle-income young people. More difficult to diagnose are those adolescents whose manner and language are not suggestive of retardation but who none theless perform at that level. Such test retardates manifest different patterns, usually according to income level. Middle-income test retardates tend to be *anxious* or *liberated,* while low-income retardates tend to be *negativistic* or *ingratiating.*

PRIMA FACIE BORDERLINE RETARDATION

A fairly typical pattern among prima facie borderline retardates is that they are exploited by friends and companions into stealing or other such delinquent acts. When they come to the court clinic, they are generally friendly and affable but fairly limited in vocabulary and in the ability to express themselves. Such young people are usually open, easy going, and quite eager to be liked, traits that often get them into trouble.

Many of these adolescents are quite sensitive about their limited intellectual abilities. Clinically this sensitivity can be seen in a reaction which is very typical of this group of borderline retardates and which is usually absent among young people with higher IQs. When confronted with the first few easy items on the information subtest of the WISC,* an almost invariable sign of the prima facie borderline retardate is laughter at items such as "from what animal do we get milk." The dynamics are clear enough. A young person with limited ability is very anxious about his intellectual prowess and fears he will reveal himself on the test. The first few easy questions flood him with relief which is then expressed in laughter. Rather typical of this group, too, is the failure to really listen to the instructions and to fully appreciate that the succeeding questions will get harder.

Borderline retardates of the prima facie variety present very special problems of placement and education. While it is clear that they need special academic programs, it is not clear what the nature of these programs should be. I do not want here to enter the debate as to whether such young people should be placed in special classes or kept with their age mates; both programs have advantages and disadvantages. The really crucial factor is the attitude of the people involved. Special classes in a total school climate that is warm and accepting will not make the children in those classes feel stigmatized. Likewise, handled with acceptance and consideration, borderline students can be integrated within a regular classroom. What counts always is the orientation of the people involved, not the structure of the program.

MIDDLE-INCOME TEST RETARDATES

In talking about middle-income test retardates, I am not talking exclusively about white teenagers; middle-income black youths demonstrate patterns comparable to those manifested by the whites. It is important to remember that the black community is every bit as diversified as the white community. In the clinic setting, socioeconomic level can be just as significant as race in determining behavior patterns. One sees the "liberated" and "anxious" patterns described below among middle-class youth

---

*The Wechsler Intelligence Scale for Children

from many different ethnic backgrounds. What they have in common is the incorporation of the middle-class value system into their own.

The liberated.   The typical liberated young person comes for testing dressed in loose-fitting, shapeless clothes and presents a rather uncombed and ungroomed appearance. Such young people are quite often defiant in a quiet and non-physical way, and it soon becomes clear that they are fighting the "system" and not just the examiner. They are interested in the tests but are quite ready to take umbrage at the questions. Indeed, the reason that liberated young people do poorly on the tests is that they often disagree with the values expressed in test questions such as "Why should criminals be locked up?" and "Why should women and children be saved first in a shipwreck?" They may reply that criminals should not be locked up and that women should not always be saved before men. These answers cannot, of course, be given credit. In many ways, therefore, the liberated young person approaches the standard intelligence test as if it were a measure of critical or creative thinking (rather than of convergent thinking) and gives a poor showing. The poor showing is in itself an expression of distaste for a social system which places value on measured intelligence.

How should such a performance be interpreted? Clearly it does not reflect the young person's true intellectual potential or even his current level of mental functioning. Rather, it reflects his attitude toward conformity and toward conventional demands. As such the test data, taken together with the clinical evidence of near-average intelligence, are still significant. They reveal, for example, why such young people are often failing in school, why they cannot get along with their parents, and why they live with friends rather than go to work. The performance of these young people on intelligence tests is a reflection of their life style, of their apparent rejection of generally accepted societal standards and values including mental testing and academic achievement. The question is whether such rejection is more apparent than real.

It must be emphasized that not all liberated young people perform poorly on intelligence tests. Rather it is just those, I suspect, who have low-average ability who go to extremes in their intelligence test performance. Their rejection of the tests is an attempt to deny that they place any value on intellectual ability. By denying that test intelligence has value, they no longer have to feel ashamed of their own limited ability. Such young people often fool themselves into believing that their rejection of society and its values is genuine. In fact, it is just as likely that they have rejected society before it has had a good chance to reject them. If they are open to it, some of these young people can be helped with counselling. But their parents must be counselled too, for unless parents can bring their demands into line with their children's modest abilities, counselling may well be undermined from the start.

The anxious. The young person who performs at the borderline level because of extreme anxiety is a much less frequent occurrence than the liberated young person. Among the anxious group the causes of anxiety are quite diverse. One young woman came in who, four years after her father's death, was still mourning him. Her depression and anxiety severely inhibited her test performance. A rather different case recently came to my attention: a fifteen-year-old girl who was slender and attractive and who did not appear to be intellectually retarded from her speech or interpersonal behavior. She had, however, been having headaches and fainting spells. EEGs had been taken and an abnormal pattern was reported. Although the girl did not show it, she was terribly concerned about losing her intellectual powers and probably had some intimation of the possibility from such signs as lapses of memory. While taking the WISC she repeatedly blocked because of her anxiety and attained a verbal IQ score of 61.

It may be said that such testing is invalid and that the obtained score is of no value. While this objection needs to be raised, I cannot agree that the finding is useless. Although it was clear to me that the girl was anxious about the testing, nothing in her appearance or manner suggested the extent of the blocking that actually occurred. Since I tried very hard to make the testing a comfortable and non-anxious situation, the extent of blocking is significant. It certainly helps explain why she was failing in school and pinpoints a major focus of her anxiety, namely, her concern over failing intellectual abilities. While it would be foolish to call this girl retarded, it would be equally foolish to throw out the diagnostic significance of her performance. In most cases, adolescents who fall into this category are very much in need of professional guidance and psychotherapy. It is also important that school personnel be made aware of the young person's special problems and that they be given guidance as to how best to help the anxious adolescent.

LOW-INCOME TEST RETARDATES

Perhaps the most frequent and diagnostically difficult cases of borderline retardation are the many young people who come from ethnic and economic backgrounds other than those presupposed by most of our mental tests. Within this group are low-income blacks, Spanish-speaking teenagers, and white youth from poverty areas. When these teenagers come in for testing, they present one of two contrasting patterns, *negativism* or *ingratition*. Sometimes the same young person will show both patterns at different times.

Regardless of whether the young person is negativistic or ingratiating, one common characteristic stands out in the testing situation: the language differences between the middle-income examiner and the lower-income examinee. There are not only differences in articulation, vocabulary, and inflection, but also more subtle differences in phrasing and emphasis. The communication problem is a very real one which complicates the testing and diagnosis.

On the WISC, for example, a black male may refuse to define the word "spade" because it happens to be a slang word for a black man. Or a low income youngster may say something like "Humb" which turns out to be Humboldt Avenue, the street on which he lives. Sometimes the misunderstanding can be amusing as in the case of the young person who makes a face when he hears "espionage" as "spinach." These language differences are very apparent to the examinee as well as to the examiner and pose an additional barrier to effective rapport and valid testing. In my own work I find that it is important to confront the issue directly, to restate words I feel have not been understood and to get the adolescent to repeat words I could not comprehend. If the young person gets the impression you really want to understand him and are not making aspersions about his speech, such little confrontations can be most helpful in aiding communication. Minor confrontations are equally effective with negativistic and ingratiating adolescents.

The Negativistic Adolescent. A great many low-income adolescents come in for testing in a rather surly mood. They tend to feel that someone thinks that they are crazy and that tests will be used against them in one way or another. They are also secretly afraid of tests as if the tests have some magical power to do things to them or to find out things about them which they do not wish to be known. The negativism is usually expressed directly in overt outbursts of anger at the examiner and diatribes against the tests ("that old stupid stuff"), or in a sullen, unbending silence.

Examples of some typical young people of this kind may help to make their negativism more concrete. One case was a fourteen-year-old black male who came to the testing against his will. He refused to take the tests saying that he did not answer "them damn questions." After his probation officer spoke to him for a few moments he agreed reluctantly to participate. On the beginning questions ("What must you do to make water boil," etc.) on the WISC he said, "Oh man, that's stupid, everybody knows that." He became increasingly angry as the items got more difficult and finally turned away and said, "I ain't gonna answer no more of that shit." As with most cases of this kind I discontinued testing and made another appointment. Almost without exception negativistic young people are much more cooperative on the second testing. It is as if having succeeded in stopping the testing the first time, they had made their point and do not need to make it again.

An example of another kind of negativism was given by a small, black girl who was fifteen years old. She came in, sat down, and said nothing in response to my greeting and initial structuring of the testing. (I routinely introduce myself, explain that I am going to give some tests, and ask whether the adolescent has ever had tests before.) After answering a few questions on the WISC, she seemed unable to answer one of the questions. When I went on to the next question, she continued si-

lent. No matter what I said or how I encouraged her, she sat
looking into her lap and not talking. Again, as in the case of the
aggressively negativistic adolescent, I terminated testing and set
another appointment. When she returned a week later, she was
cooperative and completed the tests without incident.

It should be said that the negativism shown by these young
people is, to a large extent, culturally stereotyped. Many of
these young people complain that they have a headache, are
tired, or are not feeling well. Such ploys seem to be well-learned
modes of avoiding activities they don't want to engage in. As I
indicated earlier, it is difficult to do much about this behavior
other than let it run its course and to try again another day. Not
surprisingly, these negativistic patterns seem to date back to
slavery days when such techniques were constantly in use to get
back at the "man" (Bernard, 1966).

The Ingratiating Adolescent. Much less frequent than the
negativistic adolescent are the adolescents who are ingratiating
in attitude and manner. Such young people come into the testing situation as if they were frightened and threatened. They
obey requests as if they were commands and seem to be search-
ing for cues in the examiner's facial expression and behavior as
to what is the right response. Some ingratiating adolescents are
rather outgoing and jovial, but they still reflect the eagerness to
please and the fear of offending that seem to characterize this
group of young people.

Again, this pattern of behavior appears to be a cultural
stereotype. It seems to be adopted by those adolescents who
find it difficult to be aggressive and need some mode of relating
to authority. Underneath the ingratiation is not only fear but
also hostility, which is sometimes revealed in a chance or un-
guarded remark. The ingratiating pattern also probably dates
back to the days of slavery when such patterns were the blacks'
only defense against the dominant authority of whites. But it
may be more general than that since young white people show
the ingratiating and negativistic patterns too.

The intellectual performance of the low-income test retardate,
whether the negativistic or ingratiating type, tends to show
much scatter. Consider the pattern of the negativistic young
man described earlier. He did poorly on tests of information,

vocabulary, and arithmetic, but did much better on tests of comprehension and similarities (which tend to measure ability more than content whereas the reverse is true for the other tests). His verbal IQ was 68 and his performance IQ was ten points higher. The full scale IQ was 73. On the Rorschach, the number and quality of responses were suggestive of low-average to average intellectual ability. His figure drawings, in contrast, were poor and suggested less than average ability. My clinical impression was that his potential level of ability was at least in the low-average range. This pattern of poor performance and the clinical impression of ability higher than that suggested by the attained test scores is, in my experience, common to low-income test retardates.

Another common factor in this group is an outspoken hatred of school. This hatred is *more* than lip service to a popular and conventional attitude of the high school culture. Most of the teenagers who say they hate school (but who attend regularly) really like the social world that school affords. But the low-income test retardates are habitual truants who hate school with a genuine passion. It is a place where they have experienced repeated failure, ridicule, and embarrassment. Many of these young people have developed an antipathy to formal education of any kind. One reason for the negativism of so many of these young people is that the examiner in some respects is the embodiment of the formal educational establishment they so despise.

In recent years the low-income test retardate has come into the spotlight as a consequence of the civil rights movement. The poor intellectual and academic performance of low-income youth have been used as arguments for much social and educational legislation. School integration and programs such as Headstart have been introduced to equalize the educational opportunities of low- and middle-income young people. Such programs presuppose that the test retardation of low-income youth is primarily a function of intellectual deprivation and that providing adequate intellectual nourishment will greatly remediate the problem.

Other theories, in addition to the deprivation theory described above, have been offered to explain the test retardation of many low-income youth. My argument with such theories is that those who propound them usually work from data collected by group testing. Group testing, however, is much less reliable than individual testing. This is true because in group testing there is no way to insure that the adolescents can read the items, understand them, or pay any attention to them. But a theory is only as good as the data upon which it is based. Accordingly, in the next section I want to look more closely at some of the theories that have been propounded to explain the test retardation of low-income youth. More particularly I want to look at them from the standpoint of the clinician who works on a one-to-one basis rather than with group tests.

THEORIES OF TEST RETARDATION AMONG LOW-INCOME YOUTH

It is probably fair to say that the extant theories of test retardation among low-income youth tend to be deficit models. Such models presuppose that low-income youth are deficient in a) inherited ability, b) intellectually enriching experiences, c) appropriate motivation and interpersonal skills, or d) adequate nutrition. After reviewing these theories, I would like to suggest some alternative explanations which derive from clinical and developmental considerations.

TEST RETARDATION AS A REFLECTION OF LIMITED GENETIC ENDOWMENT

In his controversial article, Jensen (1969) reviewed the extensive literature on the test intelligence of black and white young people. He notes that blacks routinely score lower than whites on IQ tests and that this difference holds true even when socioeconomic level is held constant. He concludes that there is a genetic difference between blacks and whites, and that blacks are more endowed with associative abilities while whites are more endowed with abstract abilities. More recently, Hernnstein (1971) seems to have taken a position rather close to Jensen's.

Both Jensen and Hernnstein have been criticized from many

different points of view, and I do not wish to review all of those criticisms here. Rather, I would like to approach the question from the standpoint of the testing itself. What has to be emphasized is that the administration of individual or group intelligence tests involves a number of biases. Such biases involve much more than the fact that some of the test items may be inappropriate to the low-income adolescent's experience. As the evidence presented below suggests, it is the total testing context which affects test performance, and this context is often radically different for low-income than for middle-income children. Such context effects enter into both individual and group testing and make it hazardous to use the results of such testing to make inferences about "inherited" abilities.

In the earlier discussion of the mental assessment of low-income test retardates, I suggested some of the difficulties inherent in a middle-class examiner working with a low-income examinee. The problems of communication and of cultural stereotypes are, however, only part of the problem. Studies suggest, for example, that black children perform better when tested by a black examiner than when they are tested by a white examiner (Canady, 1936; Forrester and Klaus, 1964). It is probably fair to say that many of the studies used to demonstrate race or income differences in intelligence involve examiners and examinees of different race and/or social class.

Another related factor in individual testing was demonstrated by Zigler and Butterfield (1968) with Headstart children. One finding of the study was that when the same children were given an individual intelligence test under maximizing (warm, supportive, relaxed, encouraging) and standard (cool, objective, non-reinforcing) conditions, there was an average ten-point difference in favor of the test taken under maximizing conditions. Another finding was that a comparable change occurred between standard testing of children before and after their attendance at a Headstart program. These results suggest that even when Headstart programs produce IQ changes in children, they do not change mental ability per se. What is more likely is that Headstart programs change the test orientation of low-income children. By the end of a Headstart program, children are comfortable with middle-income adults and with examination procedures. In short, one might say that Headstart makes children more motivated, comfortable, and attentive test takers.

The motivational factor is, however, but one of the contextual factors which enter into a child's performance on an individual test of intelligence. Cultural values and ethics also enter into such performance. A case in point is chronicled in an unpublished study I conducted with the Ogalala Sioux of Pine Ridge, South Dakota. I wanted to get normative data on some tests of perceptual development (Elkind, 1969) which my students and I had developed over the years. The Sioux live in a perceptually barren part of the country (near the Badlands of South Dakota) and in a relatively isolated and perceptually impoverished environment insofar as such things as books and paintings are concerned. Their performance on perceptual tests might reflect the importance of culturally provided perceptual experience for success on our tests.

Initially, the results of the testing were what I had (I confess) hoped to find. The Sioux youngsters did much more poorly on tests of figure-ground reversal and part-whole integration than did our middle- and lower-class anglo norm groups. As a clinician, however, I was dissatisfied with the way in which the children performed, and I suspected that they were not telling me everything that they had, in fact, seen. I then tried procedures similar to what Zigler and Butterfield called maximizing. I spent a lot of time talking to each child, drawing him or her out and showing that I was genuinely interested in his or her performance. With such procedures, the children suddenly opened up and performed as well or better than our middle- and low-income white children.

What I discovered when I explored this situation with some of the Indian teachers was that I was dealing with cultural and interpersonal values. Most of the children are self-conscious about their Indian names (e.g., Chief Running Fast White Water) and are afraid of being ridiculed. In addition, the Indian culture is basically non-competitive. Indeed, competition is looked at rather negatively. Consequently, even the brightest Indian children do no more than they must to get by. To do their best would be to do better than their peers, which is culturally unacceptable. In my maximizing procedures, I somehow communicated that I respected the Sioux children's names and did not see their enhanced performance as a sign of their competitiveness. Clearly the effects of such values upon individual test performance of different ethnic groups have to be taken into account when interpreting test results as reflecting inherited ability. Many other cultural factors that affect test performance were described by Michael Cole and his colleagues (1971).

There is another contextual factor which is prominent in testing low-income adolescents which I alluded to earlier. This is a cultural factor which seems to be endemic to low-income youth regardless of race or ethnic background. In general, the middle-income adolescent, whether or not he admits it, looks at the test as a challenge and overtly or covertly enjoys testing his mettle. He is also concerned about the impression he makes on the examiner. Even the hostile middle-income youth is very much concerned with "impression management."

Many, but certainly not all, low-income youth approach testing with a very different frame of mind. They seem not to have learned that "good" performance in intellectual matters is what wins adult approval. Consequently they are less ego involved with the testing and less concerned with how they appear in adult eyes than are middle-class youth. A large number of low-income youth probably see the testing situation as yet another instance where they have to find out how little they can do without getting punished (cf. Ch. 10). In other words, middle-income children are usually motivated to do well on intelligence tests, whereas low-income children are usually motivated to get by with the minimum possible performance.

If we look at group testing, the contextual factors appear to be as potent as they are in individual testing. Research on the context effects in group testing is, however, just getting under way. Rosenthal and Jacobsen (1968) argued that teacher expectancy played a considerable role in children's performance on achievement tests. Although other investigators (e.g. Fleming and Auttonen, 1971) have failed to replicate the Rosenthal and Jacobsen study, the Rosenthal work has stimulated research into the many and complex factors which affect performance on group tests.

A study of our own (Elkind, Deblinger, and Adler, 1970) highlights one factor in group testing which seems obvious but is seldom taken seriously in administering group tests. This factor is the activity which is interrupted when children are taken for testing. Our hypothesis was that children's performance on a creativity test would be enhanced if they were taken from an activity (such as social studies) which many children find uninteresting, whereas their performance on a creativity test would be impaired if they were taken for testing from an interesting activity (like gym). This follows because on creativity tests children are scored on the number as well as the quality of their responses. Children who expect to go back to a boring activity produce more responses (to avoid going back) than children who are looking forward to returning to an interesting activity.

In our study we found that the same children were twice as creative and three times more original when group testing interrupted an ongoing dull activity than when it interrupted an ongoing interesting activity.

More directly related to the question of low-income children are the findings of Long (1966), who ran kindergartens for black and white children in the rural South. While some of the children received an "enriched" program, the Stanford Binet showed no gains for any of the children. The Thurstone Primary Mental Abilities Test (PMA) did, however, reflect gains. There was some suggestion that the black children profited more from enrichment than the white children.

Another contextual factor affecting group test performance became manifest in our ongoing evaluation of an innovative inner city school. We have found that children's test performance waxes and wanes partly as a reflection of the morale of teachers and administrators. When the funding for the school was in jeopardy, performance on group tests was lower than when the future financial support for the school seemed assured.

Other studies could be cited to further document the role of contextual factors in individual and group testing. The data which have been offered, however, may suffice to show some of the sources of error in testing low-income youth. Such error, is not random but *systematic* and is therefore missed in statistical calculations for random, or error, variance. Because of such systematic sources of error in group and individual testing of middle as well as low-income children, the use of these test findings to make assertions about hereditary differences between groups seems hazardous.

It is important to add, however, that I am in no way attempting to deny that intelligence has a large hereditary component. No one could gainsay that individuals vary in intellectual ability any more than one could deny that physical traits have their origin in genetic transmission. But there is such a vast empirical and conceptual gulf between the level at which genes, chromosomes, and DNA, operate and the behavior of a child on a test that a linkage between the two must be tenuous at best. While such a linkage may be justified in studies where heredity is controlled, as in studies of identical twins, it is much less justified in comparing groups where heredity and culture are badly confounded.

In summary, we have looked at evidence for systematic bias in individual and group tests which adversely affect the performance of blacks and low-income groups. The existence of these sources of bias and the enormous gap between the genetic and behavioral levels of analysis make questionable those hypotheses about genetic differences in test intelligence between the races or socioeconomic groups. While it is undeniable that intelligence has a large hereditary component, we lack the knowledge to make specific statements about the genetic contribution to between group differences in intelligence test performance.

TEST RETARDATION AS A RESULT OF DEPRIVATION

Perhaps the most prevalent explanation for the relatively poor performance of low-income youth on intelligence tests is the concept of *deprivation*. This concept has, however, been interpreted in several different ways. Perhaps the most common interpretation is that low-income children are deprived of adequate verbal and intellectual stimulation. Another interpretation is that low-income children are deprived emotionally and interpersonally. A final interpretation is that low-income young people do poorly on intelligence tests because of nutritional deprivation. Let us look at each of these explanations in turn.

Intellectual Deprivation. The conception that low-income children are deprived of adequate intellectual stimulation is based on a variety of research findings. Numerous studies, such as that of Hess and Shipman (1965), report that low-income mothers do not engage in as much teaching and verbal interplay with their children as do middle-income mothers. Likewise Bernstein (1961) has hypothesized that low-income families have a more restricted language system than the economically advantaged families, and Bloom (1964) suggests that the cost to a child, who spends his first four years in a deprived intellectual environment—as opposed to an enriched one—is about ten IQ points.

The problem is, of course, to define what one means by a rich as opposed to a deprived intellectual environment. For example, the hypothesis that the language of blacks is less elaborated than that of whites has been challenged (Baratz, 1969). It apears now that black language is a dialect of standard English which is every bit as rich in vocabulary, inflection, and grammatical constructions as white, standard English. It is at least possible that low-income mothers are very articulate when it comes to instructing their children in things which matter to them, such as how to get along with whites without being taken advantage of by them.

These considerations make it clear that intellectual deprivation refers to the *kind* and not to the quantity of stimulation that low-income children receive. What they are deprived of is the kind of intellectual stimulation that would prepare them to take tests and to do well in public school, both of which have been designed by middle-class whites. At the same time, however, these low-income children have not been deprived of the kind of stimulation and enrichment that they need to adapt to their environment. Deprivation is thus not an accurate term to describe the intellectual experience of low-income young people. Their experience is simply *different* and not necessarily *deficient*.

This is an important point because the deprivation or deficit model has led to compensatory programs aimed at remedying deficits. Not the least of the negative aspects of such programs is the orientation it produces in adult teachers. If children are regarded as deficient, the intellectual skills and abilities they bring to the situation may not be recognized or respected. The effect is to further devalue the child's conception of himself and his family.

Let me give an analogy from my experience with the White Mountain Apache of Arizona. During a long evening's discussion with some young, college-trained Apache men, I learned a great deal about the Apache religion. It turns out to have a concept of a trinity not unlike that which underlies Christianity. The Indians felt, however, that the missionaries did not take their religion seriously. So although the Indians went to church (as much for the free food as the service) they went back to their own religion at times of crisis. Many Indian soldiers went to the reservation for a "sing" before they were shipped overseas for combat.

I would not be surprised if a good many "deprived," low-income children and their parents participate in compensatory programs with the same ambivalence experienced by Indian families attending the missionary's church. In both cases the low-income groups are ostensibly accepting a value system different from their own, but only superficially and because of the rewards involved. My guess is that the effect of compensatory programs will be minimal so long as those in charge fail to understand and respect the culture and values of the people they are attempting to serve.

That low-income children are different, rather than deficient, in the kinds of intellectual stimulation they receive is supported by cross-cultural research on Piagetian tasks. Such tasks measure basic concepts about the physical world (space, time, number, mass, weight, volume, right and left) which are required for successful adaptation. These Piagetian tasks have now been administered to children all over the world who live in widely varying environments and who come from vastly different backgrounds. And yet the results are surprisingly uniform. Children in bush Africa attain the same concepts at about the same time as children in Boston or Geneva (cf. Greenfield, 1966; Goodnow, 1969; Vernon, 1965).

To be sure, some low-income groups appear to be behind middle-income groups. Appalachian children are behind Detroit children (Sigel and Mermelstein, 1965) and children from the country are behind children from the city (Peluffo, 1962), but they all appear to go through the same sequence of stages and to attain the same abilities. It may be that some kinds of environments alter the *rate* of mental growth. On the other hand, it may be that some of the testing factors mentioned earlier penalize the low-income child on Piagetian tasks. What I want to emphasize here is that low-income children usually do better on Piagetian tasks than they do on more formal intelligence tests. Here again the implication is that their environments have not deprived them intellectually but rather have caused them to elaborate their abilities in directions other than those taken by mental elaboration in middle-income young people.

One last point must be made. Social scientists have been guilty, during the last decade, of creating new stereotypes of low-income children that are every bit as pernicious as some of the earlier "poor people" stereotypes. It is important to remember that there are more intact black families than broken ones and that within the low-income community there is tremendous diversity. There are parents who, with high aspirations for their children, provide an environment every bit as stimulating as any to be found in a home in the middle-class suburbs. The reverse is also true, and there are many suburban middle-class homes which are probably devoid of what educators might call enriching intellectual environments. In talking about low-income youth, we must be aware of the danger of homogenization, of assuming that every low-income child's experience is the same. Individual differences are every bit as varied in low-income as in middle-income youth.

Motivational and Interpersonal Deprivation. A number of studies indicate that low-income children are more deficient in achievement motivation than are more affluent children (Douvan, 1956; Lott and Lott, 1963; Mussen, Urbano, and Boutourline-Young, 1961). Achievement motivation is certainly crucial to the full elaboration of intellectual abilities and to competent performance on mental tests. Lack of achievement motivation could thus be an important factor in the borderline retardation of low-income youth. Such a lack of achievement motivation is certainly consistent with the clinical impression of low-income test retardates that I described earlier.

How is achievement motivation instilled in children? Psychoanalytic theory (Ekstein, 1966) suggests an explanation which is consistent with social learning theories such as that offered by Bandura and Walters (1963). According to psychoanalytic theory, a child's motivation for learning academic materials is not intrinsic but rather derives from his desire to win parental approval through learning. This means that the parents themselves value academic learning and reward their children for performing well at school.

Presumably, low-income parents are less impressed by academic achievement than middle-class parents. It is certainly true that low-income parents may have high aspirations for their children yet have rather low expectations (for example, want them to go to college but expect that they will work in gas stations). Such parents are not likely to demonstrate in their own behavior a taste for intellectual matters. (They are less likely to read books, go to concerts, and so on.) Hence children are given the message, "Do as I say, not as I do." Moreover, the low-income parent may be suspicious of people who are more highly educated than themselves and convey this suspicion to their offspring.

While there is probably considerable truth to these motivational deprivation explanations of test retardation among low-income youth, some reservations have to be offered. First, it is important to avoid homogenization. One must remember that many low-income parents are intellectually motivated whereas many middle-income parents are not. Second, middle-income families are smaller, hence the proportion of first-born and only children is greater than for low-income families. First-born children tend to be more competitive and achievement oriented regardless of social class. The apparently greater achievement motivation among middle-income families may in part reflect the greater proportion of first-born and only children among this income group.

Nutritional deprivation. In recent years, increasing attention has been paid to the role of nutrition in intellectual development. While much of the research has been done with animals (Barnes, 1968), a number of studies have been done on human populations as well (Cravioto, 1968). Although much more research needs to be done, some tentative conclusions seem reasonably well substantiated.

First of all, it appears that the earlier and the more prolonged the nutritional deficiency, the more severe and long-lived are the effects upon physical and mental growth. When pregnant beagles were fed a protein-deficient diet, their pups suffered greater detriment than beagle pups whose mothers had had adequate diets during pregnancy. In a study with tribal groups in Africa (Stock and Smyth, 1963), it was found that cranial circumference was significantly smaller among children whose mothers ate a nutritionally inadequate diet during pregnancy than among children whose mothers were adequately nourished.

One of the most ambitious studies of nutritional effects upon populations is the longitudinal investigations of Cravioto (1968). In his investigations Cravioto looked at the mental test performance of South American children growing up on different diets. In general he concludes that adequacy of nutrition in the early years has a significant long-term effect upon mental ability, alertness, and motivation.

The relevance of these findings to test retardation in low-income adolescents is straightforward. Low-income families by definition have relatively little money to spend on food. Protein is, moreover, quite expensive, whereas carbohydrates, fats, and starches are inexpensive. It is probably fair to say, therefore, that the average low-income child has grown up (both pre- and postnatally) on a less nutritious and balanced diet than the average middle-income child. It seems probable that in many cases of low-income test retardation a history of prolonged nutritional deficiency may play some part.

DEVELOPMENTAL CONSIDERATIONS

In the foregoing sections some deprivation models of test retardation among low-income youth have been described and critically evaluated. While such models contain some truth, they tend to unduly homogenize and stigmatize the low-income groups. The word "deprived" itself seems to cast aspersions on the quality of nurturance provided by low-income families. In fact, low-income children are deprived not of all intellectual stimulation, but of the kinds of intellectual stimulation which middle-income families regard as essential to success in our society.

It is important, in this connection, to recall the relativity of social class values. At one time social scientists described low-income mothers as permissive and middle-income mothers as strict. There was then a shift, and middle-income mothers became more permissive because this was supposed to be good for the child. Consider a more contemporary example. The unwed mother is supposed to be more common among low-income women because of their low morals, ignorance of birth control measures, and so on. But to be an unwed mother today is the height of chic among middle- and upper-class women. Many well-known women take pride in the fact that they have had a child out of wedlock. Today's low-income disgrace is tomorrow's middle-income fashion.

An approach to test retardation which avoids some of the difficulties of the deprivation models can be taken from a developmental perspective. One possibility is that low-income youth are retarded or slower in their development than middle-income youth. But my clinical impression of low-income test retardates suggests two other developmental conceptualizations of these young people. Some low-income retardates seem to have intellectual abilities which were *prematurely structured*, while others have intellectual abilities which have been *alternatively elaborated* in directions other than those taken by the intellectual abilities of middle-income youth.

Premature Structuring.†   After one of his lectures, Freud was asked what ever happens to the shoeshine boys that one sees on the street corners in Vienna. Such young men seemed exceedingly sharp-witted and verbally and socially astute. Freud thought for a moment and replied, "They become cobblers." The story illustrates the phenomena of premature structuring, which is by no means limited to low-income youth.

By premature structuring I mean that some young people are forced to apply their abilities to practical matters before those

---

†Barbara Biber (1959) has used this same term to describe the inhibition of creativity among young children due to too early introduction of formal education.

abilities are fully realized or elaborated. The effect is to stunt or limit growth. An analogy would be the pruning of a tree to make it assume a particular shape. Such pruning affects the ultimate limits of tree growth as well as shape. In the case of low-income children the same may hold true. Out of necessity, many such children may have to assume responsibility for their siblings at an early age and direct their intellectual abilities to practical issues. This early application of mental abilities to real life matters may inhibit future growth.

To be sure many middle-class children have chores (such as mowing the lawn or taking out garbage) and possibly have a paper route. Such chores are usualy underwritten and backed by parents (who may even deliver the papers in inclement weather). But middle-class children also exercise their mental abilities through activities (such as collecting coins, stamps, and rocks, or playing games of cards, monopoly, and chess) which have no practical end. In this way they exercise mental abilities without forcing them into particular molds.

My guess is that premature structuring is most likely to occur when a child has little or no opportunity to play with his mental abilities. Such play is, in my opinion, crucial to further mental elaboration of abilities (Elkind, 1972). The low-income child who has to deal with storekeepers, landlords, little children, bullies, and drunks has to use his abilities in very practical ways, and few low-income children have the wherewithal to collect coins, rocks, stamps, or to purchase elaborate games. Because of his practical orientation, spending time on apparently frivolus games or collections may appear nonsensical. Consequently, academic subjects may seem only another kind of useless play to the prematurely structured child, on a par with collecting coins or stamps.

In my clinical experience, prematurely structured test retardates show a limited fund of interests which seem to be focused upon eating, sleeping, a job, a few simple recreations, and nothing else. They show little or no appreciation for such things as science or even the important community issues which affect them personally. Such young people seem to pass through life with few distractions. To other people, such adolescents come across as narrow and constricted.

Alternate Elaboration.   One young man of the ingratiating variety exemplifies the alternate elaboration model of test retardation. He came to the court clinic because he was not going to school, and was suspected of pushing dope and of having a couple of girl friends doing "tricks" for him. He was well-dressed and smooth-talking with a vocabulary rich in the argot of the street and the underworld. He was alternately amused and annoyed at the test questions and did best in arithmetic and least well on the test of general information and vocabulary.

His poor performance on information and vocabulary does not reflect deficiency but rather alternate elaboration. This young man was far from lacking in general information. Indeed, his fund of information in many areas was much greater than mine. The same was true for his vocabulary which was rich in words not found on intelligence tests. To call this young man deficient in ability would be a gross error. On the contrary, his (at least) average intellectual abilities were elaborated in a subcultural domain that is virtually unknown to the middle-class test maker and user.

Individuals who manifest alternate elaboration of intellectual abilities are sometimes thought to be malingering. A black adolescent who was not drafted because of his low IQ was taken into custody for running a crap game. When playing craps he demonstrated rather remarkable mathematical acumen in figuring odds. The probation officer was sure this young man had failed the Army IQ test on purpose to avoid the draft. But he failed the intelligence test quite honestly. His mathematical abilities were elaborated in a different way than they are for most young people.

An analogy should help clarify the notion of alternate elaboration. During the first two years of life the infant's linguistic prowess is infinitely malleable. He will learn any language to which he is systematically exposed. Once he learns one particular language, however, it becomes progressively more difficult for him to learn a second as he grows older. After about the age of twelve, according to Lennenberg (1967), the critical period for language learning is at end. It is possible that something similar occurs in cognitive development. The young man who elaborates his abilities in the underworld subculture acquires a kind of cognitive language which may make it difficult for him to elaborate his abilities or to learn academic material in a traditional school setting.

The concepts of premature structuring and alternate elaboration are offered here as alternatives to the deficit models which have been proposed to account for the test retardation of low-income youth. These concepts have been derived primarily from my clinical experience with delinquent young people; they could, however, serve as a starting point for more systematic investigations. In the meantime, these concepts of premature structuring and alternate elaboration might prove useful if only to divert us from the value-laden terms of "deprived" and "disadvantaged." From a developmental standpoint, the mental growth of some low-income youth may simply be different in direction and elaboration than for the offspring of more well-to-do parents.

SUMMARY

I have tried here to do three things: a) describe some varieties of borderline retardation observed in clinical practice; b) critically evaluate some of the theories that have been offered to account for the test retardation in low-income youth, and c) offer an alternative developmental conceptualization of test retardation. In this closing section I want to reemphasize some of the points made earlier and to mention some possible practical implications of the foregoing discussion.

One of the dangers social scientists must constantly work to avoid is that of homogenization, or treating a group of individuals as if they all exhibited exactly the same traits. It is useful to talk about low- and middle-income youth and to point out features which are more common to one group than another. But as I have tried to indicate, there are many individual differences within groups. Test retardation appears in both middle-income and low-income young people although the patterns are somewhat different. Among middle-income youth the liberated and anxious syndromes are most common, whereas for low-income youth the antagonistic and ingratiating are most common.

A second point to be emphasized is the danger of interpreting intelligence test data as if it reflected specific genetic factors. While the contribution of heredity to intelligence is assuredly considerable, we are far from understanding the interactions between these two very different levels of observation and analysis. Moreover, the many systematic contextual biases that affect the performance of subcultural groups on these tests lessens their usefulness in making inferences about group differences in ability. In short, there is no more reason for attributing the test retardation of low-income adolescents to heredity than there is for attributing the test retardation of middle-income youth to heredity.

Likewise, since test retardation occurs in both middle- and low-income youth, environmental deprivation is probably not a major factor in test retardation. Rather, what seems to be the case for both middle- and low-income youth is that test retardation is produced not by the quantity but by the quality of experience as well as by such factors as motivation and role models available for imitation. The complex of factors that make for test retardation may be more common in low-income families, but they are certainly not their exclusive province.

From the clinical point of view taken in this chapter, some test retardation can be conceived as involving alternate directions of mental growth. One such direction is premature structuring, the other is alternate elaboration of mental abilities. What low-income circumstances produce, therefore, are not young people who are deficient in mental abilities, but rather young people who have elaborated their intelligence in directions that are different from the middle-class norm.

REFERENCES

Bandura, A., & Walters, R.H. *Social Learning and Personality Development.* New York: Holt, Rinehart & Winston, 1963.

Baratz, J.C. A bi-dialectal task for determining language proficiency in economically disadvantaged Negro children. *Child Development,* 1969, *40,* 890–901.

Barnes, R.H. Behavioral changes caused by malnutrition in the rat and pig. In D. Glass (Ed.) *Environmental Influences.* New York: Rockefeller University Press, 1968, 52–60.

Bernard, J.S. *Marriage and Family Among Negroes.* Englewood Cliffs, N.J.: Prentice-Hall, 1966.

Bernstein, B. Social structure, language and learning. *Educational Research*, 1961, *3*, 163–76.

Biber, B. Premature structuring as a deterrent to creativity. *Am. J. Orthopsychiatry*, 1959, *29*, 280–90.

Bloom, B.S. *Stability and Change in Human Characteristics*. New York: Wiley, 1964.

Canady, H.B. The effects of rapport on the IQ: A new approach to the problem of racial psychology. *J. Negro Education*, 1936, *5*, 209–19.

Cole, M., Gay, J., Glick, J.A., & Sharp, D.W. *The Cultural Context of Learning and Thinking*. New York: Basic Books, 1971.

Cravioto, J. Nutritional deficiencies and mental performance in childhood. In D.C. Glass (Ed.) *Biology and Behavior: Environmental Influences*. New York: Rockefeller University Press and Russell Sage Foundation, 1968, 3–151.

Douvan, E. Social status and success strivings. *J. Abnormal and Social Psychol.* 1956, *52*, 219–23.

Elkind, D. Developmental studies of figurative perception. In L. Lipsitt and H.W. Reese (Eds.) *Recent Advances in Child Development Research*. New York: Academic Press, 1969, 1–28.

Elkind, D. Teacher child contracts. *School Review*, 1971, *79*, 575–89.

Elkind, D. Cognitive growth cycles in mental development. In D. Katz (Ed.) *Nebraska Symposium on Motivation, 1971*. Lincoln: University of Nebraska Press, 1972, 1–31.

Elkind, D., Deblinger, J., & Adler, D. Motivation and creativity: The context effect. *Am. Educational Research Association J.*, 1970, *7*, 351–57.

Ekstein, R. *The Challenge: Despair and Hope in the Conquest of Human Space; Studies of the Psychoanalytic Treatment of Severely Disturbed Children*. New York: Appleton Century Crofts, 1966.

Fleming, E.S., Auttonen, R.G. Teacher expectancy as related to the academic and personal growth of primary age children. *Monographs of the Society for Research in Child Development*. 1971, *36*, 1–31.

Forrester, B.J., & Klaus, R.A. The effect of race of examiner on intelligence test scores of Negro kindergarten children. *Peabody Papers on Human Development*, 1964. *2*, 1–7.

Goodnow, J. Problems in research on culture and thought. In D. Elkind and J.H. Flavell (Eds.) *Studies in Cognitive Development*. New York: Oxford University Press, 1969, 439–64.

Greenfield, P.M. On culture and conservation. In J.S. Bruner, R.R. Olver, and P. Greenfield (Eds.) *Studies in Cognitive Growth*. New York: Wiley, 1966, 225–56.

Hernnstein, R. IQ. *The Atlantic*, 1971, *228*, (September), 43–64.

Hess, R.D., and Shipman, V.C. Early experience and the socialization of cognitive modes in children. *Child Development*, 1965, *36*, 869–86.

Jensen, A.R. How much can we boost IQ and scholastic achievement? *Harvard Educational Review*, 1969, *39*, 1–123.

Lennenberg, H. *Biological Foundations of Language*. New York: Wiley, 1967.

Long, E. The effect of programmed instruction in special skills during the preschool period on later ability patterns and academic achievement. *U.S. Office of Education Prog. No. 1521*. University of North Carolina, 1966.

Lott, A.J., & Lott, B.E. *Negro and White Youth*. New York: Holt, 1963.

Mussen, P., Urbano, P., and Boutourline-Young, H. Esplorazione del motivi per mezzo di un reattivo: II Classi sociali e motivazione fra adolescenti di origine Italiani. *Arch. Psicol. Neuro. Psichiat.*, 1961, 22, 681–90.

Peluffo, N. Les notions de conservation et de causalite chez les enfants provemant de differents milieux physiques et socio-culturels. *Arch. Psychol.*, Geneva, 1962, 38, 75–90.

Rosenthal, R., & Jacobsen, L. Self-fulfilling prophecies in the classroom: Teachers' expectations as unintended determinants of intellectual competence. In M. Deutsch, I. Katz, & A.R. Jensen (Eds.) *Social Class, Race and Psychological Development*. New York: Holt, 1968, 219–53.

Sigel, I.E., & Mermelstein, E. The effects of nonschooling on Piaget's conservation tasks. Paper read at American Psychological Association, Chicago, 1965.

Stock, M.B., 9 Smyth, P.M. Does undernutrition during infancy inhibit brain growth and subsequent intellectual development? *Archives Disorders of Childhood*, 1963, 38, 546–52.

Vernon, P.E. Environmental handicaps and intellectual development. *British J. of Psychol.* 1965, 35, 1–12; 117–26.

Zigler, E., & Butterfield, E.C. Motivational aspects of changes in IQ test performance of culturally deprived nursery school children. *ChiLd Development*, 1968, 39, 1–14.

17
COGNITIVE DEVELOPMENT AND PSYCHOPATHOLOGY
OBSERVATIONS ON EGOCENTRISM
AND EGO DEFENSE

At each stage of intellectual development there are characteristic constructs which reflect the limitations of the intellectual structures at these age levels. These "egocentric" constructs help to explicate some of the "ego defenses" postulated by psychoanalysis. This chapter first describes the development of egocentric structures, then details their relation to ego defenses and to the age-related appearance of some psychopathological syndromes.

Over the past decade and a half, American research on the cognitive development of children has received its greatest impetus from the work of Jean Piaget (e.g. Piaget, 1963). Most of this research started from Piaget's later studies and theories concerned with the evolution of rational thought. Much less attention was paid to Piaget's early work (e.g. Piaget, 1929) on egocentrism, but it is this work which seems most closely related to psychopathology and thus warrants more study than it has heretofore received. This chapter will explore the evolution of egocentric structures in children and adolescents and their relation to ego defenses.

E. Schopler and R.J. Reichler (eds.) *Psychopathology and Child Development*. New York: Plenium, 1976, 167–184.

THE STUDY OF EGOCENTRISM: BRIEF HISTORY

The study of egocentrism in children grew out of the interest in nonrational thought that was one of the preoccupations of the new disciplines of psychology, cultural anthropology, and psychoanalysis that emerged around the turn of the century. Much of this work, with the exception of Freud's, was carried out within a Darwinian framework which suggested that rational thought evolved from nonrational thought much as man evolved from the apes. Cultural anthropologists sought, and found, evidence of primitive thinking among esoteric peoples living in remote and isolated places. Cultural historians likewise found evidence for primitive ideas in earlier eras of western society. Freud noted primitive "primary process" thinking in the dreams, fantasies, and free associations of normal as well as disturbed adults. And early-developmental psychologists found evidence of nonrational thought among children.

The early work on nonrational thought was primarily descriptive and contrasted these modes of thought with those of rational discursive thought. In a series of classic studies, Jean Piaget (1929; 1948; 1951) dealt with nonrational thought from a perspective that was at once empirical and philosophical. Piaget was cognizant of the epistemological questions raised by the discovery of primitive thought and tried to answer some of these questions with his early investigations. Basically he was concerned with the question, How is primitive, nonrational thought possible?

The discovery of primitive thought seriously challenged traditional theories of knowing. If esoteric peoples, children, and even normal people could entertain false notions about the world, then experience could not be the sole source of knowledge. Experience could not be the source of both true and false pictures of the world. Where then do such erroneous notions as animism come from? The appeal to the innateness of these ideas is also unsuccessful. Young children have primitive ideas, but give them up as they grow older. Since by definition innate ideas are fixed and unchanging, they cannot be the source of developmentally malleable primitive ideas.

Spurred on by such questions and by the results of his researches, Piaget was led to a *constructivist* epistemology. This epistemology insists that children actively construct reality out of their experience with the environment. We can never know the environment directly, but only indirectly, through our intellectual constructions which approximate the environment but are never identical to it. As children grow older and their intellectual abilities mature, they progressively construct a series of realities which move ever closer to the reality of adults. But the reality of adults is also only an approximation and continues to change and be modified with the accumulation of new knowledge and new reconstructions of reality.

From this point of view the designation of a particular mode of thought as primitive (or egocentric) is necessarily relative since it is unshared and unsocialized thought; it lacks what Sullivan (1953) called *consensual validation*. In this sense, the animism of primitives was not egocentric because it was a mode of thought that was consciously shared by a given society. In the same way, the heliocentric theory was not egocentric at the time it was held because it was socially shared and agreed upon. In contrast, the animistic ideas of the preschool child are implicit and unconscious in his thinking and are not agreed upon or shared by adults within the society. In short, egocentric thought and concepts are those which lack social articulation and consensus.

In Piaget's view, egocentric thought progressively declines in importance as children grow older and their intellectual abilities mature. Rational, discursive thought gradually predominates in the thinking of older children and adults. After his initial concern with egocentric thought Piaget turned to his major work, the mechanisms by which the child constructs progressively more socialized realities. This is not, however, the place to review the stages Piaget delineated in the child's conquest of objective socialized reality, for our concern is with the fate of egocentric thought.

Although Piaget soon lost interest in egocentric thought as he began to deal with the evolution of logical thought, other investigators did not. The gifted Russian psychologist Vygotsky (1962), for example, took issue with Piaget regarding the fate of egocentric thinking. For Vygotsky, egocentric thought did not disappear but rather became successively internalized and transformed into private, inner speech and thought. These two interpretations have continued to interest investigators who have tried to devise investigations to decide between them. The research as of this date (cf., e.g. Kohlberg et al., 1968) remains ambiguous as to the fate of egocentric thought in general.

Other investigators have looked at egocentrism with respect to its relation to communication (Flavell et al., 1968) or to pathology (Anthony, 1956) or to delinquency (Chandler, 1973). In all of these approaches, egocentric thought is regarded as a stage of mental development which can be overcome by movement to the next higher level of development. In particular, movement to concrete operations and the ability to take another person's point of view, required for the socialization of thought, are regarded as crucial to overcoming the egocentric stage of thought. By helping children take the point of view of others, it is hoped that children will move out of their egocentricity.

From the perspective of this chapter, egocentrism is not limited to a particular stage of development but is present at each stage, though in different degrees and in different forms. At each stage of development, the child's new forms of thinking enable him to overcome early forms of egocentrism but also ensnare him in new, more complex varieties of unsocialized thought. In general the sphere of egocentric thought diminishes with age and pertains to more specific and more abstract aspects of the physical and social world. These more advanced forms of egocentric thinking are less well-known than those of the preschool period but are equally important. Indeed, the last section of this chapter will argue that many defenses and symptoms can be described in terms of the egocentric structures characteristic of childhood and adolescence.

Egocentric concepts are formed because there is a lag between the development of ability to form concepts and the ability to check or test their social validity. Hence the preschool child has the ability to form causal concepts such as animism before he has the logical abilities (the concrete operations which appear at six and seven) which are necessary to test them. In fact, most veridical concept formation at a particular stage is the correction of erroneous concepts formed at the previous stage.

That is to say, much of the concept formation activity of a

particular stage of development is directed not so much at realizing the potentials of the abilities of that stage as at correcting the erroneous conceptions formed at previous stages. This is why egocentrism diminishes with age: as the individual is more and more concerned with reconstructing his previous erroneous conceptions of space, time, causality, and so on, he has less time to form totally new concepts that would bring his egocentrism into play. But when he does use his conceptual powers in new situations, egocentrism is likely to emerge, at least temporarily.

EGOCENTRIC STRUCTURES IN CHILDHOOD AND ADOLESCENCE

At each stage of development, egocentric structures reflect the child's cognitive abilities of the moment and his attempts to make sense out of his world. Egocentric concepts are, in essence, assumptions about some aspects of the environment which the child takes as given because he lacks the ability to challenge or test them. Egocentric ideas are given up as the child attains the prerequisite mental abilities to test them and as his ideas are challenged by social interactions. Knowing this, it is possible to identify the kinds of assumptions made at each major stage of development.

EGOCENTRIC STRUCTURES AT THE PREOPERATIONAL STAGE

Between the ages of three and six children acquire the symbolic function: the ability to create symbols and to learn signs that can represent their experience and their concepts. But the young child's ability to create symbols and to learn signs far outstrips his ability to comprehend them in socially accepted ways. Because this discrepancy pervades the young child's thinking, egocentrism is rampant during this stage. His egocentrism covers his attempts to discover all aspects of his world and justifies our calling this stage one in which the child behaves according to *assumptive philosophies:* a global set of beliefs as to how the physical and social worlds operate.

Many assumptions of young children's philosophies are by now well known. One assumption is that the world is *purposive,* that everything has a purpose or cause and that there is no possibility of chance or arbitrary events. Another assumption is *artificialism*, that everything in the world is made by and for man. Still another assumptive philosophy is *nominal realism*, the belief that names are essential components of the objects they designate and cannot be separated from them or changed. Finally, although it does not exhaust the list, there is the assumption of *animism*, the belief that nonbiological objects are alive.

What is typical of the egocentric concepts of this and later stages is a fundamental confusion between what comes from without and what from within the child. Such confusion is to be expected if reality is in fact constructed and is neither copied from some fixed and separate world, nor simply remembered as if it were an innate idea. But this epistemological confusion takes different forms at different age levels and reflects those respective levels of conceptualization.

At the preschool level, the confusion is between what the child's knows concretely of himself, his feelings, his intentions, his sensory experiences, and what he knows concretely of the world, namely, its tangibility and its objectivity. In effect, what the young child does is construct his psychic world on the model of the physical world and construct the physical world on the model of his psychic reality. Hence the young child believes that his dreams come in through the window at night, that other people can feel his toothache, and that the wind, moon, and sun are alive. Again these ideas are egocentric, not of themselves, but in the context of a society where they are not acceptable to the adult mind.

EGOCENTRIC STRUCTURES IN CHILDHOOD

At about the age of six or seven, in Piaget's view, new mental abilities emerge which take the child far beyond what he was capable of doing at the preschool level. These new mental abilities—concrete operations—resemble the operations of arithmetic in their mode of activity, and function as a system rather than in isolation. Thus if a child knows that the class of children minus the class of boys equals the class of girls (C − B = G), one can infer, with reasonable certainty, that he also knows that the class of children minus the class of girls equals the class of boys ($C - G = B$). These operations also enable the child to grasp the notion of a unit which is at once like every other unit in being a unit, and different in order of enumeration or seriation.

Concrete operations thus enable the school-age child to progressively comprehend many of the verbal representations he acquired but understood only egocentrically at the preschool level. He begins to grasp, for example, that "right" and "left" are relations and not absolute properties of things. And he comes to appreciate that changes in the appearance of quantities does not mean a change in their amounts. The concrete operations of middle childhood thus progressively overcome the egocentric notions found at the preschool level.

But concrete operations also engender new egocentric concepts in their own right. With his new mental abilities, the school-age child can now mentally represent various possible courses of action. The preschool child, in contrast, was able to represent only properties and things. The new ability to represent possible courses of action appears in many different ways. For example, when a preschool child is presented with a finger maze he proceeds by immediately putting his finger to the maze and succeeds, if he does, by trial and error efforts. A school-age child will, in contrast, survey the maze and mentally represent various paths until he discovers the right one. Only at that point will he put his finger to the maze.

In the maze situation, the ability to internally represent actions works quite well because there is immediate and unequivocal feedback as to the correctness of the representation. But in many other situations, there is no mental way to test which of several possible courses of action will succeed. In such circumstances an experimental frame of mind is required that permits one to hold several hypotheses in mind while testing each in succession. The ability to do this is, however, only made possible by the formal operations of adolescent intelligence. Consequently the school-age child is in the position of being able to conceptualize alternate paths of action but not being able to test these alternate paths in systematic ways.

The school-age child is thus in the same position with respect to representing possible courses of action that the preschool child was with respect to representing classes, relations, and units. In both cases there is a lag between the ability to represent experience and the ability to test out the social validity of the representations. In the school-age child, as in the preschool child, the result is the formation of egocentric conceptions. Again, at this stage these egocentric conceptions deal with assumptions about the world, but the assumptions have to do with possible courses of action in the real world and might be called *assumptive realities.*

As in the case of the assumptive philosophies of the preschool child, the assumptive realities of the school-age child reflect a confusion between the mental and the physical, between the reality of mind and the reality of matter. When the school-age child arrives at a possible course of action, a hypothesis, or a strategy which cannot be immediately tested, he often mistakes this *conceptual possibility* for a *material necessity.* Once he has adapted this egocentric position he proceeds to make any disparate facts fit the hypothesis rather than the reverse. This mode of egocentric thought is not unfamiliar at the adult level and is epitomized in folk sayings such as "Love is blind" or "No mother has a homely child."

Consider some of the following examples of assumptive realities in operation. In one study, Peel (1960) gave children and adolescents a passage describing the rock formations at Stonehenge without revealing their supposed function. The subjects were asked to decide whether the formations were used as a fort or as a religious shrine. The children (nine years old) made their decision on the basis of a few facts and, if given contrary information, rationalized this to fit in with their hypothesis. Adolescents, in contrast, based their hypothesis upon multiple facts and if given sufficient contrary information, changed their hypothesis.

In another experiment, Weir (1964) had five- to seventeen-year-old children work on a probability task. The apparatus was a box with three knobs and a payoff chute. One knob was programmed to pay off (in M&Ms or tokens) 0 per cent of the time, another was programmed to pay off 33 per cent of the time, and a third was programmed to pay off 66 per cent of the time. Subjects were instructed to find a pattern of response (knob pressing) that would produce the most rewards. The solution was to press only the 66 per cent knob inasmuch as it paid off more times in any hundred pressings than any other knob.

The results, plotted as number of trials to a successful solution, showed an inverted U curve with respect to age. Young children, who were getting M&Ms, did not waste time and quickly learned which button gave them the most candy. Adolescents approached the task with many complex hypotheses and tried out multiple complex patterns. In the process they discovered the fruitfulness of the 66 percent knob and eventually stuck to pressing it. But the seven- to nine-year-old children had great trouble. They adapted a "win stick, lose shift" strategy which they assumed was correct and blamed the machine for being wrong. This is a good example of the assumptive realities of the school-age child.

Other examples could be given (e.g. Elkind, 1966) but these few may suffice to illustrate the character of egocentric thought at the elementary school level. Whenever children are in a position to form possible courses of action in their heads, without immediate and unequivocal evidence of their correctness, the stage is set for assumptive realities. The child mistakes his hypothesized course of action for the real or necessary course of action and attributes more weight to it than to contrary bits of evidence. Such assumptive realities are egocentric because the child lacks the means to check them against the facts.

Clearly, if the child is given the correct solution in these problems or in other situations, then the assumptive reality is given up, because the child can then see the relation between the correct course of action and the result. The preschool child also can be shown that a particular object like a stone does not have feelings. These specific discoveries do not abolish the egocentric mode of thought, but only an egocentric concept in a particular situation. Egocentric concepts will emerge again when the child is in a situation where he can represent more than he can comprehend.

EGOCENTRIC STRUCTURES IN ADOLESCENCE

Roughly coincident with the onset of puberty is the appearance of new mental structures which Piaget calls formal operations.

Like concrete operations, formal operations function as a system but extend the young person's intellectual powers far beyond what they were in childhood, allowing the preadolescent to represent his own representations. Formal operations are to concrete operations as algebra is to arithmetic: a second-order, higher-level symbol system. While concrete operations make it possible for the child to conceive possible courses of action in the real world, formal operations make it possible for the adolescent to conceive of possible representations (which include theories, ideals, metaphors and so on). Formal operations also enable the young person to hold many hypotheses in mind while testing each one systematically: they make possible experimental thinking.

Formal operations enable the child to be aware of his hypotheses as hypotheses, as mental constructions, and permit him to test these against the evidence. In this way, formal operations enable the child not only to overcome his egocentric assumptive realities, but also to represent his own and other people's feelings and thoughts. Although he has the mental ability to test out these assumptions, the young adolescent lacks the motivation to do so. He is so preoccupied with the changes in his physical appearance and with his new feelings and emotions that he has little interest in checking out his assumptions about what other people think and feel. For a few years, therefore, the young adolescent operates on the basis of *assumptive psychologies* about himself and other people.

As in the case of assumptive philosophies of preschool children and assumptive realities of elementary school children, the assumptive psychologies of the young adolescent represent a confusion between the child and his world, but now on a psychological plane. What happens is that the young adolescent takes what is unique to himself as being universal to mankind, but also believes that what is universal to mankind is unique to himself. Such assumptive psychologies are sometimes gratifying and sometimes painful, and it is often the painful assumptions that eventually cause young people to test out their assumptions about how other people think and feel.

To illustrate some assumptive psychologies, consider the attractive young woman with a minor facial blemish. At this stage (early adolescence), she is convinced: a) that everyone notices and thinks about it, b) that everyone regards it as horribly ugly and detestable, and c) that it is the sole criterion on which people judge her as a person. Hence the conclusion, "Everybody thinks I am ugly. I must be ugly." In this familiar instance, the young person mistakes a personal, idiosyncratic appraisal of herself for one that is a uniform, consistent appraisal of mankind.

The reverse is also true: young people also mistake what is universal as being unique to themselves. A young man who has been saving up to buy an electric guitar feels that no boy in the world has ever wanted a guitar as much as he. But boys growing up all over the world want horses, boats, or even bows and arrows as signs of their maturity. Far from being unique, the desire for a symbol of adult male status is probably universal to male adolescents. In the same way, the young woman who is in love for the first time feels that her feelings are unique and that no one has ever experienced the exquisite pain she is enduring. "Oh Mother, you don't know how it feels"; and yet most mothers, and fathers, have at one time or another felt the same way.

These are but a few of the assumptive psychologies of adolescence, the egocentric ideas which permeate this age period. Again these ideas are egocentric only because the individual assumes they are shared by others when in fact they are not, or that they are not shared by others when in fact they are. Many of the interpersonal interactions among young adolescents are governed by assumptive psychologies, which can account in part for the self-centeredness of these interactions.

EGOCENTRIC STRUCTURES AND EGO DEFENSES

The delineation of the defense mechanisms of the ego evolved primarily out of the clinical work of Freud (1957) and his followers who worked for the most part with adults. When the developmental aspect of ego defenses was discussed, as in the work of Anna Freud (1946), it was primarily in connection with the psychosexual stages of development. These stages, the oral, anal, oedipal, latency, and adolescent periods (together with their substages), were defined primarily in terms of the vicissitudes of the child's developing sexual orientation. In Freudian theory, therefore, structural changes in cognitive functioning are derived from "geographical" changes in sexual orientation.

With the advent of psychoanalytic ego psychology (cf. Rapaport, 1960, for a historical summary) and the postulation of autonomous ego functions, a path was opened between psychoanalytic and cognitive theories of development. Much of the work on cognitive styles (e.g. Klein, 1958) was an attempt to show how autonomous ego functions could be related to personality dynamics. But the work on cognitive styles has been, for the most part, nondevelopmental. Styles such as "field independence-dependence" (Witkin et al., 1962) and "impulsivity/reflectivity" (Kagan, 1966) are present at all age levels, although perhaps to different extents. Cognitive styles appear to be more closely relted to long-standing affective orientations than to changing cognitive structures.

The work on cognitive styles evolved before much was known about cognitive development and was based on the assumption that thought did not change qualitatively with age once secondary, rational thinking appeared. But the work of Jean Piaget (1963) has demonstrated that rational thought is not of one piece, but rather evolves in a series of stages that are related to age. These stages were briefly described earlier. Piaget's work thus forces a reconsideration of cognitive styles in general and of ego defenses in particular. The present discussion attempts such a reconsideration of ego defenses within a cognitive development framework.

Because ego defenses were derived from dynamic considerations, and without regard to cognitive development, they do not always make sense from a Piagetian standpoint. Rather than try to reinterpret ego defenses from the standpoint of cognitive growth, I propose to describe cognitive structures available for defensive purposes at successive age levels. Traditional ego defenses, such as denial, can then be defined in terms of cognitive structures at a particular age level and in this way lose some of their ambiguity. Because of the wide scope of such a project, only a brief introduction to what might be accomplished will be presented here.

EGOCENTRIC STRUCTURES AND DEFENSES AT THE PRESCHOOL LEVEL

In the earlier discussion, it was suggested that the egocentric structures of the preschool period have to do with assumptive philosophies. One of these assumptive philosophies is *phenomenalistical causality,* the belief that events which happen together cause one another. Such thinking is in evidence when a child who sees the sun appear when the window shade is raised believes that raising the shade causes the sun to rise. Phenomenalistic causality is involved with animism and artificialism, both of which reflect a confusion between the psychic and the physical.

Although phenomenalistic causality is a general characteristic of young people's thinking, it can also be used for defensive purposes. To illustrate, the work on father absence (Herzog and Sudia, 1973) suggests that such absence or separation is most detrimental when it occurs before the age of six or seven. Clearly this is an important period of identification, particularly for the boy. In addition, however, it is also the period of phenomenalistic causality thinking. Boys who may fantasize the father gone may find that he has gone in fact. The chance association of fantasy and fact leads the child to believe that one caused the other. This is what is usually called *magical thinking.* But magical thinking is merely a special case of phenomenalistic causal thinking which is derived from the preoperational mental functions.

Phenomenalistic or precausal thinking does not disappear as children mature: it continues to appear even at the adult level. A salesman who makes an unexpected sale after crossing his fingers may cross his fingers prior to the next sale in hopes it will "work" again. The popularity of the television show "Bewitched" for both adults and children suggests the ease with which both age groups fall back into the magical thinking mode.

A very common instance of phenomenalistic causality thinking occurs in the children of divorced couples. Such children, particularly at the early elementary school level, are likely to believe that some misbehavior on their part brought about the separation. The magical thought, which grows out of guilt feelings, further aggravates the guilt feelings and hence leads to the perpetration of the magical thought. Since such children are capable of more mature thought, their difficulty is primarily emotional rather than rational. A therapeutic approach aimed at their feelings, rather than at their magical thinking, would probably be most helpful.

EGOCENTRIC STRUCTURES AND EGO DEFENSES IN CHILDHOOD

During childhood, the egocentric structures that are in prominence derive from concrete operations and amount to assumptive realities, wherein the child mistakes a possible course of action (a mental construction) for the real or actual course of action or events. As a consequence, the child views his mental construction as necessary and defensible against contrary evidence. While such assumptive realities are normal to most children at one or another time, they can become defenses when strong emotions are involved.

Elsewhere (Elkind, 1973) I have described some of the defensive egocentric structures in childhood and I will briefly review some of those structures here. One of these structures I have called *cognitive conceit*. During the preschool years the child believes his parents are all-powerful and all-knowing. With the advent of concrete operations and elementary reasoning abilities, the child has the intellectual capacity to detect the fallacies in parental logic and the gaps in their knowledge. Once a child has the revelation that a parent, a grownup, can be in error, he jumps to the conclusion that he knows more than the adult and that the adult is stupid. This belief that he is clever and that adults are stupid is a cognitive conceit of the school-age child.

Cognitive conceit is common to children in greater or lesser degrees. It is embodied in their language and lore and is exemplified in jokes and riddles wherein adults are made to look stupid. That is one reason children at this age prefer stories in which children outwit adults (Shlager, 1974). When children play games with adults, cognitive conceit becomes apparent in their boasting when they win and in their rationalizations when they lose. Children seek evidence to bolster their cognitive conceit and often delight in tripping up adults when they can catch them in error.

Another assumptive reality common to the elementary school

period is the *tall tale*. Children often make assumptions about the world which add to their sense of adventure. They may assume that there is buried treasure in the backyard and proceed to dig up a flower bed in search of it. Or they may skulk about following a "suspicious-looking" stranger whom they are sure is a spy or gangster. Although at some level children understand that the tall tale is just that, they also maintain it cognitively and rationalize a good deal of information to preserve such assumptive realities intact.

From an ego-defense point of view, assumptive realities and their maintenance relate to what has been called *denial* and *rationalization*. Denial is seldom, if ever, a passive nay-saying. Rather it is a reconstruction of reality for defensive purposes. It is a hypothesis about reality which the subject mistakes for reality itself. A common example of assumptive reality as denial occurs when a child is accused of stealing or lying. In this situation the child may, even though aware of having taken something or told an untruth, reconstruct his memory of the event in such a way that he appears innocent and uninvolved. He then treats his memory reconstruction as a veridical memory and asserts his innocence to his parents' great consternation.

Rationalization goes hand in hand with assumptive realities and is the use of reason to defend an assumptive reality. It is the modification of facts to fit the hypothesis rather than a modification of hypothesis to fit the facts. When a child denies his guilt by memory reconstruction, he must also rationalize a good deal of evidence that is in conflict with that reconstruction. Accordingly, from a developmental point of view, denial (in the sense of memory reconstruction) and rationalization (in the sense of reasoning to make the facts fit the hypotheses) are ego defenses that make their appearance during childhood and in connection with the egocentric assumptive realities that mark this period.

EGOCENTRIC STRUCTURES AND EGO DEFENSES IN ADOLESCENCE

At about the age of puberty, the gradual emergence of formal operations makes possible the conceptualization of thought and of other people's thinking. The egocentric structures of this age period amount to assumptive psychologies—beliefs about other people's thoughts and feelings. As indicated earlier, the young adolescent confuses the universal with the unique and the unique with the universal. The assumptive psychologies of the early adolescent period give rise to the characteristic structures described below.

One of these structures is an *imaginary audience* (cf. Ch. 8), an assumption that other people are as interested in the young person as he is himself. The imaginary audience derives from a confusion between what is important to the young person and what he believes is important to others. The young adolescent believes that other people are observing and evaluating his appearance and his clothing because he mistakes his unique concern for himself, engendered by all the changes of adolescence, for a concern that is common to everyone. The imaginary audience grows naturally out of the characteristic self-other confusion of this age period.

Coupled with the imaginary audience is a complementary egocentric structure, the *personal fable* (cf. Ch. 8). Just as the youth mistakes what is unique to himself for what is common to everyone, so too does he mistake what is common to everyone as unique to himself. Most adolescents find it hard to conceptualize their own death and believe that while everyone else in the world may die, they will live on forever. Each adolescent feels in addition that the belief is unique to himself, even though it is practically universal even among older age groups. The personal fable is the story each individual tells himself about his own immortality and specialness which happens not to be true. While each individual is indeed unique and special, it is not in the ways that are embodied in each individual's personal fable.

If we look now at these egocentric structures from the standpoint of ego defense, they appear to be comparable to what is usually called *projection*. Dynamically, projection is defined as the attribution to others of one's own feelings, impulses, and thoughts. But such attribution must, of necessity, wait upon the child's ability to conceptualize the thoughts, feelings, and impulses of others. This does not appear until adolescence. Projection is, therefore, another name for assumptive psychologies.

But assumptive psychologies, such as the imaginary audience

and the personal fable, move in two directions: the attribution of what is unique to the self as common to others and the attribution of what is common to others as unique to the self. In the latter case, the individual fails to attribute to others what is characteristic of them. This latter process is a form of *intellectual narcissism,* a refusal to accept that what is true of the self might also be true of others: "No one else feels with the intensity and sensitivity that I do." Projection and intellectual narcissism are, in the sense defined here, characteristic of the adolescent period and of the formal operations that generally emerge with the advent of puberty.

SOME CLINICAL IMPLICATIONS

The foregoing discussion is a beginning attempt to relate cognitive development to the construction of ego defenses. The analysis offered here suggests that magical thinking derives from the preschool period, that denial and rationalization derive from the elementary school period, and that projection and intellectual narcissism (as defined here) are the outcomes of the formal operations of adolescence. In view of the preliminary nature of this discussion, it would not be in order to advance a detailed presentation of clinical implications. It does seem appropriate, however, to mention a few issues that appear to warrant further research.

First of all, it might be possible to relate traditional clinical syndromes to the age when the cognitive component of their characteristic defenses emerge. While the dynamic underpinnings for the use of these defenses may well appear earlier in development, the defensive pattern itself will not appear until the appropriate structures are available. This type of analysis would suggest that more consideration must be paid to the ages when the cognitive structures of various syndromes emerge.

The obsessive-compulsive neuroses, for example, are often traced to fixations at the anal stage of development (one to two years old). But what characterizes the obsessive-compulsive is the prevalence of a few assumptive realities about the danger inherent in loss of control and environmental disorder. As in the case of all assumptive realities, evidence to the contrary is no way to combat them. The point is that assumptive realities are the product of concrete operations which do not appear until after the age of six or seven. According to this analysis, obsessive-compulsive symptomatology should not appear until middle childhood, except in intellectually precocious children. This is an hypothesis which might be tested.

A similar case could be made for paranoia not appearing, in symptomatic form, until adolescence. At the cognitive level, paranoia involves projection of feelings and thoughts onto others. It also involes the form of intellectual narcissism known as meglomania. In theory, however, such projection and narcissism cannot occur until the advent of formal operations. Indeed, the imaginary audience and the personal fable could be the normal analogs to delusions of persecution and of meglomania. The fact that paranoia does not usually appear until adolescence and that it generally occurs in individuals of better than average intelligence would support the argument that formal operations are required for the realization of this syndrome. Again, this is a matter that could be put to test.

A final example may add further support to the approach suggested here. Although some forms of mild depressive states are observed in children, true depression is not usually observed until adolescence. It is generally recognized that the central dynamic of depression is the loss of or separation from a loved object. When separation occurs early in life, when no defenses are hossible, the infant shows anaclitic depression. But when the separation or loss occurs during childhood, the young person can use assumptive realities—denial and rationalization—to deal with the separation. In the case of divorce, for example, the assumptive reality of the eventual parental reunion is often maintained regardless of the parent's animosities and even in the face of their remarriage to others.

With the emergence of adolescence and formal operations, separation and loss are experienced with full cognitive force. The young person can no longer cling to assumptive realities that deny the facts. The recognition that there will be no parental reunion can result in deep depression.

Moreover, once the young person can conceive how other people think about him, a new kind of loss or separation becomes possible, namely, the loss of face or of reputation, the good will toward us held in the minds of others. Momentary social lapses are excruciatingly painful to adolescents who are now aware of "audience reactions." Adolescent depressions and suicides are frequently the direct result of such reputational or image losses that are only possible to individuals who can conceptualize the way others think about them.

The cognitive dimension of depression is seen most dramatically and tragically in young people who have suffered from a physical defect or handicap. During childhood, due to assumptive realities such as "I will get better," they often appear as happy children. When adolescence and formal operations arrive, however, these children sometimes experience severe depressions. The assumptive realities must be given up. Moreover, the young person can now conceive the thoughts of others and so believe they reject his defect as emphatically as he does. Such children no sooner gain a sense of the potential esteem of others than they lose it, in imagination, due to their defect. In such instances, cognitive development is the precipitating factor in the depression.

These few examples of the relation between egocentric structures, ego defenses, and psychopathology are merely suggestive. Much more theoretical, clinical, and research work needs to be done before we can be more sure about the tentative ideas presented here. I do hope, however, that this material suggests the potential fruitfulness of cognitive developmental theory for the study of psychopathology.

SUMMARY

The study of cognitive development has, for the most part, been concerned with the evolution of rational, socialized thought. The evolution of egocentric, nonrational thought has, on the other hand, been neglected. This chapter has concerned itself with the development of egocentric thought and its relation to ego defenses, first tracing the history of the study of egocentric thought to the early anthropological studies of primitive thinking in esoteric peoples and to the psychological studies of primitive thinking in children and adults. The advent of ego psychology in some ways blocked further study of the development of egocentric thinking.

The second section describes the evolution of egocentric thinking from the perspective of Piagetian theory. Egocentric thinking occurs because there is a discrepancy between the growing individual's ability to form hypotheses and his ability to test them. Egocentric concepts are those which, at any level of development, the child can form but not test. These concepts amount to assumptions about the self and the world which take different forms at different age levels. At the preschool level, the child forms assumptive *philosophies;* at the school-age level, he forms assumptive *realities;* while at the adolescent level, he forms assumptive *psychologies.*

A third section details some of the particular egocentric structures at each age level and relates them to familiar ego defenses. At the preschool level, the assumptive reality of phenomenalistic causality was related to the defense of magical thinking. Among the egocentric structures of the school-age child are the notions of cognitive conceit and tall tales. The ego defenses most closely related to the egocentric structures at this age period are denial and rationalization. From the standpoint of cognition, denial is a false reconstruction of past events with rationalization brought in to support it. At the adolescent level, the egocentric structures of the imaginary audience and the personal fable resemble ego defenses of projection and intellectual narcissism.

In the concluding section, some possible implications of the discussion for research and practice are suggested. It was hypothesized that the obsessive-compulsive neuroses should not appear until childhood and the emergence of assumptive realities. In addition it was suggested that paranoia and depression must wait upon the assumptive psychologies of adolescence for their emergence. These suggestions do not presuppose that the dynamic anlage of those syndromes could not be laid down earlier in development. It does suggest that a certain level of cognitive organization must be present before certain psychopathological syndromes can become manifest.

REFERENCES

Anthony, E. J. The significance of Jean Piaget for child psychiatry. *British J. of Medical Psychol.*, 1956, *29*, 20–34.

Chandler, M. J. Egocentrism and antisocial behavior: The assessment and training of social perspective-taking skills. *Developmental Psychol.*, 1973, 9, 326–32.

Elkind, D. Conceptual orientation shifts in children and adolescents. *Child Development*, 1966, 37, 493–98.

Elkind, D. Cognitive structure in latency behavior. In J.C. Westman (Ed.) *Individual Differences in Children.* New York: Wiley, 1973, 105–17.

Flavell, J., et al. *The Development of Role-taking and Communication Skills in Children.* New York: Wiley, 1968.

Freud, A. *The Ego and the Mechanisms of Defense.* New York: International Universities Press, 1946.

Freud, S. *The Ego and the Id.* London: The Hogarth Press, 1957 (originally published in 1923).

Herzog, E., & Sudia, C. E. Children in fatherless families. In B.M. Caldwell & H.N. Ricciuti (Eds.) *Review of Child Development Research.* Chicago: The University of Chicago Press, 1973, 141–232.

Kagan, J. Reflection-impulsivity: The generality and dynamics of conceptual tempo. *J. of Abnormal Psychol.*, 1966, 71, 17–24.

Klein, G. S. Cognitive control and motivation. In. G. Lindzey (Ed.) *Assessment of Human Motives.* New York: Rinehart, 1958, 87–118.

Kohlberg, L., Yaeger, J., & Hjertholm, E. Private speech: four studies and a review of theories. *Child Development*, 1968, 39, 691–736.

18

THE CURRICULUM-DISABLED CHILD

Learning disabilities are always a product of child-curriculum interaction. When the disability results from introducing young people to the curriculum too soon or from materials that are ambiguous and confusing, we can speak of a curriculum-disabled child. This paper presents examples of curriculum disabilities, describes the consequences of curriculum-induced school failure for children's self-appraisal, and offers suggestions to mental health professionals who deal with curriculum-disabled children.

This chapter is concerned with a rather large group of children who are often ignored in contemporary discussions of children with special needs. Such children are of average intellectual ability and have no serious physical or emotional problems. Yet they experience failure in the first few grades of school. In such children, school failure can be traced to several different factors. One of these is the too early introduction of formal instruction, say in reading, before the children are perceptually and cognitively mature enough to profit from such instruction. Other children find the learning materials so confusing or so boring

Invited address, Divisions 7–15, American Psychological Association, San Francisco, 1977.

that they cannot invest themselves in the task of learning. Gifted children, by the way, often fall within this category. Still other children have learning styles or strategies that conflict with those demanded by the school program. It is a mistake, or so it seems to me, to call such children learning disabled. For these children, school failure is not attributable to some malfunction in their brains. It *is* attributable to a mismatch between the child and the curriculum. Accordingly, I propose to call such children *curriculum disabled.* That is to say, for these children school failure is as much the fault of the school system as it is of the children.

In adding another phrase to the mental health lexicon, I am well aware of some of the dangers that this entails. Children of the sort to be described here have long been recognized so that the phenomenon, if not the terminology, is well known. Perhaps more serious is the possibility that, by adding another phrase to describe children, the practice of labeling children (which has already gone much too far) will be abetted. Nonetheless, it is sometimes necessary to fight fire with fire, and the term "curriculum disabled" has the advantage that it focuses upon the child-curriculum interaction rather than upon the child in isolation. And it is just this interactional perspective that is so lacking in contemporary discussions of learning disabilities.

In this discussion I would like to document how children can be disabled by the curriculum, describe some of the psychological problems created by curriculum-induced school failure, and, finally, to suggest a new professional orientation for dealing with these problems. Unfortunately, many of these problems could be averted by an early critical evaluation of educational practices and materials.

TWO MYSTIQUES REGARDING CURRICULUM

In contrast to teachers and school administrators, who are constantly under attack, either from parents or other teachers, the curriculum is rarely criticized. When the curriculum is attacked, it is usually in terms of the content of certain materials or books that are regarded as unfit for tender minds. But parents do not challenge instructions that are so complex that they confuse rather than enlighten, or exercises and illustrations that hinder rather than help children's learning, or subject matter that is way beyond the children's level of comprehension.

We do not challenge the curriculum for a number of reasons. One is the *mystique of the printed word*. Print lends authority to subject matter, and even those of us who should know better are often taken in. When we find stupidities in the curriculum material we assume that they are there for a reason, that there is an intelligent rationale that we, as laymen, simply do not appreciate. In fact, however, there is often no intelligent rationale and many times the materials are in fact as stupid as they appear.

In addition to the mystique of print, there is also a mystique of *challenge*. Whenever I talk to groups of parents and/or teachers about modifying the curriculum so that it is in greater harmony with children's mental abilities, I get asked the same question. "If we make things easy for children as you suggest, don't we deprive them of the challenge that will stimulate their thinking?" My answer to this question is that we have to distinguish between intelligent and unintelligent challenge. By intelligent challenge I have in mind materials that are novel but within the child's level of comprehension. Applying one's mental powers to novel problems is the essence of human intelligence. On the other hand, unintelligent challenges are those that present children with novel problems that are beyond the range of their mental capacities.

Let me give you some illustrations of intelligent and unintelligent challenges. In one first grade classroom that I like to visit, children spend a week working on each letter of the alphabet (in addition to their usual math, reading, etc.). If the letter is "M," then they find words, pictures, objects and places that begin with "M." They think of foods that begin with "M" and bring them to class. They find games that begin with "M" and play these too. By the end of the week they have a pretty good concept of "M," not only of its various sounds but also of the many words of which it forms a part. Finding different kinds of words that begin with "M" Provides an intelligent challenge because the child is dealing with novel material (new words) that are at his or her level of comprehension.

On the other hand, I recently sat with another first grade class while they watched a brief, eight-minute film about cotton. In the course of eight minutes they saw cotton growing, they watched it being harvested, threshed, baled, and transported to mills where it was converted to thread, dyed, and then made into cloth. Trains and trucks transported the cloth to factories where it was made into clothing. The last shots of the film showed people in a clothing store buying the shirts that had been made in the factory. It did not surprise me a bit that the children's response to the teacher's question about how cotton was made into cloth ended up in a debate as to which of the shirts in the store was the "prettiest" or "nicest." The film was an unintelligent challenge to these children because it presented too much information, too fast, and at too high a level of abstraction for them to fully comprehend.

WHY CURRICULUM ERRORS PERSIST

The curriculum error described above, far from being the exception, is unfortunately quite common. I have recently detailed a variety of such curriculum errors in all of the elementary school subjects (Elkind, 1976). But the question that needs to be asked is why these curriculum errors persist. The reasons are many and complex. They involve historical, political, sociological, and psychological factors among others. For example, in the past hundred years there has been a repeated alternation between subject oriented and child-centered curricula. The dynamics of this alternation are instructive and show the interplay of forces that determine curriculum priorities and direction.

What has happened in the last two decades in America is a case in point. During the 1950s, there was a reaction to the teacher written, child-centered curricula then in use. This reaction was intensified by the launching of the Russian Sputnik in 1957. During the late 1950s and the 1960s curriculum development was in the hands of the academics who gave us the "New Math," along with new curricula in science, in reading, and in social studies. In terms of subject matter these new curricula were quite up-to-date, but in terms of being appropriate for the child's intellectual abilities, they were far too complex and abstract. In the 1970s the reaction has been against these new curricula and back to basics has become the catchword of the latter half of this decade. What back to basics means, to anyone who looks at the "new" new curricula carefully, is back to the kinds of materials that were prevalent in the early 1950s! Materials today, like those of that time, are increasingly teacher written and child centered. The pendulum has come full swing again.

Even the "new" new, more child-centered materials, however, still reflect many mistakes from a child development perspective. The problem arises because even child-centered teachers involved in writing the "new" new curricula are not fully acquainted with the knowledge about children's thinking that has been made available to us largely from the work of Jean Piaget. Piaget's work has given us powerful new tools with which to analyze curriculum materials and so insure that they are appropriate to the intellectual level of the children for whom they are prepared. What is most disturbing about the "new" new curricula is that they are much worse than they need to be given our existing knowledge about children's thinking.

I do not believe, however, that the answer to this problem is to give curriculum development over to the academics again because this would simply reinitiate the cycle that has repeated itself too often in the past. What is really needed is a new breed of curriculum writer. People who write curriculum should be steeped in child development *and* in the subject matter they are writing about. Until we get this sort of person into the curriculum field, we are almost certain to have these perpetual swings from content-centered to child-centered curriculum materials, neither of which is entirely satisfactory. It is time, now, to give some examples of how curriculum errors, fostered by either approach, can produce learning disabilities.

EXAMPLES OF CURRICULUM DISABILITIES

In actuality, all of us are curriculum disabled in certain respects. Our woefully deficient artistic skills are a case in point. By the age of nine or ten, most of us give up trying to draw, paint, or sculpt. There is such a discrepancy between what we want to do and what we are able to do, that we simply give up the effort. Important veins of self-expression are, in effect, closed to us for the remainder of our lives unless we make special efforts to get individual and expert instruction. This curriculum disability is a direct consequence of the poor art instruction that is provided in most schools. To be sure, artistic creation of the first rank is as much a matter of talent as it is of training. On the other hand, many, many people play and enjoy music who are not concert artists. Music is simply taught better than is art. But, in principle, as many people could enjoy their art work as now enjoy playing an instrument alone or in groups.

Even a curriculum that is quite good, however, can still produce curriculum disabilities in children for whom it is inappropriate. This is most obvious in children who are confronted with a curriculum for which they are not yet ready. Children, for example, whose birthdays fall in October, November or December, but who nonetheless begin school in September, are often disabled by the curriculum. This is true because the kindergarten curriculum presupposed a level of maturity that these children often do not yet possess. If such children proceed to first grade they are many times even less prepared for the formal instruction in reading and in math that is offered at that level. If a child with a late birthday is having trouble and is not kept back in kindergarten or in first grade, his or her difficulties become increasingly more severe as the child progresses through the grades. Such children make up a considerable proportion of curriculum-disabled children.

It should be said that this problem was noted and dealt with organizationally several decades ago. In the thirties and forties, for example, there were A and B classes. A child with a late fall birthday began school in January rather than in September. He or she would then continue to complete the grade the following fall and begin a new one the following January. Although it was awkward, this system attempted to match curriculum more exactly with the developmental level of the children to whom it was directed. The system was dropped because of its awkwardness. In its stead we have an even more cumbersome evaluation system, varying from state to state, for determining at what age or stage children should be permitted to enter kindergarten when they have a fall birthday.

There is another group of children who are disabled not so much by their time of entry into the curriculum as by endless ambiguities and needless complexities of everyday curriculum materials. These children have the mental ability to learn the skills to be mastered, but are hindered on every side by curriculum errors. Usually these children are of average or slightly below average intelligence. Such children have to work very hard to learn the material and curriculum errors make their task that much harder. For these children, curriculum materials designed to facilitate learning often have the opposite effect.

Some commonplace examples may help to illustrate this point. A very frequent error, that occurs in almost every single workbook (of whatever publisher) for beginning reading, is to be found in the illustrations. A usual workbook exercise is to show a series of pictures of common objects, beneath each of which is the first letter of the name of the object, followed by a series of dashes over which the child is to complete the name of the object. The problem is that the pictures are often quite ambiguous. For example, the picture might be of a ball while beneath it is the following: R - - - -. The word required is "Round," but the word that comes most readily to the child's mind is "ball." Consequently, the child may have difficulty with the item not because he or she does not know the word "round" but because the item itself was misleading.

Other common curricular errors are instructions that confound rather than instruct. Instead of asking a child to find the sum of the following numbers, $2 + 2 = $ ____, the child is asked, in some math series, to "Make this sentence true." Such an instruction introduces analogies (between math and language and math and logic) that intrude extraneous and irrelevant concepts and concerns into what is basically a mathematical problem. Such instructions confound and confuse rather than instruct children by presupposing levels of reasoning and conceptualization that are far beyond the level of the children to whom they are presented.

Unfortunately, our curriculum materials are full of roadblocks to learning of this sort. The bright child, or the self-confident child of average ability, can usually take such curriculum errors in stride. But for children who lack good ability and/or self-confidence, the curriculum errors add immeasurably to his or her difficulties. Clearly, the child is disabled by the curriculum in part by his or her prior propensities. But for many of these children school plays a very pivotal role in whether the child succeeds academically or becomes a school failure. For such children curriculum errors make a very real difference in the outcome of the child's efforts to attain tool skills. Some children do fail primarily because of curriculum errors and I want now to detail the consequences of school failure for children in general and for curriculum disabled children in particular.

PSYCHOLOGICAL CONCOMITANTS OF CURRICULUM DISABILITY

Contemporary psychology and psychiatry recognize the role of self-esteem in mental health and in mental illness. Individuals with chronically low self-esteem show a variety of neuroticlike behaviors, ranging from extreme shyness, withdrawal, and depression to gross exhibitionism and aggressive bullying. Low self-esteem can be traced to many different sources, but most often derives from early and repeated negative appraisals from others. The self, at least initially, is based primarily on the appraisals of others, and when those are predominantly negative so too is the individual's self-concept.

Consider the role of school achievement in the child's sense of self-esteem. In our society, particularly at present, enormous weight is placed upon successful performance in school. Children are well aware of how much value their parents place on school achievement and how attuned parents are to each telltale sign of school success or failure. "Oh, you can read this book, great!" or "Oh, you can't do that easy problem!" Such expressions tell children how important school success is to their parents. And children also "overhear" their parents brag or complain to friends about how well or how poorly their children are doing in school.

What happens to a child who experiences school failure?

When the other children understand what the teacher means, this child doesn't understand—try as hard as he or she may. The whole business, say, of reading is a great mystery. Unfortunately, many of these children reason, "But if the other children can do it and I cannot then there must be something wrong with me." School failure is a very public failure that occurs day after day, week after week. It is not surprising that one seven year old who was not reading told me, "I guess I am a flop in life."

School failure in the early grades is particularly harmful because at that age children do not distinguish clearly between what I have called the *transient* and the *abiding* self. The transient self has to do with momentary appearances: a bad haircut, soiled or torn clothing, a momentary clumsiness. The abiding self has to do with qualities such as intelligence, energy level, and competence. What happens in early elementary school children is that they often mistake what is transient for what is abiding and vice versa. School failure is not seen as a transient event but rather as a reflection of the abiding self.

What also happens, and what makes the consequences of school failure so pernicious, is that the child begins to look upon any school success as a success of the transient self. Hence, even if a child who has been experiencing school failure is given some success experiences, these may be read as chance occurrences with no meaning for the abiding self. Once a child begins to feel badly about himself or herself, it becomes a reality to which all facts, no matter how discrepant, are made to conform. The child develops a sense of *cognitive ineptitude* which becomes all pervasive.

There is another important consequence of early school failure. Remember that the school age years are those which Erikson (1950) describes as significant for the establishment of a sense of *industry* in the child, a sense of being able to do a job competently and well. By instructing children in a skill that they are not yet capable of acquiring, we not only cause suffering and frustration, we may also undermine the child's sense of industry and reinforce a sense of inferiority about academic matters which will stay with the child for the rest of his or her academic career. Recall that Bloom (1964) demonstrated that a child's academic achievement at age seventeen could be predicted with fifty per cent accuracy from his or her academic achievement at grade three. The early grades of school, not the preschool years, are the critical ones in the determination of long-term academic achievement.

In summary, early school failure can do serious injury to the child's sense of self-esteem and of industry and can, eventually, give rise to serious emotional disturbance. This happens because school failure can negatively affect the child's interactions with parents and peers. In such cases it would be a mistake to take the family problems as the cause of the school failure. In fact, these problems may center about the child's learning difficulties. I contend that in many families, early school failure is not a symptom but the *primary cause* of emotional disturbance in the child and of familial disharmony.

CHALLENGE FOR MENTAL HEALTH PROFESSIONALS

If curriculum-disabled children become emotionally-disabled children, this has implications for mental health practitioners. Ideally, of course, we would want to eliminate the cause of such disabilities and introduce materials appropriate for children into the schools. But we are a long way away from that situation. In the meantime, we will have to deal with children whose emotional problems derive, at least initially, from school failure. Before I make a practical suggestion, however, we need to look at a phenomenon that has blinded us, in the mental health professions, to the problems of curriculum disabilities.

I believe that when psychiatrists, psychologists, or social workers deal with school related problems, we are guilty of a *mental health egocentrism*. Egocentrism always involves seeing the world from our own point of view and failing to see it from the other person's perspective. Consequently, in our programmatic preventive and individual remedial efforts, we focus on matters that seem most important to us, but which may in fact be unimportant or of little consequence to children and to teachers.

Some of the current programs in affective education are a case in point. There are now programs in the elementary school for "value clarification," for "sensitivity training," for learning "interpersonal problem solving skills," and many others. Some of these programs are genuinely helpful in promoting better communication between children and teachers. But some of them are every bit as bad as some of the academic curricula. This is true because we know, both from clinical experience and research, that seven to eleven year old children are not willing or very able to reflect upon and talk about their feelings and thoughts. And yet that is just what some of these "affective curricula" require children to do.

But the affective curricula, even the good ones, reflect mental health professionals' egocentrism. Communication and feelings are our stock in trade. When schools tell us that there are problems in the classroom, we immediately assume that the teachers and the children are not communicating and are not expressing their feelings. If they can be trained to do this, everything will be all right again. But the failure to communicate and express feelings may be a symptom and not a cause. Moreover, in these affective curricula neither the teacher nor the children are ever encouraged to express feelings or to communicate about what may really be bothering them: namely, curriculum materials that are often both unteachable and unlearnable.

In an active classroom (Elkind, 1976), one that is truly child centered and in which the curriculum materials are teacher- and child-made and suited to the children's interest and level of mental development, there is no need for special affective education. Curricula that are appropriate to the child's conceptual level open up avenues of communication between child and child, and child and teacher, that are closed when the child cannot elaborate upon the material from his or her own experience and within his or her own conceptual system. Moreover, in a truly active classroom where children take some responsibility for their own learning and for their own discipline, they develop both respect for themselves and respect for others. And isn't that really what affective education is all about?

The separation of affective education from sound educational practice is a mistake, and one that we mental health professionals have foisted upon the schools. Not only have we artificially separated the cognitive and the affective, we have diverted attention from the source of many of the difficulties that children and teachers encounter in the school, namely, the curriculum. It is time, I believe, that we move out of our egocentrism and recognize the child is a totality and that it is only we, the professionals, who split that totality into cognitive and affective components.

To take account of this totality means that, when dealing with curriculum-disabled children, we give up the clinical bifurcation between the cognitive and the affective. Traditionally, the remedial teacher busies himself or herself with a child's academic problems and regards the emotional ones as outside of his or her province of activity. The therapist concerns himself or herself with the child's emotional problems and ignores or pays scant attention to the academic ones. This separation may make sense (although I am not convinced) with children whose primary problem is rooted in a familiar form of family pathology, but for curriculum-damaged children such a bifurcated approach is totally inappropriate.

There are several reasons why this is true. First, it reinforces the child's devaluation of education and of schooling. This is most obvious in a children's ward at a hospital. Children are very much aware of the status hierarchy in such places; they know that the doctor is on top and the teacher is on the bottom of the status ladder. This supports the children's defensive attitude that school is not important and that talking about feelings and problems is the most important thing.

And yet, for these young people, the devaluation of schooling as supported by the system is antitherapeutic. For them, schooling *is* important; it is of central concern to them and to their emotional difficulties. The avoidance of school related discussion by therapists thus helps these young people to avoid their most serious problem. And, of course, they really do not want to avoid the topic. I recall visiting an adolescent ward recently, and when I spoke of these matters, one therapist told me, with some embarrassment, that her patient often wanted to show her his school work and she never paid much attention to it!

The division between affective and cognitive, between education and therapy, is inappropriate for curriculum-disabled children for a second reason. Learning the tool skills of reading, writing, and arithmetic is socially rather than intrinsically motivated. Learning to read, for example, is an extraordinarily difficult task for most children and does not begin to be enjoyable in its own right until it is fairly well developed. What motivates the majority of children to learn the three R's is attachment to adults who model, reward and praise their efforts.

Consider the therapist who has established a good relationship with a patient but who deals only with the young person's interpersonal relationships. The value of that attachment as a motivator for school achievement is lost. And the teacher, who sees many children together, can seldom have the same significance for the child or adolescent as the therapist. For the curriculum-disabled child, the separation between therapist and teacher dissipates the value of the therapist's attachment as a motivating force in the child's learning.

I am not saying that every therapist has to be a teacher and vice versa. I am saying that with curriculum-disabled children, the roles of teacher and therapist have to be combined for the most effective treatment. Obviously, the therapist cannot become a trained teacher, but there are some basic skills in teaching reading and math that can be mastered quickly. Likewise the teacher of children with learning problems does not have to be a trained therapist to acquire some skills for handling emotional problems as they come up.

I know that some readers will object that the blurring of professional boundaries may be difficult for children to deal with. After all, don't children need clear cut role definitions? No, for older children and adolescents this is really not necessary. Children can deal quite well with a science teacher who is also a coach or a music teacher who also conducts the orchestra. I believe that it is we professionals, not the children we work with, who are concerned about role diffusion.

In working with curriculum-disabled children, then, one and the same person should help the child with his or her school problems as well as his or her emotional problems. Only in this way can we avoid the devaluation of schooling inherent in our traditional separation of the affective and the cognitive. And it is only in this way that we can help the curriculum-disabled child deal, in a focused way, with the central concern of his or her existence. To avoid or to deny the central role of school failure in the emotional disturbance of a child of this sort is to deny the child's reality and to make it subservient to our own.

SUMMARY

I have argued here that, in our society, school failure can be a significant factor in the emotional disturbance of children. In many cases, however, school failure is not a consequence of something wrong in the child as much as it is a result of the child's interaction with the curriculum. Curriculum disabilities occur when the curriculum is poor, when children are introduced to an adequate curriculum too early, and when curriculum errors present unnecessary roadblocks to children who do not learn as easily as most.

The consequences of school failure are a lowered sense of self-esteem and an impaired sense of industry. Unfortunately these early, negative evaluations interact with cognitive dynamics which push children into believing that they are permanent misfits and that their learning failures are part of their abiding self. The child's school failure can produce family disharmony as well. But it is important to remember that such disharmony is often a symptom rather than a cause of school failure.

We in the mental health professions have to overcome our egocentrism and to recognize that *our* concerns may not be the same as those of teachers and of children. Rather than introduce "new" affective curricula that are as bad as the school curricula, we need to help children with the school curricula itself. In dealing with curriculum-disabled children, we need to ignore professional boundaries and combine the roles of teacher and therapist. Otherwise we actually help children avoid the issue that is at the root of their problem, namely, school failure. We cannot eliminate school failure, but we can take it seriously as do curriculum-disabled children.

REFERENCES

Bloom, B. *Stability and Change in Human Behavior.* New York: Wiley, 1964.
Elkind, D. *Child Development and Education.* New York: Oxford, 1976.
Erikson, E. H. *Childhood and Society.* New York: Norton, 1950.

19

THE ACTIVE CLASSROOM AND CHILDREN WITH SPECIAL NEEDS

AFFECTIVE AND SOCIAL DIMENSIONS

The active classroom is one that is organized and adapted to the developmental level of the children it serves. Although the primary focus of the active classroom is to facilitate intellectual growth and academic attainments, it has affective and social dimensions as well. This chapter describes three such dimensions and how they make the active classroom well suited for assimilating some children with special needs.

An active classroom is one that is geared to the developmental level of the children it serves and which permits children to use the various modes of learning of which they are capable (Elkind, 1976). Children learn some things by imitation and repetition, other things by active inquiry, and still others through expressive activities such as writing and painting. An active classroom provides the materials and the opportunities for all three kinds of learning. Although the active classroom is usually thought of in terms of its emphasis on cognition, it has some affective/social dimensions as well. This chapter is concerned with this "hidden side" of the active classroom with particular reference to children with special needs.

Before all else, it is important to recognize that children, re-

S.J. Mersels (ed.) *Open Education and Children with Special Needs.* Baltimore: University Park Press, 1978.

gardless of their handicap or disability, are children first of all. There is a danger in thinking of a "blind child" or a "deaf child" or a "retarded child" because one tends to think of the handicap first and the child second. What must be kept in mind is that children are first and foremost children, and only secondarily individuals with one or another handicap.

Moreover, not every child with a special need should be "mainstreamed," i.e., incorporated into a regular classroom. Although integration is a worthwhile ideal, it does not always make sense in practice. By far the majority of classroom teachers are ill prepared to deal with children with special needs. Without adequate support services, a teacher taking in a child with special needs could well find himself or herself overburdened and thus rendered ineffective. Nor is it clear that mainstreaming is the best experience for all children with special needs. Done well, mainstreaming could do much for the self-esteem of a child with special needs. Done poorly, it could make such a child miserable.

Accordingly, this chapter does not advocate that all children with special needs be incorporated into regular classrooms, rather that some children can be so incorporated. Very likely, since the active classroom is designed to respond to children's affective and cognitive abilities, it can adapt to children with special needs somewhat more readily than other types of classroom orientation. The active classroom's recognition of the personal curriculum, of the attachment dynamism, and of interpersonal frames gives it the affective/social dimensions required by children in general and by children with special needs in particular.

THE PERSONAL CURRICULUM

In general, a curriculum can be regarded as a set of priorities concerning what-is-to-be-learned-when. Unfortunately, there is not one but at least three different curricula with which the teacher must contend. First, there is the *developmental* curriculum determined by the interaction of the child's mental abilities and his or her need to make sense out of the physical world in which he or she lives. The attainment of number, space, time, and causality concepts in a predictable sequence, as discussed by Piaget (1950), is one manifestation of this developmental curriculum. A second curriculum with which the child has to cope is the *school* curriculum, the sequence of attainments in math, science, language arts, social studies, and fine arts that is mandated by society.

In addition to the developmental and school curricula there is a third curriculum with which the teacher must deal; this might be called the *personal* curriculum. The personal curriculum, the child's individual learning priorities, is determined both by the developmental curriculum and by his or her own individual needs, interests, abilities, and talents. As in the case of the other curricula, personal curricula are both transient or short-range and abiding or long-range. An ideal educational program, one that is seldom found, occurs when the short-range as well as the long-range priorities of all three curricula coincide. This occurs, for example, when children want to read and do math (coincidence of the personal and school curricula) and are allowed to do so at their level of mental ability (coincidence of the developmental and the school curricula).

Sometimes, more often than we would like, the various curricula come into conflict and one or another has to give way. Which one does the giving often cannot be decided in advance and sometimes priorities must be set as the situation demands. Recently, for example, there was a theft at the Mt. Hope School, the laboratory school of the University of Rochester. The children did not actually witness the theft, but they were aware it had occurred. The youngsters were excited and a little frightened by the event and their feelings about the theft constituted a personal curriculum priority. It seemed important enough that the teachers gave up their school curriculum priorities and encouraged the children to write about and draw their impressions of this critical incident.

Of course there are other situations in which personal curricula cannot be allowed to become the first priority. This is true, for example, when children engage in playing games in the Eric Berne (1950) sense. Such games are frequently played by children with special needs as a way of avoiding school work. In playing a game, the child puts forth a *con* (a statement) that ties into a teacher's *gimmick* (her desire to be helpful, to be successful as a teacher). Then the child pulls a *reverse* which produces *payoffs* for the child (the glee at having outsmarted the teacher) and for the teacher (the frustration at having been taken in).

A child who plays games has personal curriculum needs that are at variance with the school curriculum priorities. He or she wants to engage in interpersonal games that are not constructive or helpful to himself, herself, or others. When a game-playing child is encountered, therefore, his or her personal-curriculum objectives cannot be allowed to hold sway because they are self-destructive. Once a game-playing child is detected, the games can be aborted by the teacher not being hooked by the con. For example, the child who cannot find his pencil: "Sounds like you don't really want to do that right now, why don't you do reading now and come back to writing later." And to the child who says, "I can't do it" when there is evidence that he can, the teacher has to say, "I believe you can do it. Why don't you try."

For children with more severe special needs, personal curriculum problems are of a somewhat different order. It is hard for adults to appreciate the emotional trauma undergone by a child who day after day must be in a situation where he or she cannot do what others do, or who can only do it badly. Playing a poor game of tennis, golf, or softball can elicit the same feelings temporarily in an adult. One has to multiply this feeling a hundredfold to appreciate what the child experiences in the classroom day after day. To be sure, young children lack some of the cognitive structures adults have and they are better at rationalizing and fooling themselves than adults are. Nonetheless, the experience is sufficiently traumatic to severely damage self-esteem and self-confidence.

In a sense, the child's personal curriculum can be said to involve his or her need to enhance, defend, and maintain self-esteem, the sense of being a worthwhile person. At each stage of development the modes of satisfying these personal curriculum needs differ, but the basic needs remain the same. During the early years of schooling, when children have what Piaget calls concrete operations,* they are capable of learning adult imposed

---

*A system of mental abilities which in their manner of operation are similar to the basic operations of arithmetic and which permit children to engage in syllogistic reasoning and higher order classifications.

rules and are still needful of adult approval and ratification. Indeed, the tool skills of reading, writing, and arithmetic are acquired largely to win social approval rather than because of their intrinsic interest or worth to the child. Much of the "spontaneous" learning of children is already very much socially conditioned.

Many children with special needs cannot satisfy their personal curriculum needs in a developmentally appropriate fashion, i.e., through the acquisition of tool skills. Since they cannot enhance self-esteem through the acquisition of these skills, they seek to defend it by what often turns out to be socially disruptive and self-defeating behavior. What a child of this sort needs, first and foremost, is an interpersonal relationship in which friendship and approval are not contingent upon academic achievement. This is more easy to accomplish in an active than in a traditional classroom.

In the first place, learning in the active classroom is individualized and children work at their own pace on materials adapted to their developmental level. In such circumstances it is easy for the teacher to casually put his or her arm around the child, say something to the effect that "you look especially nice today" or "thank you for helping with the clean-up" without embarrassing the child. Secondly, because of the flexibility inherent in individualization, the teacher can permit the child with special needs to rearrange the days work when he or she is "out of sorts." Finally, in an active classroom there is a "quiet corner" where all children, including children with special needs, can retreat to listen to records, read, or simply daydream for a bit. In short, the individualization and flexibility of the active classroom makes it easy for the teacher to accommodate to children's personal curriculum needs, whether these be of average or special children, without disrupting the classroom as a whole.

THE ATTACHMENT DYNAMISM

There is now a good deal of evidence (Bowlby, 1973; Ainsworth, 1969) that the attachment of the infant to particular adults comes about during the last trimester of the first year of life, and that this attachment increases during the second year of life when fear of strangers and strange places is inordinate. By and large the infant remains attached to only a very small coterie of adults, usually his mother, father, and perhaps a caretaker. The adults to whom the child is attached are his or her primary source of self-esteem and, hence, they wield considerable power over the youngster without always being aware of this fact. It is this attachment of the child to significant adults which is one of the most powerful motivations for the elaboration and utilization of mental abilities. Although the phenomenon of attachment is quite familiar, its importance for the child's learning of the school curriculum has largely been overlooked, particularly in special education.

The importance of attachment in learning the school curriculum can be demonstrated in many different domains, but its importance can be illustrated in two practical situations. These situations are the teaching of reading to normal children and the teaching of tool subjects to youngsters with special needs. In both of these contexts, the role of attachment is often ignored, and those concerned with instructing children in these situations may be primarily concerned with curriculum materials and instructional techniques rather than with interpersonal relationships. It is often assumed that the selection of the right curriculum materials and instructional techniques will release the child's "innate" curiosity and eagerness to learn. But as I have already suggested, I do not think one can hope to build upon intrinsic motivation in every learning situation. Indeed, I am very much afraid that what appears to be intrinsic motivation is, in a good many cases, social motivation derived from the adults to whom the child is attached.

Learning to read is a case in point. Unlike walking and talking, reading is not something a child acquires spontaneously as a part of his normal, expectable adaptive apparatus. Learning to read is a difficult task and, in addition to having the requisite mental abilities and experiences, children need powerful motivation to learn to read. In the majority of cases, this motivation comes from attachment to adults who encourage and reward the child's efforts at learning to read. In our studies of children who read before coming to school (Briggs & Elkind,

1973; 1977), we found that many youngsters who read early had a close friend (either an older child or adult) who spent a great deal of time helping the child to read. And, in the biographies of successful people who grew up amidst poverty and adversity, one often reads of particular adults or teachers who recognized and encouraged their abilities and talents. Attachment to adults who encourage and reward academic achievement is probably of major significance in the lives of most individuals who succeed at school.

A more concrete example of the role of attachment in academic achievement might help to strengthen the argument for its importance. I have been supervising, at the University of Rochester, an undergraduate practicum wherein college students tutor children with special needs for an entire year. Among the many things we learned in the course of running this program was that remedial work could not be introduced or used effectively until an emotional relationship, an attachment, occurred between the tutor and the child. After this occurred, the child's behavior began to change at home and at school. Once children began to feel that they were worthy of an adult's liking and respect, there ws a kind of *spread of affect*– which made them feel good about themselves and their abilities to learn in a variety of domains.

It seems to me that this spread of affect phenomenon is of crucial importance in working with children with special needs. Whatever the child's physical, neurological, or physiological handicaps, his or her impaired sense of self-esteem always plays a part in his or her difficulties with learning. When such a youngster is made to feel better as a person, from the attention, concern, and liking of another person, he or she feels better about himself or herself in general and about his or her capacity to cope with new learning situations in particular. We have often observed how children in our program begin to do better

---

†In learning theory there is a principle which is called spread of *e*ffect, referring to the generalization of reinforcement effects upon behavior. But the spread of *a*ffect has to do with feelings. It has to do with the fact that when we have a rewarding experience, we have an overall good feeling that colors our behavior in many different situations.

work at school and begin to be more tractable at home as a result of the nonacademic, self-esteem bolstering experience of our program.

To test the effects of attachment and spread of affect more directly, we opened a full-time school, the Mt. Hope School, in the fall of 1974. We took underachieving children of average, or slightly below average, intelligence. Some of the children were thought to be brain injured, others presented behavior patterns unacceptable in traditional classroom settings. In our program we emphasized one-to-one relationships between students and children and between teachers and children. The small size of the group (2 teachers, 15 children and 15 undergraduates) made this possible. The teachers were present full time, the undergraduates a day or two a week.

During the first few months the children were quite unmanageable: they fought, destroyed materials, and seemed unable to concentrate or sit still. As the interpersonal relationships developed, however, a transformation took place. The children began to settle down to work at reading and math. With a lot of individualized instruction they began to have success experiences and this further motivated them to continue. Where before we had trouble getting them to read and do math, it then became almost impossible to stop them. The classrooms were beehives of children eager to read, write, play math games, and interact verbally with others. Once they returned to their regular schools, 80 percent of the children maintained their gains over a three year period.

The experience at the Mt. Hope School has strengthened our belief in the importance of the attachment dynamism for learning in general and for children with special needs in particular. Although our situation was somewhat ideal in that we had a large number of aides, attachment can be fostered by the organization of the active classroom even in the absence of such aides. For example, many active classrooms have vertical grouping wherein the same children stay with the same teacher for two years (usually K-1 or 1-2). This facilitates children's attachment to the teacher and makes him or her a more potent figure than he or she might otherwise be.

There are other features of the active classroom which also help foster the attachment between children and teacher. In the active classroom the teacher does not sit at the head of the room with the children behind him or her in rows of desks. In most active classrooms it is hard to tell where the teacher's desk is. The teacher in the active classroom is mobile in the sense that he or she is usually sitting with one or another child or a group of children as they work. This mobility facilitates one-to-one interactions and thus more close attachments between teacher and child. In summary, the organization of the active classroom is particularly well suited to the attachment between teacher and child that is beneficial to all pupils but particularly to children with special needs.

There is one type of child who may not benefit from attachment. We call such youngsters *impossible* children. Every teacher occasionally encounters a child who he or she does not like and who the other children do not like either. It is not unusual to discover that the child's parents also have trouble liking the youngster. Such children seem to do everything in their power to annoy, often in little ways, the adults and children with whom they interact. They are usually poorly dressed, and personally not well cared for. Often they discover and play upon the little sensitivities that each of us has and that thoughtful, caring people take pains to avoid. But the impossible child steps on everyone's toes and always seems to know which ones are the most tender and painful.

Impossible children are difficult to teach and often have problems learning. This is true even when they have good native ability and can catch on to difficult material quickly. But they are often so involved in their interpersonal machinations that they have little incentive or inclination to concentrate on school work. Such children are frustrating because nothing seems to work with them. If one tries to be loving, they reject this effort or make a mockery of it. If one is harsh, they play the helpless victim and feel sorry for themselves. If one is indifferent they make their presence known in obnoxious ways and if they are punished for being too loud they will proceed to be too soft and will not speak even when spoken to. For these children, interpersonal relations present a perpetual chess game in which each move must be countered with another determined by the previous move.

By definition, impossible children are difficult to understand.

246

THE CLINIC

But this is true because their symptoms are misleading and disguise the real issue. The situation is not unlike school phobia, wherein the child's manifest reaction, fear of school, conceals the real fear that is quite different, namely, fear of separation from the parent. However, in some respects impossible children are the opposite of school phobics. Whereas the school phobic is afraid of separation, *impossible children are afraid of attachment.* Impossible children are afraid of love and acceptance and ward it off with all the powers at their command. Such children are impossible because they reject the aspirin of contemporary humanism, namely, love, acceptance, and freedom.

In some ways, the impossible child proves the power of the attachment dynamism. Strange as it seems, the impossible child makes himself or herself impossible in order to please or satisfy the parents' often unconscious wish. If the parent needs an objectionable child to reject without social disapproval (no one else likes the child either), the child will unconsciously comply to satisfy the parental need. To be sure, something in a particular child will provoke rejection on the part of the parent, but the child's objectionable behavior reflects the power of the attachment dynamism and how easily it can become perverted.

In line with these unconscious dynamics, the conscious assumptive realities (cf. Ch. 17) of impossible children—the hypotheses that the child formulates and assumes to be part of reality rather than assumptions about it—can take many different forms. Some believe that if they like someone else it will hurt or destroy that person. These children have to avoid liking other people in order to protect those people. Other children just assume that everyone is evil and that if you look hard enough or long enough you can find the evil in everyone. Still other impossible children seem to believe that the world owes them something and that they do not need to do anything in return because everyone has it so good while they have it so bad. These assumptive realities account for some of the varieties among impossible children, but the basic dynamic, fear of attachment, is common to them all.

In dealing with impossible children it is important to be accepting but not overly loving and friendly. As in the case of school phobics who, though afraid of separation, generally want to be more independent, impossible children really want to be liked and to like others, but their anxieties get in the way. Sometimes these anxieties have to be verbalized to help the child deal with them realistically. "I think you are working very hard not to like me and for me not to like you. It's okay to like people." While some impossible children can be helped in the classroom, some may benefit from the help of mental health professionals. For our purposes, the main point about impossible children is that the attachment dynamism operates in them as it does in all children, albeit in a somewhat different form. Even in an active classroom, which takes heed of the importance of attachment in learning, some children cannot be helped in the classroom and additional professional assistance is required.

Still a third affective social dimension of the active classroom is its recognition of the importance of situational "frames" which are different from social roles and which children need to learn if they are to be successful at school.

THE COGNITIVE FRAME

As it is employed in contemporary sociology (e.g., Goffman, 1974; Bernstein, 1971), a frame is a repetitive social situation which embodies a set of implicit rules, expectancies, and understandings that govern behavior in those situations (cf. Chs. 6 and 12). When people follow the constraints of the frame, an emotional equilibrium is maintained. If, however, someone breaks the rules of the frame, the equilibrium is disrupted and some sort of remedial work has to be done to restore the equilibrium. The disruption of a frame is not catastrophic but it is uncomfortable, and that is why individuals work hard to restore frame behavior.

A familiar frame situation is the waiting room, whether a doctor's office, a busy bakery where one takes numbers, or an airport gate waiting area. In such situations one is expected: to take one's turn; not to push into line; not to attend too closely to other people's dress or conversation; not to speak too loudly and to follow the instructions of whoever is vested with authority in that situation. Anyone who violates these rules immediately becomes a focus of attention and sometimes the object of a cutting remark. Thus the man who pushes into line while other passengers are waiting patiently to board an aircraft is looked upon with distaste and may be told, "What's your damn hurry?"

In educational settings there are many different frames, each with its own set of rules, understandings, and expectancies. There is, for example, a group-reading frame in which children come together as a group to read. Each child may read a part of the story and then is expected to read along silently while other children take turns reading aloud. Ordinarily children learn the frame rules of the educational setting quite easily and these are more or less background to their foreground learning activities. But the rules are there nonetheless and constitute what might be called *learning frames.*

Now what often happens in the case of many children with special needs is that the learning frame becomes the foreground (the center of attention) and the learning activity moves into the background. That is to say, a child who is having difficulty in school begins to break frame rules. He or she may get up and noisily roam about when other children are at work. When such behavior occurs, it is wrong to assume that the child does not understand the frame rules that are in play—that you don't disturb other children who are at work. Indeed, the "misbehavior" is a reflection of the fact that the young person is now attending to the frame rules in order to avoid the learning task. He or she has effectively reversed figure and ground and wants to do battle on frame rules rather than upon learning tasks.

Accordingly, when a child deliberately breaks frame rules, there is little point to reiterating them since he or she knows them very well already or he or she wouldn't be breaking them. What the child is saying, in effect, is that the social disapproval of breaking frame rules is to be preferred to the social ridicule for displaying school failure. The proof of this analysis is given by the fact that when such a child finds something interesting he is permitted to do it, he or she obeys the frame rules very nicely indeed. To be sure, there are some hyperkinetic youngsters who cannot, for physical reasons, obey frame rules, but such children may be fewer than we suppose. And some retarded children may not understand the frame rules and may need to be instructed in them.

Another difficulty children with special needs encounter with frames has to do with discriminating between child-child and child-adult frames. For most children the rules for dealing with children are different from the rules for dealing with adults. For example, even young children shift verbal registers and use different grammatical forms when they switch from talking to children to talking to adults (Shatz & Gelman, 1973). More generally, among young children, communication by pushing, shoving, pulling, pinching, etc. is regarded as an appropriate means of getting one's message across. Such communication is, however, generally not permitted in child-adult frames. Expressive adults may communicate to children by touching, patting, or caressing, but children are not expected to return these actions in kind. Between children, physical communication is a symmetrical relation whereas between children and adults it is asymmetrical.

One consequence of the experience of continuous failure of the child with special needs is that there is a blurring of the child-child and child-adult frame rules. Such a child may, for example, poke, shove, and pull at the teacher to get his or her attention much as the child might to other children. In the same way, an emotionally troubled child may use words with the teacher that most children would reserve for child-child frames. On the other hand, sometimes troubled children become excessively angry at other children for pushing and shoving them as if they were the adult and as if the other child were breaking the child-adult frame rules.

The situation here is just the reverse of that wherein the child is violating the rules of the learning frame. In that situation the youngster knows the rules and that is why he or she is breaking them. But in the case of the disturbed child's violation of child-child and child-adult frame rules, the young person fails to discriminate which rules are appropriately in operation. Interestingly, when children break child-child or child-adult frame rules, it is generally assumed that they understand the rules and are deliberately breaking them. In this situation the child's violation of frame rules is attributed to personal traits such as need for attention and immaturity. In fact when a child breaks adult-child or child-child frame rules, what he or she needs is help in discriminating which rules apply where. To such children it is appropriate to say, "You and your friends can push and shove one another, but it is not okay to push and shove me. I am a grownup."

Unfortunately, a troubled child's difficulty in discriminating child-child and child-adult frame rules is compounded by a *negative spread of affect*. The anxiety, fear, and frustration that such a child experiences in the classroom becomes associated with all aspects of the school setting. Classrooms, desks, and workbooks all become signs of unhappy experience and produce emotional states that make appropriate frame discrimination difficult. These negative associations can be mitigated to some degree by the spread of positive affect that proceeds from the attachment dynamism, but other things can be done as well. Recognition of these frames and frame difficulties in an active classroom facilitates helping children to deal with them more effectively.

In an active classroom it is recognized that children with problems occasionally need to be removed from the learning environment, to go for walks, to play ball with a tutor, or to visit a local craftsperson. The active classroom itself is set up so as to suggest a more informal, relaxed setting. Plants and animals, large comfortable pillows on the floor, really good art work, all add to the sense of a rich, interesting environment that has much to offer besides academic failure. By creating a comfortable and interesting environment, the emotional "feel" of the place will inhibit the negative spread of affect that the troubled child experiences in more traditional classroom settings. In the informal setting of the active classroom, with some of the negative affect reduced, it is easier for the child to discriminate between child-child and child-adult frame behaviors.

SUMMARY AND CONCLUSION

Given the affective and social dimensions of the active classroom, it is possible for the teacher to facilitate the assimilation of children with special needs. Basically, an active classroom is one responsive to the children's level of development and is a setting which encourages a variety of learning modes. In addition, an active classroom pays particular attention to each child's, as well as the group's, personal curriculum needs. It also recognizes the importance of emotional attachment in academic achievement and fosters such attachment by its organization. There is recognition of the implicit rules, understanding, and expectancies, that is, frames, that form the background of all learning situations. A recognition of the difficulty children with special needs have with frame rules helps the teacher in the active classroom to ease such children's learning problems. While the active classroom is usually thought of as facilitating cognitive development, its recognition of the personal curriculum, of the importance of attachment, and the pervasiveness of frames enables it to support the child's affective and social development as well. And, it makes such classrooms particularly well suited for assimilating children with special needs.

REFERENCES

Ainsworth, M.D.S. Object relations, dependency and attachment: A theoretical review of the infant-mother relationship. *Child Development*, 1969, *40*, 969–1025.

Berne, E. *Games People Play*. New York: Ballatine, 1964.

Bernstein, B.B. *Class, Codes and Control*. London: Routledge & Kegan Paul, 1971.

Bowlby, J. *Separation*. Basic Books, 1973. (Attachment and Loss, Vol. II).

Briggs, C., and Elkind, D. Cognitive development in early readers. *Developmental Psychology*, 1973, *9*, 2, 279–280.

Elkind, D. *Child Development and Education*. New York: Oxford, 1976.

Goffman, E. *Frame Analysis*. Cambridge: Harvard University Press, 1974.

Piaget, J. *The Psychology of Intelligence*. London: Routledge & Kegan Paul, 1950.

Shatz, M., and Gelman, R. The development of communication skills: modifications in the speech of young children as a function of listener. *Monographs of the Society for Research in Child Development*, 1973, *38*, Serial No 152.

THE CHURCH

20
THE STUDY OF SPONTANEOUS RELIGION IN THE CHILD

In the course of growing up, children construct spontaneous conceptions about religion which differ from the acquired conceptions taught by institutional religion. In this chapter a method for studying the spontaneous religion of the child is described and illustrated with material from investigations into the children's conceptions of their religious identity.

For research purposes it is convenient to distinguish between the spontaneous and the acquired religion of the child. The child's spontaneous religion consists of all those ideas and beliefs that he has constructed in his attempts to interpret religious terms and practices that are beyond his level of comprehension. For example, upon hearing that God was everywhere, a boy refused to occupy his favorite chair for fear of "sitting on God" and thus revealed his spontaneous conception of God's omnipresence. In contrast to these spontaneous mental constructions, there are many religious ideas and beliefs that the child acquires directly from adults either through imitation or through instruction. A child's recitation of the standard definition of theological terms or of particular prayers would thus reflect acquired rather than spontaneous religion.

J. for the Scientific Study of Religion, 1964, 4, 40–46.

It is fair to say that by far the majority of research on religious development has concerned itself with acquired rather than with spontaneous religion. For example, in many of the studies dealing with the God conception (Barnes, 1892; Tanner, 1906; Bose, 1929; MacLean, 1930; Mathias, 1943), questionnaires were employed which either asked children to choose among standard conceptions of the Deity or required them to complete sentences which strongly suggested the standard conceptions (e.g. "God, where is He?"). While such studies of acquired religion are of value for assessing the degree to which children profit from religious education, they do not reveal the full nature of religious development. Indeed, they can be misleading! In all of the studies mentioned above, none of the investigators noted any marked age differences in the God concept even when a considerable age span (four to fourteen) was sampled in the study. Yet, developmental psychology has repeatedly shown (Reichard et. al., 1944; Welch and Long, 1940 a; b; c; Piaget, 1928; 1929; 1930; 1952) that children's spontaneous conceptions follow a regular sequence from concrete to abstract conceptualization between early (four to six) and late childhood (ten to twelve).

This is not to say that results from the traditional questionnaire studies of religious development are wrong, but only that the acquired religion revealed by these results does not follow the same developmental course as spontaneous religion. Since even the young child can memorize definitions of religious terms, it is not surprising that when children are tested on these definitions, the young children do about as well as the older children. If, on the other hand, the *understanding* of these definitions were to be evaluated, it is likely that significant age differences would be found because the understandings would reflect the child's spontaneous and not his acquired ideas. Only the child's spontaneous ideas follow the sequence from the concrete to the abstract that we have come to expect in developmental studies of concept formation.

As yet, however, we have little information about the spontaneous religion of the child, and the purpose of the present paper is to describe and illustrate (by means of a completed investigation) a method for exploring the child's own interpretations of religious terms and practices. The method to be described is the semi-clinical interview devised by the Swiss psychologist, Jean Piaget.

THE SEMI-CLINICAL INTERVIEW

BACKGROUND OF THE METHOD

Piaget was one of the first investigators to realize that the child's spontaneous remarks were more than amusing errors and that they reflected forms of thought that were different from those used by adults. In order to investigate children's spontaneous thought, Piaget was forced to devise his own method inasmuch as this aspect of thought had not been previously recognized, much less explored. The specifications for such a method, however, were exceedingly stringent and apparently contradictory. For what Piaget required was a method with sufficient flexibility to enable him to follow the meandering stream of any particular child's thought and yet with sufficient standardization to enable him to reach the same destination with many different children at different age levels.

The only method which met the first of these specifications was the psychiatric interview, while the only method which met the second specification was the mental test. This being the case, Piaget combined the standard questions of the mental test with the free inquiry of the psychiatric interview and labeled the result the semi-clinical interview. The union of standard question and free inquiry was a happy one and led to the now classic findings concerning children's conceptions of physical causality (1930), of the world (1929), and of judgment and reasoning (1928).

Despite the proven fruitfulness of the semi-clinical interview, however, it has seldom been employed by American psychologists and, with one exception (Elkind, 1961; 1962; 1963), has never been brought to bear on the study of religious development. The reasons for this neglect of Piaget's method are several, including the amount of time and skill required of the examiner and the difficulty involved in interpreting the obtained data. While these objections are well-taken, they do not out-weigh the potential value of the method for exploring spontaneous religion.

In the first place, although the interview is more time consuming than the questionnaire, the obtained data will be much more complete and therefore more revealing than that obtained by more rapid group-testing procedures. In the second place, while skill in conversing with children is required, most investigators dealing with children have the basic requirements for a good interviewer: a liking for children, a respect for their individuality, and patience. As for the difficulty in interpreting responses, this is present no matter what method is used and, in fact, Piaget has given particular attention to this problem and has worked out techniques and criteria for discriminating between the significant and the trivial in children's verbalizations. So, on this point, the Piaget method is actually superior to the questionnaire wherein no such discriminations can be made. There are no really good reasons for not using the interview techniques in studying religious growth.

CONSTRUCTION OF INTERVIEW QUESTIONS

Since the construction of appropriate questions is one of the most difficult features of the semi-clinical interview, an illustration of how the author proceeds in formulating such questions might be helpful to prospective investigators. In general, one begins with a remark that suggests the presence of a spontaneous conceptualization. For example, after the tragic death of President Kennedy the author heard a child say, "Are they going to shoot God too?" This remark suggested that the child identified God with famous persons in high offices and opened up a whole new path of inquiry. If we desire to follow this lead we might begin formulating some questions about God and high offices. For example we might ask, "Can God be president of the United States? Why or why not?" Furthermore we might ask about how God obtained his position. For example one might ask, "Who chooses the president? Who chooses God, or how did God become God?"

If this line of inquiry proved unfruitful, we might go back to the original remark and note that it also suggests that God is conceived as a person. This notion leads to quite another line of questioning (Can God dance, talk French?). Should this line of inquiry prove barren, we might approach the problem from the fact that the term "God" is a name and ask such things as "How did God get his name? Does God have a first name?" The only requirement in formulating questions is that they be so absurd, to the adult way of thought, that one can be reasonably certain children have not been trained one way or the other regarding them. Trial and error with various questions proposed to one's own or to neighbor children will soon reveal which questions are the most productive of unstereotyped, spontaneous replies.

INTERVIEW TECHNIQUE

Once a group of related questions about a given topic has been gathered, the actual interviewing can begin. The child should be seen in a quiet place where there are few distractions and at a time when he does not desire to be somewhere else. As soon as the examiner has won rapport with the child—most easily accomplished by asking the youngster a few questions about himself—he can begin putting his interview questions. After the child has replied, it is usually necessary to ask additional questions to clarify the meaning of the response. It is in this free inquiry part of the interview that the most skill is required because the examiner must direct the child's thought without, at the same time, suggesting an appropriate answer. There is no better preparation for this part of the examination than a course in Rorschach testing because in the Rorschach examination non-suggestive questioning is developed to a fine art.

INTERPRETATION OF RESULTS: VALIDITY

Both during the examination and afterwards, in analyzing the data, the most important question is to what extent the child's response truly reflects his own mental constructions. To this end Piaget has described five types of response that need to be distinguished in any examination of the child. When the child is not at all interested in the question and is bored or tired, he may simply answer with anything that comes into his head just to be relieved of the burden of having to answer. Piaget speaks of such responses as *answers at random*. When a child fabricates or invents an answer, without really reflecting about the question, Piaget speaks of *romancing*. On the other hand, when the child does attend to the question but his answer is determined by a desire to please the examiner or is suggested by the question, Piaget speaks of *suggested conviction*.

In contrast to the three foregoing types of reply, which are of little value to the investigator, the following two types are of very great significance. When the child reflects about a question which is new to him and answers it from the reservoirs of his own thought, Piaget calls this *a liberated conviction*. And when the child answers quickly, without reflection, because he has already formulated the solution or because it was latently formulated, it is called by Piaget *a spontaneous conviction*.

Since the investigator is primarily interested in the liberated and the spontaneous conviction, it is important to have ways of separating them from answers, at random, romancing, and suggested convictions. This can be done at two points in the investigation, one during and the other following the interview. If, during the interview itself, the examiner suspects that a reply is other than a spontaneous or a liberated conviction, he can check this in several ways. First, he can offer counter suggestions to determine how firmly rooted the idea is in the child's thought. A true liberated or spontaneous conviction will withstand counter suggestion whereas romancing, suggested convictions, and answers at random are easily changed by counter suggestions. Secondly, he can ask about related issues. If the idea is truly a conviction of the child's, it will fit a pattern or system of ideas that follow a general principle or rule which Piaget calls a *schema*. If the child's response fits the general trend or schema of his thought, this is a good indication that it is either a spontaneous or liberated conviction.

The second point at which one can determine whether or not replies obtained in the interview represent genuine convictions occurs after the data have been collected and age trends can be examined. First of all, if the majority of children at the same age level give similar replies, this is evidence that the responses reflect a form of thought characteristic of that age. If the answers were random, suggested, or romancing, there would be no reason to expect such uniformity. Secondly, if the responses show a gradual evolution with age in the direction of a closer approximation to the adult conception, this is another evidence that the replies reflect a true developmental trend. Finally, a valid developmental sequence must give signs of continuity in the sense that traces of concrete ideas held at early age levels (adherences) are present among the abstract conceptions of older children and in the sense that foreshadowings of abstract ideas typical of older children (anticipations) are present among the concrete expressions of the young children.

The use of counter suggestion and varied questioning during the interviewing of individual children and of the three group criteria during the analysis of the data from all children provides a good basis for determining whether the obtained responses are indeed liberated or spontaneous convictions. Piaget has thus provided several means for checking the validity of the data obtained by his semi-clinical interview.

INTERPRETATION OF RESULTS: RELIABILITY

Although Piaget has always been concerned about the validity of his observations, he has almost ignored the question of their reliability, i.e., their repeatability. A possible reason for this neglect is that Piaget's training in biological science has led him to assume that a characteristic found in the individual can automatically be taken as characteristic of the species. Such a position is less defensible for the complex human species than it is for lesser organisms, however, and reliability measures probably should be made when using the Piaget method. Two such measures are needed. One is a measure of the consistency with which individual children respond to interview questions at different times. This measure can be obtained by retesting each of the subjects, preferably not before a month and not later than six months after the original examination. The correlation of initial and retest responses will provide an index of response reliability.

The second index of reliability that should be obtained relates to the categorization of responses into stages or sequences of development. That is to say, it is necessary to determine whether the responses are sufficiently distinctive that independent workers will classify them in similar ways. If several persons independently categorize the responses and a measure of their agreement is determined, this measure will serve as an index of the reliability of the categorization. These steps to insure the reliability of response, together with the fulfillment of Piaget's criteria for determining validity, should suffice to ensure that investigations employing the semi-clinical interview will be acceptable to even the most hardheaded experimentalist.

To make the use of the semi-clinical interview concrete, a study in which the method was applied to the development of religious identity will be briefly described and summarized.

THE DEVELOPMENT OF RELIGIOUS IDENTITY

Religious identity can be defined in terms of the spontaneous meanings children attach to their religious denomination. A developmental study of these meanings was undertaken by the writer who investigated the growth of religious identity among Jewish (Elkind, 1961), Catholic (Elkind, 1962), and Congregational Protestant (Elkind, 1963) children.

In these studies the children were individually interviewed and asked six novel questions about their denomination. The questions were, with the appropriate denominational term inserted: a) Is your family . . . ? Are you . . . ? Are all boys and girls in the world . . . ? b) Can a dog or a cat be . . . ? c) How do you become a . . . ? d) What is a . . . ? e) How can you tell a person is . . . ? f) Can you be . . . and American at the same time? In order to clarify the meaning of the child's responses and to insure that these were firmly rooted in his thought, additional questions, following no set pattern, were asked.

These questions had their origin in a child's spontaneous question which the author happened to overhear. The child asked whether a dog that ate kosher food became Jewish. From this remark it was clear that the child did not really understand the word "Jewish" in the adult sense but had his own spontaneous conception, namely, that you became Jewish by eating kosher foods. It seemed to the author that such spontaneous religious conceptions were probably not unique to this child and that an exploration of age changes in the child's spontaneous conceptions of his denomination might reveal material of interest to the developmental psychology of religion. Since a denominational term is basically a class concept, it seemed reasonable to frame questions which would tap various aspects of this class notion but in ways novel to the majority of children. Accordingly, questions a, b and e get at the child's understanding of the extension of the concept, i.e., the groups to which it is appropriately applied and the external signs by which group membership can be recognized. Questions c and d, on the other hand, tap the child's grasp of the intension of the concept, i.e., the property or properties that distinguish members belonging to a particular group. Finally, question f was designed to test the child's conception of multiple group membership.

In each denominational group at least 30 children at each age level from 5 to 11 (among the Jewish children) and 6 to 12 (among the Protestant and Catholic children) were interviewed so that more than 700 children were examined. No attempt was made to control for liberal/conservative status, church attendance, etc., in the belief that uniformities which appeared despite a great deal of uncontrolled variation would be further support for the view that maturation as well as experience plays a part in religious development.

Piaget's (1929) criteria for interpreting children's responses as liberated or spontaneous convictions were applied to the interview materials. The results met all three criteria, and there was: a) uniformity of ideas at a given age level which often extended over several year levels; b) an increasing correctness (conformance with adult conceptions) of children's ideas with increasing age; c) adherences of ideas from an earlier year level as part of, or added to, the more advanced ideas given at a later age level and also anticipations of later conceptions in the remarks of younger children. Analysis of the age changes in response made it possible to distinguish three well-marked stages in the attainment of religious identity which held true of Jewish, Protestant, and Catholic children.

At the first stage (usually ages five to seven, the child had only a global, undifferentiated conception of his denomination as a kind of proper name. Although he acknowledged being a Jew, Protestant, or Catholic, he confused these names with the terms for race and nationality, for example:

Sid (6-3)* What is a Jew? 'A man." How is a Jewish person different from a Catholic? "Cause some people have black hair and some people have blond."

Mel (5-9) What is a Jew? "A man." How is a Jewish person different from a Catholic? . . . "He comes from a different country." Which one? "Israel." Furthermore, at this stage the child regarded having a denominational name as incompatible with possessing a racial or national designation. For example, it was common for the child at this stage to reply, in answer to the question about being an American and a Jew (Protestant, Catholic) at the same time that, "You can't have two." That is to say, because you can't have two names.

Children at the second stage (usually ages seven to nine) have a concretely differentiated conception of their denomination. Their conception was concrete in the sense that they used observable features or actions to define their denomination, and their conception was differentiated because they discriminated among different behaviors in order to distinguish persons belonging to different denominations. For example:

Mae (7-9) What is a Jew? "A person who goes to Temple or Hebrew school."

Bill (8-10) What is a Catholic? "He goes to mass every Sunday and goes to Catholic school."

Ron (7-9) Can you be a Catholic and a Protestant at the same time? "No." Why not? "Cause you couldn't go to two churches."

Unlike the first-stage children, young people at the second stage said they could be an American and their denomination at the same time. The reasons given in explanation were concrete and personal to the effect that "You can live in America and go to church" or "I'm an American and I'm a Protestant."

Third-stage children (usually ages ten to twelve) demonstrated an abstract, differentiated conception of their denomina-

---

†Numbers in parentheses indicate the child's age in years and months.

tion. It was an abstract conception in the sense that these children no longer defined their denomination by mentioning names or observable activities but rather by mentioning nonobservable mental attributes such as belief and understanding. For example:

Bi (12-0) What is a Catholic? "A person who believes in the truths of the Roman Catholic Church." Can a dog or a cat be Catholic? "No, because they don't have a brain or intellect."

Sed (11-10) What is a Jew? "A person who believes in one God and doesn't believe in the New Testament."

When third-stage children were asked the question as to whether they could be American and their denomination at the same time, they replied that one was a nationality and the other was a religion and that they were two different things.

In summary, the results of this study dealing with children's conceptions of their religious identity have shown that identity is at first vague and undifferentiated and has no more significance than a proper name. Gradually the child comes to think of his religious identity in terms of certain religious practices and sacred objects, and since these differ from religion to religion, he now has a means for discriminating between children of different religions. It is only at the age of eleven or twelve, however, that a majority of children come to think of their religious identity in terms of particular beliefs for it is only at this age that the child can reflect on his own thought. To the writer it seems that these interesting findings regarding the development of religious identity would not have been found if a pencil and paper technique had been used.

POTENTIAL APPLICATIONS

The foregoing sections have described a method for exploring the spontaneous religion of children and the results of a study in which this method was applied to the problem of religious identity. In this concluding section it remains to suggest the range of problems to which the method might be applied and also to suggest the importance of the findings which could result.

With regards to the problems to which the semi-clinical interview could be appropriately applied, they are the traditional ones of the developmental psychology of religion. Conceptions of God, belief, prayer, sin, morality, and many others all deserve to be looked at from the point of view of spontaneous religion. It would be fascinating, too, if someone were to undertake a study of children's theologies and cosmologies, of children's confusions between magic and ritual, and of children's attempts at integrating moral and religious ideas. For the study of these issues and of many more like them, the semi-clincial interview is a necessary starting point.

The results to be obtained from the study of such issues will be of more than theoretical interest and will pertain directly to religious education. A knowledge, for example, of the erroneous interpretations children are likely to attach to religious conceptions at different age levels would suggest ways of teaching these concepts so that they would not be misunderstood. More importantly, perhaps, the educator's awareness of the ideas children inevitably associate with religious terms and practices will change his orientation. The awareness of spontaneous religion carries with it the implication that teaching must be more than writing on a tabula rasa, and that it must be instead the replacement of the correct for the incorrect, the substitution of the proportionate for the exaggerated, and the inculcation of the essential in lieu of the trivial. To attain this orientation the religious educator must be conversant with the spontaneous thought of the child.

There are then potent reasons for exploring the spontaneous religion of children and hence for the use of the semi-clinical interview in the study of religious development.

SUMMARY

This chapter has described Piaget's semi-clinical interview and illustrated its application with a summary of research on the child's conception of his religious identity. The semi-clinical interview combines features from the psychiatric interview and the mental test, adding flexibility to the latter and uniformity to the former. Beginning with a set of questions that derive from children's own spontaneous remarks, the interview follows the course of the child's thought. Five types of response are distinguished: answers at random, suggested conviction, and romancing are responses that do not reflect the child's true thought. Spontaneous and liberated convictions, in contrast, reveal children's own mental constructions.

Using this method to explore children's conceptions of religious identity revealed three stages of conceptualization. Among the youngest children religious affiliation was regarded as a name comparable to other names, such as nationality and family names. At the second stage (seven to ten years old), children had a more differentiated conception and distinguished religious groups by the activities that characterize those groups. Only at the third stage (early adolescence), subjects talked about religious identity in terms of different belief systems. These findings held for Catholic, Protestant, and Jewish children.

It was concluded that the semi-clinical interview is a powerful tool for exploring many different facets of the spontaneous religion of children.

REFERENCES

Barnes, E. Theological life of a California child. *Pedagog. Semin.*, 1892, 2, 442–48.

Bose, R. S. Religious concepts of children. *Relig. Educ.*, 1929, 24, 831–37.

Elkind, D. The child's conception of his religious denomination I: The Jewish child. *J. Genet. Psychol.*, 1961, 99, 209–25.

Elkind, D. The child's conception of his religious denomination II: The Catholic child. *J. Genet. Psychol.*, 1962, 101, 185–93.

Elkind, D. The child's conception of his religious denomination III: The Protestant child. *J. Genet. Psychol.*, 1963, 103, 291–304.

MacLean, A. H. *The Idea of God in Protestant Religious Education.* New York: Teachers College, Columbia University Press, 1930.

Mathias, W. D. *Ideas of God and Conduct.* New York: Teachers College, Columbia University Press, 1943.

Piaget, J. *Judgment and Reasoning in the Child.* London: Routledge & Kegan, Paul, 1928.

Piaget, J. *The Child's Conception of the World.* London: Routledge & Kegan Paul, 1929.

Piaget J. *The Child's Conception of Physical Causality.* London: Routledge & Kegan Paul, 1930.

Piaget, J. *The Child's Conception of Number.* London: Routledge & Kegan Paul, 1952.

Reichard, S., Schneider, M., and Rapaport, D. The development of concept formation in children. *Am. J. Orthopsychiatry,* 1944, *14,* 156–62.

Tanner, A. E., Children's religious ideas. *Pedagog. Semin.,* 1906, *13,* 511–13.

Welch, L., & Long, L. The higher structural phases of concept formation in children. *J. Psychol.,* 1940, *9,* 59–95. (a)

Welch, L., & Long, L. A further investigation of the higher structural phases of concept formation. *J. Psychol.,* 1940, *10,* 211–20. (b)

Welch, L., & Long, L. The genetic development of the associational structures of abstract thinking. *J. Genet. Psychol.,* 1940, *56,* 175–206. (c)

21

THE ORIGINS OF RELIGION IN THE CHILD

Religion is here regarded as an externalized adaptation which serves both the individual and society. It is argued that the four major elements of institutional religion—the God concept, Scripture, worship, and theology—provide ready-made solutions to adaptive problems engendered by four cognitive need capacities—the search for conservation, representation, relation, and comprehension—which emerge in the course of mental growth. It is concluded that while religious elements such as the God concept may have arisen, in part at least, out of confrontations between cognitive need capacities and physical or social reality, the religious elements are nonetheless *sui generis* and are not reducible to the needs and the phenomena that produced them any more than these needs or phenomena are religious of themselves.

Every social institution, whether it be science, art, or religion, can be regarded as an externalized adaptation which serves both the individual and society. From the point of view of the group, social institutions provide the ground rules and regulations which make society and social progress possible. Looked at from the standpoint of the individual, social institutions afford

Review of Religious Research, 1970, *12*, 35–42.

ready-made solutions to the inevitable conflicts with social and physical reality which the individual encounters in his march through life. Social institutions, therefore, originate and evolve out of the adaptive efforts of both society and the individual. It follows that any complete account of the origins of religion must deal both with individual and social processes of adaptation.

In the present chapter, I propose to treat the origins of religion solely from the perspective of the individual and not from that of society. It is not my intent, therefore, to give a comprehensive account of the origins of religion in general nor in any way to negate the central importance of social factors in the origination and historical evolution of religion. All that I hope to demonstrate is that religion has an individual as well as a social lineage and that this individual lineage can be traced to certain cognitive need capacities which emerge in the course of mental growth. To whatever extent religion derives from society's efforts to resolve the conflicts engendered by these individual need capacities, we are justified in speaking of the origins of religion in the child.

Briefly stated, this chapter will describe four cognitive need capacities with respect to the age at which they first make their appearance, the problems of adaptation which they engender, and the corresponding resolutions offered by religion. A concluding section will take up the question of the uniqueness of religious adaptations from the point of view of the individual.

EMERGENCE OF COGNITIVE NEED CAPACITIES IN THE CHILD

In describing the mental development of the child, this chapter will lean rather heavily upon the work of the Swiss psychologist, Jean Piaget.* For more than forty years Piaget has been studying the mental development of the child. He has evolved a general theory of intelligence, wherein he derives the thinking of adults from the gradual elaboration of mental abilities in the child. In effect, Piaget argues that each new mental capacity carries with it the need to realize itself through action and that,

---

*For a comprehensive and detailed summary and interpretation of Piaget's work, see Flavell (1963). A briefer introduction is provided by Elkind (1967).

in the course of such realization, the individual comes into conflict with social and physical realities. The resolution of each such conflict results in structural changes which we call growth and which in turn pave the way for new conflicts and further growth in an unending dialectic.

Although Piaget's theory would seem to have rather direct implications for religious development, he has not himself, except for a few early papers (Piaget, 1923; 1930), dealt with the problem at length. It seems to me, however, that the major elements common to most religions provide comfortable solutions to some of the conflicts which Piaget's cognitive need capacities engender in the course of their realization. I must emphasize, however, that this is my way of viewing the problem and is not necessarily the way in which Piaget would deal with the issue, were he to attack it.

Before proceeding to the discussion of the cognitive need capacities themselves, it might be well to give a few concrete illustrations of the way in which their efforts at realization result in problems of adaptation. Once the child acquires language and a rudimentary understanding of causality, for example, he enters the notorious "why" stage. He soon discovers, however, that parents do not appreciate such questions, particularly when they are endlessly repeated. The child's attempts to realize his capacity for causal understanding thus bring him into conflict with the adult world. In the same way, when the child of four or five years begins to realize his emerging capacity to deal with quantitative relations, he again comes into conflict with others. His constant concern with "who has more" fails to endear him either to his parents or to his siblings. In short, every cognitive capacity is in itself a need which prompts behaviors that can create discord between the child and his social and physical milieu.

INFANCY AND THE SEARCH FOR CONSERVATION

During the first two years of life, the human infant makes truly remarkable progress. From an uncoordinated, primarily reflex organism, he is within the course of a short two-year period transformed into an upright, talking, semisocialized being, more advanced intellectually than the most mature animal of any species. Of the many accomplishments during this period, perhaps none is as significant nor of such general importance as the discovery that objects exist when they are no longer present to the senses; that is to say, the discovery that objects are *conserved*.

To the adult, for whom the world and the self are clearly demarcated, it is hard to envision the infant's situation. The closest we can come to it is in a state of reverie or semiconsciousness when the boundaries of awareness waver and we are imbedded in the very pictures we are sensing. This is the perpetual state of the infant for whom all awareness can hardly be more than a series of blurred pictures following one another in an unpredictable sequence. Only gradually does the child begin to separate his own actions from things and to discriminate among different things, such as the human face. Even when the response to the human face occurs, usually in the second and third months of life, there is still no awareness that the face exists when it is no longer present. An infant, for example, who is smiling delightedly at an adult peering at him from the side of the crib will turn his head away immediately if the adult ducks out of sight. The infant does not cry; he behaves as if the adult drops out of existence when he disappears (Piaget, 1952).

Only toward the end of the second year and as a consequence of a series of progressive learnings and coordinations does the infant give evidence that for him objects now exist and have a permanence of their own quite independent of his immediate sensory experience. At this age, for example, the young child will search for objects, such as candy or a toy, which he saw hidden from view. This awareness of the permanence or conservation of objects comes about when the progressive coordinations of behavior give rise to internal representations or images of absent objects. It is the two-year-old's capacity to mentally represent absent objects which results in their conservation.

The construction of permanent objects is important because it is a prerequisite for all later mental activity. All of our concepts start from or involve objects in one way or another, so the recognition of their permanence is a necessary starting point for intellectual growth in general. Object permanence, however, is just the first of many such permanences or conservations which the child must construct. As his mental capacities expand, he encounters new situations which parallel, though at a higher level of abstraction, the disappearance of objects. Illusions are a case in point. A spoon in water looks bent or even broken and the moon appears to follow us when we walk, just as the sun appears to revolve around the earth. Similar problems present themselves on the social plane. The child must learn to distinguish, for example, a true invitation to stay at a friend's home from an invitation which is, in fact, a polite dismissal. In all of these cases the child has to distinguish between appearance and reality, between how things look and how they really are. Infancy thus bears witness to a new mental ability, the capacity to deal with absent objects, and to a corresponding need, *the search for conservation*, a life-long quest for permanence amidst a world of change.

One of the problems of conservation which all children eventually encounter, and to which they must all adapt, is the discovery that they and their loved ones must ultimately die. In contrast to the conservation of the object, which is first transient and only later permanent, the child begins by assuming that life is everlasting and is shocked when he finds out that it is transient. After the initial recognition, often accompanied by intense emotional outbursts, the child seeks means whereby life can be conserved, a quest which continues throughout his existence.

In many cases, the conflict between the search for conservation and the inevitability of death does not arise with its full impact until adolescence. Religion, to which the young person has already been exposed, offers a ready solution. This solution lies in the concept of God or Spirit which appears to be religion's universal answer to the problem of the conservation of life. God is the ultimate conservation since He transcends the bounds of space, time, and corporality. By accepting God, the young person participates in His immortality and hence resolves the problem of the conservation of life. Obviously, whether in any particular case the young person will accept the religious solution will be determined by a host of personal and sociocultural factors. All that I wish to emphasize here is that religion offers an immediate solution to the seemingly universal human problem posed by the search for conservation of life and the reality of death.

EARLY CHILDHOOD AND THE SEARCH FOR REPRESENTATION

As was true for the period of infancy, the preschool period is one of rapid mental growth and of wide-ranging intellectual accomplishments. Foremost among these is the mastery of language. With the conquest of language, the child goes far beyond the representation of things by mental images. Language is a series of conventional signs which bear no physical resemblance to that which they represent. The child must now painstakingly learn to represent all of those objects which were so laboriously constructed during the first years of life. The child is not, however, limited to representing things by language; he can now also employ symbols which bear some semblance to the objects which they represent. At this stage, the child creates his own playthings and transforms pieces of wood into boats, pieces of paper into airplanes, and odd-shaped stones into animals (Piaget, 1951). It is at this stage, too, that the child dons adult clothes and plays house, store, and school. Both these behaviors—the mastery of language and the engagement in symbolic play activities—bear witness to a new cognitive capacity, the ability to use signs and symbols, and to a new cognitive need, *the search for representation*.

The search for representation, which makes its appearance in early childhood, like the search for conservation, continues throughout life. At each point in his development, the young person seeks to represent both the contents of his own thought and those of his physical and social environment. As his knowledge of himself and his world grows more exact, he seeks more exacting forms of representation. Not only does his vocabulary increase at an extraordinary rate, but he also begins to acquire new tools of representation, such as mathematics and the graphic arts. Yet, the more exacting the child becomes in his search for representation, the more dissatisfied he becomes with the results. One reason, to illustrate, why children usually give up drawing in about the fourth or fifth grade is their disgust with the discrepancy between what they wish to portray and what they have actually drawn. In the same way as the child matures, he gradually realizes that language is a lumbering means at best for conveying his thoughts and is hopelessly inadequate for expressing his feelings.

For the young person who has accepted God, the search for representation poses special problems. If religion provided only a concept of God and nothing else, he would be at a loss to represent the transcendent. How, after all, does one signify that which is neither spatial, temporal, nor corporeal? Religion, however, affords more than a simple God concept; it also provides representations of the transcendent. In primitive religions the representations were totems or idols, whereas in modern "revealed" religions, the transcendent finds its representation in scripture. Here again, however, as in the case of the concept of God, the individual's acceptance of the religious solution is multidetermined and difficult to predict in the particular case. What must be stressed is that once the individual accepts the concept of God, the question of His representation is an inevitable outcome of the search for representation in general.

CHILDHOOD AND THE SEARCH FOR RELATIONS

The school-age period is one of less rapid intellectual growth than was true for the preceding two periods. During this epoch in the child's life he is, for the first time, exposed to formal instruction and must acquire a prescribed body of knowledge and special skills such as reading and writing. The acquisition of a prescribed body of knowledge, however, presupposes a mental system which is, in part at least, comparable to the mental systems of adults who transmit the knowledge. Such a system does come into being at around the sixth or seventh year, the traditional "age of reason." Research on children's thinking has shown that this is in fact quite an appropriate designation of the accomplishments of this age period. It is only at about the age of six or seven, for example, that the child manifests the ability to make logical deductions (i.e., to recognize that if A is greater than B, and if B is greater than C, then A must be greater than C even if he has not compared A and C directly); to nest classes (i.e., to recognize that, say, boys + girls = children, and children − boys = girls), and to seriate relations (to group elements systematically so that A>B>C>D<E<F, etc.) (Piaget, 1952; Elkind, 1961; 1964).

One general feature of this new ability to reason in a logical manner is that the child now tries to relate phenomena in the world about him in a systematic manner. The youngster at this stage wants to know how things work, how they are put together, where they come from, and out of what they are made. Moreover, his concepts of time and space have broadened, and he can now grasp measured time and conceive of such distant places as foreign countries. It is the age period during which Robinson Crusoe has his greatest appeal, because Crusoe describes in marvelous detail all the building, planting, hunting, and fishing activities in which he engages. In a very real sense, then, the child is trying to relate things to one another with respect to time, space, causality, and origin. It seems appropriate, therefore, to speak of the new ability that surfaces at school age as *the capacity for practical reason* and of the corresponding need as *the search for relations*.

The search for relations, which makes its appearance in childhood proper, continues throughout life. As the young person matures, he seeks to relate himself to his social and physical milieu and to relate the things and events in his world to one another. While this search for relations is often gratifying, it is also on occasion disheartening. There are many events in life which cannot be related to one another in any simple rational way. The quirks of fate and accident are of this kind and defy man's rational efforts. There is often no simple rational answer to the question, "Why did this happen to me?" So, while the quest for relations helps man to understand himself and his world better, it also makes him aware of how much he cannot know and understand.

Within the religious sphere, the young person who has accepted the concept of God and His scriptural representation is confronted with the problem of putting himself in relation to the Transcendent. Here again, in the absence of a ready-made solution, the young person might flounder and his resolution of the problem would be makeshift at best. Religion, however, affords a means whereby the individual can relate himself to the deity, for it offers the sacrament of worship. By participating in worship, the young person can relate himself to the Transcendent in a direct and personal way. To be sure, the young person's acceptance of religion's answer to the problem will again be determined by a variety of factors. Indeed, some of our research (Elkind and Elkind, 1962; Long, Elkind, and Spilka, 1967), suggests that many young people reject the formal worship service but nonetheless engage in individual worship in the privacy of their rooms. In any case, for the adolescent who has accepted God and His scriptural representation, the question of relating himself to God is an inevitable one, no matter how it is resolved.

ADOLESCENCE AND THE SEARCH FOR COMPREHENSION

The physical and physiological transformations so prominent in adolescence frequently obscure the equally momentous changes undergone by intelligence during the same period. As a consequence of both maturation and experience, a new mental system emerges in adolescence which enables the young person to accomplish feats of thought that far surpass the elementary reasonings of the child. One feat that makes its appearance is the capacity to introspect, to take one's thought and feelings as if they were external objects and to examine and reason about them. Still another feat is the capacity to construct ideal or contrary-to-fact situations, to conceive of utopian societies, ideal mates, and preeminent careers. Finally, in problem solving situations the adolescent, in contrast to the child, can take all of the possible factors into account and test their possibilities in a systematic fashion (Inhelder and Piaget, 1958).

Implicit in all of these new mental accomplishments is the capacity to construct and think in terms of overriding theories which enable the young person not only to grasp relations but also to grasp the underlying reasons for them. To use a biological analogy, the child is concerned with "phenotypes," whereas the adolescent focuses his attention upon the "genotypes," the underlying laws and principles which relate a variety of apparently diverse phenomena. It seems reasonable, therefore, to characterize the mental ability which emerges in adolescence as the capacity for theory construction and the corresponding need as *the search for comprehension.* . . .

As in the case of the other need capacities we have considered, the search for comprehension persists throughout life, although it takes different forms at different stages in the life cycle. The search for comprehension is also like the other need capacities in the sense that it never meets with complete success. Whether it be in the field of science, art, history, or government, each new effort at comprehension uncovers new puzzles for the understanding. The same holds true on the personal plane. Although the adolescent, to illustrate, now has a conception of personality which enables him to understand people in depth, he still encounters human foibles and eccentricities which defy his generalizations. And, though his newfound capacity for comprehension enables him to hold a mirror to his mind, he still frequently fails to understand himself.

In the domain of religion, the problem of comprehension arises naturally to those who have accepted God, His scriptural representation, and the sacrament of worship. Many young people often seek such comprehension on their own with the result that they become bewildered and disheartened by the failure of their efforts. Religion again provides a solution. Every religion contains a body of myth, legend, and history which provides a means for comprehending God in His various aspects.

In modern religions, the resolution to the problem of comprehension is provided by theology. It may be, however, that the ferment within present-day theological discussions makes it more difficult than heretofore for the young person to accept the religious solution to the problem of comprehension. Be that as it may, for the individual who has accepted God, His representation, and His worship, the problem of comprehension must be faced regardless of how it may be resolved.

SUMMARY

I am aware that the foregoing discussion probably raises many more questions that it has answered. All that I have tried to do is to present a scheme to illustrate the extraordinary fit between certain basic cognitive need capacities and the major elements of institutional religion. It is probable that this fit is not accidental and that religion has, in part at least, evolved to provide solutions to the problems of adaptation posed by these need capacities. To the extent that this is true, we are justified in speaking of the origins of religion in the child.

Psychologists who have concerned themselves with religious phenomena (e.g., Allport, 1960; Dunlap, 1946; James, 1902) are in general agreement with respect to one point, namely, that there are no uniquely religious psychic elements. Insofar as anyone has been able to determine, there are no drives, sentiments, emotions, or mental categories which are inherently religious. Psychic elements, it is agreed, become religious only insofar as they become associated with one or another aspect of institutional religion. Nothing which has been said so far contradicts this position, with which I am in complete agreement.

Nonetheless, the view that there are no uniquely religious psychic elements does not preclude the possibility that there may be uniquely religious *adaptations*. Adaptations, by definition, are neither innate nor acquired but are instead the products of subject- (individual or society) environment interaction. Every adaptation is thus a construction which bears the stamp of both nature and nurture, yet is reducible to neither one. The same holds true for religious adaptations. The concept of God, Spirit, or more generally, the Transcendent, cannot be reduced to the search for conservation any more than it can be traced to the phenomenon of death. On the contrary, neither the search for conservation nor the phenomenon of death is in itself religious, although it may well take part in the production of religious elements. Like a gestalt, such as a painting or a melody, the Transcendent is greater than the sum or product of its parts.

As suggested above, once the concept of God or Spirit is accepted as the ultimate conservation, it necessarily entails genuinely religious problems for the other emerging need capacities. These problems can, in turn, be immediately resolved by the ready-made constructions afforded by institutional religion, such as scripture, worship, and theology. From the standpoint of the individual, therefore, the concept of God or of the Transcendent lies at the very core of personal religion. At the same time, however, whether the concept of God is a personal construction or one acquired from institutional religion, it is always superordinate, transcending the particular individual or social needs as well as the phenomenal facts out of which it arose.

REFERENCES

Allport, G. W. *The Individual and His Religion.* New York: Macmillan, 1960.

Dunlap, K. *Religion: Its Function in Human Life.* New York: McGraw Hill, 1946.

Elkind, D. The development of quantitative thinking. *J. of Genet. Psychol.,* 1961, *98,* 37–46.

Elkind, D. Discrimination, seriation and numeration of size and dimensional differences in young children. *J. of Genet. Psychol.,* 1964, *104,* 275–96.

Elkind, D. (Ed.) *Six Psychological Studies by Jean Piaget.* New York: Random House, 1967.

Elkind, D. & Elkind, Sally F. Varieties of religious experience in young adolescents. *J. for the Scientific Study of Religion II,* 1962, 102–12.

Flavell, J. H. *The Developmental Psychology of Jean Piaget.* New York: Van Nostrand, 1963.

Inhelder, Barbel, & Piaget, J. *The Growth of Logical Thinking from Childhood Through Adolescence.* New York: Basic Books, 1968.

James, W. *Varieties of Religious Experience.* New York: Longmans, 1902.

Long, Diane, Elkind, D., & Spilka, B. The child's conception of prayer. *J. for the Scientific Study of Religion,* 1967, *VI,* 101–09.

Piaget, J. *La Psychologie et les Foi Religieuses.* Geneva: Labor, 1923.

Piaget, J. *Immanentisme et foi religieuse.* Geneva: Robert, 1930.

Piaget, J. *Play, Dreams and Imitation in Childhood.* New York: Norton, 1951.

Piaget, J. *The Child's Conception of Number.* New York: Humanities Press, 1952.

Piaget, J. *The Construction of Reality in the Child.* New York: Basic Books, 1954.

22
LIFE AND DEATH
CONCEPTS AND FEELINGS OF CHILDREN

Children understand death differently than do adults. This
chapter describes the stages in the evolution of the child's conception of death and some of the consequences of children's
limited understanding for their behavior in relation to death. A
final section offers suggestions for talking with children about
death either in response to the death of a loved one or in response to a child's natural curiosity about the topic.

Life and death are topics of great interest to children because
they pose such interesting problems and riddles. "Why can't
the bird fly anymore?" and "Why do they have to kill the tur-
key?" are the sort of questions that parents and teachers are
inevitably asked by young children. Death, however, is a particularly difficult topic to discuss, in part at least because of our
own, adult emotional attitudes toward the subject. It is helpful,
therefore, to know something about how children at different
ages think and feel about death in order to deal with the subject
at their level. The purpose of this chapter is to review the evolution of children's conceptions of life and death with two aims in
mind: to help us better understand children's behavior in connection with death, and to help us in talking about death with
bereaved and nonbereaved children.

Day Care and Early Education, January/February, 1977.

EVOLUTION OF CHILDREN'S CONCEPTIONS OF LIFE AND DEATH

A number of different investigators have explored the evolution of children's conceptions of life and death and have arrived at quite comparable conclusions. Most investigators agree that conceptions of life and death evolve in stages that are roughly related to age. The stages are approximately as follows: from about the age of three to five, children do not understand the meaning of death and do not regard it as discontinuous with, nor in opposition to, life. At the second stage, usually ages six to nine, children begin to think of death as discontinuous with life but as reversible and not applicable to everyone. Then at the last stage, beginning at about the age of ten or eleven, children begin to view death as irreversible and in medical/biological terms (e.g. Anthony, 1940; Gesell, 1956; Melear, 1973; Nagy, 1948; Wallon, 1946).

In order to do full justice to the evolution of children's conceptions of life and death, however, we need to put the conceptions in the context of the general systems of thought which characterize intelligence at different age levels. For this purpose, the more general stages of intellectual development described by Piaget (1950) are appropriate. Piaget's stages have to do, in part, with how children conceptualize space, time, and causality, all of which are central to the child's understanding of death. For example, only when the child begins to appreciate future time does the anticipation of death appear frightening. It seems reasonable, therefore, to present a detailed description of children's conceptions of life and death in the context of their more general conceptions of the world.

THE PREOPERATIONAL CHILD

Children at the preoperational stage of development, usually ages three to six, tend to see the world in *anthropomorphic* terms (Piaget, 1929). The young child believes that many physical objects are alive and that they have feelings, intentions, and purposes. Moreover, trees, plants, and animals, as well as houses and automobiles are regarded as having been made by and for man. And every event—rain falling, clouds moving—is regarded as having a purpose. In the world view of the young child there is no such thing as accident or chance. Past and future are barely grasped at this stage and the here and now looms very large in the thinking of the young child.

It is not surprising then, that death in the sense of the termination of life is not really understood by children. Since they cannot really conceive of the distant future, nor of the absence of life, death in the adult sense is not really appreciated. The responses of some of Anthony's (1940) young children, when she asked them what to be dead meant, reflect the thinking at this stage. Children at this level said that to be dead meant that you "didn't have any supper" or that you "go to sleep." At best, preschool children understood death as a kind of change of state, being hungry or asleep, but as nonetheless continuous with life.

THE CONCRETE OPERATIONAL PERIOD

At around the age of six or seven, most children acquire what Piaget (1950) calls concrete operations. These operations are an internalized set of actions that allow school-age children to do in their heads what before they had to do with their hands. In playing checkers, for example, the concrete-operational child examines the various paths before moving his man. The preschool child, in contrast, seems to play by trial and error, moving his pieces in one direction then another. Concrete operations also make possible the understanding of space, time, and quantity as measurable dimensions. These operations give rise to a *pragmatic* orientation toward the world which is reflected in many different aspects of elementary school children's behavior including their conceptions of life and death.

Two characteristics mark the concrete operational child's conceptions of life and death. One is the notion that while death is the end of one life, it is also the beginning of another. This reincarnation theme appears in all of the studies of children's conceptions of life and death. Here are some examples:

> The child has just viewed a coffin and says, "Of course the person who went away (in the coffin) will become a baby." What makes you think so? "Of course he will, won't he?" I

don't know. "When John (the child's baby brother) was
born someone must have died."

(Anthony, 1940, p. 169)

What happens when you die? "You don't feel anything."
Anything else? "There are many people who go there."
And when they go there what happens? "Sometimes they
become an animal." How does that happen? "There is a
force, a force which changes you into an animal after you
have been in a cemetery."   (Wallon, 1947, p. 372)

The other idea characteristic of this stage is that while death
happens to some people, it does not happen to everyone. Which
people are to die and which are to live is not always clearly
thought out in the child's mind. Here are some examples of this
mode of thought:

(The child accepts the idea that people will be put in
graves.) And will they put me in a grave one day? "No!
[laughs]." Why don't you believe they will put me in a
grave? "I don't know." Who is it who dies? "The parents,"
and then? "the women." And then? "The orphans." And
who will die then, will I die then? "Yes." And you? "Yes."
And your Papa? "Yes." Is it good or bad to die? "Bad."

(Wallon, 1947, pp. 373–74)

In this instance the child seems to believe that there is a hierarchy and that some classes of people die before others. Death is
regarded as a sort of bad "place" where people go perhaps in
their order of wickedness with the least wicked going last. Other
children see certain classes of people as exempted from death:

Are there people who never die? "Some times." Who are
the people who never die? "The parents." Why don't they
die? "Because they take care of the children... and the
policemen too." Why the policemen too? "Because they
take us to prison and put handcuffs on." And they never
die? "No." Would you like to be a policeman? "No, I would
like to be a teacher." Would some of your friends like to be
a policeman? "I don't know." If some of your friends became policemen would they not die? "There are some
people who die and some people who don't."

(Wallon, 1947, p. 375)

Sometimes children associate death with old age or with ill
health and assume that, since neither of those eventualities will

happen to them, they are exempt from death. I had the following conversation with a young man of seven:

> I am afraid that the goldfish is dead. It happens sometimes. "Yes, fish die but children don't die." Oh? "Yes, children don't die unless they drown or get run over." I see, children only die by accident. "Right, I won't die. When you are old you die. I won't get old so I won't die."

The concrete operational child thus displays a number of contradictory ideas about death. Sometimes it is thought of as reversible, sometimes as the fate of special groups. Toward the end of this period, however, the child discovers death in a very personal sense. It suddenly occurs to the child that he or she will die and this comes as a startling and terrifying revelation. So traumatic is this experience that many grownups still remember it quite vividly. Death is suddenly understood to be discontinuous with life. And the child fears death because of the value he or she now places on life.

THE FORMAL OPERATIONAL PERIOD

Beginning at about the age of eleven or twelve, children acquire what Piaget calls formal operations. These operations make possible new modes of thought and the acquisition of more abstract conceptions of space, time, and causality. In adolescence young people can begin to comprehend notions of historical time, of celestial space, and of probabilistic causality. And young people can grasp metaphor and simile and engage in intellectual discussions about ideals, values, and attitudes. At this stage young people arrive at a *scientific* view of the world that is reflected in their conceptions of life and death.

At about the age of eleven and twelve, young people begin to define life and death in biological/medical terms. In Anthony's (1940) study, children at this age level defined death as: "A body that has no life in it" or "When you have no pulse, no temperature, and can't breathe." Adolescents, then, appear to accept death as a fact of nature without undue upset or concern. They know that they themselves and their loved ones will die. But their sense of time is such that they also recognize that these events are, in all probability, far in the future and need not be worried about now. In addition, formal operations allow adolescents to shift perspectives and to look at death from the religious, dramatic, and other points of view. This ability to shift perspectives, together with the young person's newfound sense of temporal duration, makes the consciousness of his or her own mortality much more easy to bear than when it was first discovered at the end of the concrete operational period.

BEHAVIORAL CONSEQUENCES

These findings regarding the way in which children come to understand the ideas of life and of death can help to explain children's real and fancied reactions to the death of a loved one. To adults such reactions often seem callous and insensitive. In fact, however, the child's emotions are structured by his cognitions. Because the child cannot conceive of death in the adult sense, he does not experience grief or remorse in the adult way. Grief and remorse require cognitive structures that would enable the child to order past memories and anticipate the future. But such structures are not available until late childhood.

An investigation of children who had lost a father supports this observation. The youngest children in the study (under five years) did not seem to react to bereavement in any noticeable way. And children between the ages of five and nine years apparently took death in stride and remarked about it in a seemingly callous way: "My daddy's gone to heaven, hasn't he?" These same children, however, were tearful and anxious. Older, adolescent children reacted in different ways. Some responded with anger whenever the dead father was mentioned, some became solitary and withdrawn. Others tried not to show their feelings and became solicitous of their mothers (Marris, 1958).

There are other types of evidence to show that young children do not suffer severe grief reactions on the death of a parent. In one study, adults were asked to recall their reactions to the death of a parent which occurred when they were children. When the bereavement occurred before the child had reached the age of nine, almost none of the adults recalled any feelings of grief which they themselves had. Women could remember their mothers' reactions quite clearly while men remembered the events, particularly the funeral arrangements. When the death of a parent occurred after the offspring were eleven years of age or older, they recalled mainly their own grief and not that of their mother or father.

In talking about the young child's relative lack of reaction to bereavement, it needs to be said that there are sometimes delayed-reaction effects. In one study, the long-term effects of losing a parent seemed to be most negative if the parent died during the child's third or fourth year. There is some possibility that this relation may occur because the dead parent deprives the child of an appropriate figure to identify with at a crucial point in the formation of self-concept. In this regard, death of the same-sexed parent during the early years was an important factor in psychiatric disturbance of adult women but not of adult men (Rutter, 1962).

Death of a parent or sibling may also have long-term, negative effects if the child, because of magical thinking, feels in some way, responsible for the death. Here is a case described by Wolff (1969):

> Allan, a five-year-old boy, had been deserted by his father in infancy. His mother had then married a farmer and there was now a stepbrother aged two. Allan adores his step-father and one day when he was running to join him in the rambling shed, the younger brother followed. Allan shouted back at him to stay behind, as he himself climbed over a low wall to reach the shed. The brother, however, toddled after him over the wall, fell into a well and was drowned. Allan's behavior now changed completely. He became a very aggressive child, frequently in fights with other children at school, and was unable to concentrate on his lessons. He climbed dangerously and sustained several bad falls so that his mother was constantly afraid he would injure himself. He became accident prone.
>
> (Wolff, 1969, p. 87–88)

This clinical example could be interpreted at many different dynamic levels. What it suggests is that a child's magical think-ing can produce serious emotional reactions, which the death of a relative in and of itself does not. Allan may have wished his brother dead (in the sense of not being around), and when this actually occurred, he felt responsible. When he was old enough to fully understand death, his reaction was even more severe. *Even though children may not fully understand the death of parent or sibling when it occurs, the appropriate emotional dynamics may come into play once the young person attains conceptual understanding of the event.*

Children who have not experienced bereavement (like some of those who have) often talk about death in what appears to be a cruel and insensitive way. Here again the children's verbalizations have to be understood from the child's perspective and not the adult's. Young children, for example, sometimes talk about the death of parents or other relatives with some equanimity. This usually occurs in the context of what the children will inherit or get from the parents or the relatives. When our children were small they sometimes argued about which one would get our summer cottage (a much coveted place) when we, the parents, were dead. Such apparent hard-heartedness really reflects the young child's failure to fully comprehend the significance of death.

The following poem illustrates the same idea because in it the child is focused upon the personal enhancement that results from a death.

> My father's friend came once to tea,
>   he laughed and joked and spoke to me,
> But in another week they said,
>   that friendly, pink-faced man was dead.
> How sad they said, the best of friends,
>   so said I too, how sad, but then,
> Deep in my heart I thought with pride,
>   I know a person who has died.

Remnants of this sort of thinking are found even in adults. Some college students fantasize that a parent will die and thus provide an acceptable excuse for them not to take their final exams.

Some of the jibes and taunts that children hurl at their siblings also have to be understood as reflecting a nonfinal conception of death. When children say they wish their brother or sister "would get sick and die," they are expressing the wish that the siblings were far away, not that they should die in the biological sense. In this instance it is an analogue to the adult expression "Drop dead" which is usually employed in the sense of "Get lost!'' Again we find a parallel construction arising from quite different mental processes. In the child, wishing someone dead arises from a failure to understand death, whereas in adults, it arises from a figurative use of the term.

IMPLICATIONS: TALKING WITH CHILDREN ABOUT DEATH

There are two different sets of circumstances under which it is useful and necessary to talk about death with children. One set of circumstances is that in which the child has actually suffered the loss of a loved one, witnessed a death, or in other ways come into personal contact with the death of another person. Another set of circumstances arises when children become curious about death for any number of different reasons—because adults or children talk about it, it occurs on television and so on. The crucial difference between the two sets of circumstances is the emotional state of the adults and children in question.

When a real death occurs, the adults' attitude and posture communicates as much or more as their words. Death raises many issues and feelings in adults that children may not have experienced before. When, for example, a grandparent dies, a usually outgoing, energetic Daddy may, for a time, become quiet and lethargic. The child is thus aware that something has happened even without being told. If the child is not informed about a death of a near relative (including a parent), frustration and anger is always the result, because the child senses that something is wrong and is left to imagine the worst possible events.

How, then, should one talk with a child about the death of a loved one? Unfortunately there are no magic formulas and circumstances, and individuals differ so greatly that the same words are not appropriate for every situation. There are, however, some simple rules that can serve as guidelines. As I indicated earlier in the discussion, children do not really understand death in the adult sense. What they react to at the time of bereavement is the emotional climate that prevails. In speaking with children about death, therefore, the first rule is to speak to their emotions and not to their intellect.

Children who experience a death in the family also experience a turmoil in their familiar world. People they know and love behave in strange and difficult ways. The usual sources of emotional support are absent and children begin to fear that their accepting and comfortable world is about to fall apart. They need to know that while the adults in their world are unhappy and upset now, this will pass. They need to hear that the adults in their world will continue to love them and that there will be no major changes in their way of life (if indeed there will not be any). In short, what children need to hear most, at the time of bereavement, is that their immediate world—most especially the love and protection of the parent(s)—will continue.

A second general rule on talking with children about death is to avoid figurative language. Often, what is meant to provide emotional reassurance has just the opposite effect and ends up causing additional fear and anxiety. This is true because children do not understand figurative language and often take it quite literally. A child who is told that "Grandma has gone to sleep and won't wake up" may develop a dread of going to sleep for fear he or she won't wake up either. Likewise a child who is told "Jesus took Daddy because he was so good" may decide never to be good for fear of being taken by Jesus. In the same way a child who is told that "Grandpa died because he was sick" may associate all sickness with death and become terrified of catching a cold. And, finally, a child who is told that his mother has "gone on a long trip" may believe that he or she has simply been abandoned.

In effect there is no way to explain death to young children because the concept itself, as we saw earlier, is foreign to the young child's way of thinking. Even a child who has been told his father is dead, has witnessed his father's funeral, and observed the unhappiness of those around him, still does not appreciate death in the adult sense. John F. Kennedy's son John-John is a case in point. When the family returned from the funeral service (during which John-John saluted his father's casket), John-John saw his father's secretary and asked, "When is Daddy coming home?" We cannot really communicate a concept to a child when he lacks the conceptual system to assimilate and understand it.

This does not mean that the issue of death is to be avoided, but only that we avoid confusing or misleading children. In this regard it may be appropriate to admit that we have no explanation, that "Daddy loved us and we love him and I don't know why he had to die. I just know he would want us to love each other and to be happy." It is appropriate to use the words "dead" and "death" at such times because the child understands these terms better than any others. Whatever words are used, it is important to be honest, direct, and simple. In talking with bereaved children, reassurance about the continued quality of life is more important, and should be given more weight, than explanations about death.

It remains to say something about talking with children about death when there is no immediate personal involvement by adult or child. In such circumstances the discussion is usually generated by questions that children ask themselves. But the review of research on children's spontaneous conceptions of life and death suggests that they already have implicit answers to the questions they ask. A reasonable first step, therefore, when children raise such questions, is to ask the children their opinion on the matter. As an illustration, consider the following discussion I had with our then five-year-old son Ricky a couple of weeks after we had found a dead bird which I placed in a plastic bag and put in the garbage can.

> Ricky: "Why do they bury dead people in the ground?"
> D: "Oh, for a lot of reasons. Where do you think we should put dead people?"
> Ricky: "In the garbage can."
> D: "Why in the world in the garbage can?"
> Ricky: "Well, it's easier to get out of and it's cleaner, you don't get all muddy and stuff."

Clearly, for Ricky, death was a temporary going away and from that standpoint a garbage can makes more sense than a hole in the ground.

Sometimes, of course, children are insistent and some sort of direct answer is warranted. But it is important to put the answer in terms that children will understand. For example, if I had answered Ricky's question directly, I might have said something like "To make room for all the new babies that are being born into the world." This answer speaks to the real point of the child's question, namely, *for what purpose* do we bury people in the ground? Such answers are really not bad pedagogy. First, because the child would not really understand a biological answer anyway. And second, because answering the intent of the child's question communicates that the adult understands the child's intention and can respond appropriately. In my opinion, it is much more important for young children to feel that they can communicate meaningfully with an adult than that they learn some empty verbal formula about death. In talking with children about death, under nonemotional circumstances, it is still necessary to be more concerned with life than with its termination. What children learn about death is far less important than what they learn about life from those who continue to love and care for them.

SUMMARY

The child's conception of death evolves in a series of stages that are related to age. Among preschool children death is thought of as a "going away" which is temporary rather than permanent. At the next stage, roughly the early elementary school years, the child's conception of death includes the notion of reincarnation and the belief that not everyone dies. There is thus a beginning notion of death as termination but it is alleviated by the potential for return from, or selective susceptibility to, death. Finally, toward the end of the elementary school years, young people understand death in biological-medical terms and as holding for everyone.

Because young children do not understand death in adult terms, they may seem callous and heartless in their discussions of the topic. Likewise children who lose a parent by death may not show much in the way of immediate grief or mourning. This is because death is not understood as a permanent state. It may be, however, that the effects of early bereavement are delayed in their expression and only appear when the young person reaches adolescence or later.

In talking with young people about death, it is important to be tuned to the child's feelings. A child who has lost a loved one wants to be reassured about the continuity of life; he or she does not really want to hear a treatise on death. What has to be avoided, in talking with children about death, are evasions that are at best misleading. Using simple direct language, including the word death, and acknowledging our own grief and inability to understand why people die when they do, can help children deal with death honestly and on their own terms.

REFERENCES

Anthony, S. *The Child's Discovery of Death.* New York: Harcourt Brace, 1940.

Gesell, A., Ilg, F. L., & Ames, L. B. *Youth: The Years from Ten to Sixteen.* New York: Harper & Row, 1956.

Marris, P. *Widows and Their Families.* London: Routledge & Kegan Paul, 1958.

Melear, J. D. Children's conception of death. *J. of Genet. Psychol.*, 1973, *123*, 359–60.

Nagy, M. The child's theories concerning death. *J. of Genet. Psychol.*, 1948, *73*, 3–27.

Piaget, J. *The Child's Conception of the World.* London: Routledge & Kegan Paul, 1929.

Piaget, J. *The Psychology of Intelligence.* London: Routledge & Kegan Paul, 1950.

Rutter, M. *Illness in Parents and Children.* M. D. Thesis. University of Birmingham, England, 1962.

Wallon, H. *Les Origines de la Pensee chez L'enfant.* Paris: Paris Universitaires de France, 1946.

Wolff, S. *Children Under Stress.* London: Penguin Press, 1969.

CONCLUSION

In these essays I have shared some of my experiences and efforts at conceptualizing the child's interactions with different facets of society. As these essays suggest, the interactions of children and society are not static but rather are constantly changing. In this concluding discussion I want to suggest some directions the interactions of child and society, child and family, child and school, child and clinic, and child and church may be taking in the decades to come. I have no special claims to clairvoyance, however, and simply believe that the best guide to the future is a careful consideration of the past.

THE CHILD AND SOCIETY

Although divorce rates continue to increase, they will probably soon level out and even decrease. Americans are basically marriage and family oriented, and this cultural value is not likely to dissipate. My guess is that we will soon see a new conservatism with respect to sexuality and morality and that some of the excesses of the past will be redressed. I do not mean that we will go back to a new puritanism but only that we will reach a more mature, accepting attitude about sexuality without having to flout it.

This new conservatism will probably have, on balance, positive benefits for children. Marriages and commitments will be more stable and the excesses of some of the more extreme psychologies of "live for thyself alone," suggested in the chapter on "Culture, Change and Children," will be redressed by more socially oriented and more interpersonally responsible systems. Parents are already moving toward firmer discipline, toward more regulation of television watching, and in general are trying to recover some of the responsibilities of parenting that, for awhile, seemed more and more given over to outside agencies.

The new conservatism is having impact in the civil rights field as well, not always positively. Efforts on behalf of blacks have lessened somewhat, but this may be positive as well as negative. Blacks are beginning to question whether traditionally "liberal" practices, such as higher minimum wages, actually benefit blacks. The new civil rights wisdom suggests that what is good for the economy as a whole may also be good for blacks and that blacks may actually be disadvantaged by programs designed specifically for their behalf.

The same, it seems to me, is occurring at the level of education. It is increasingly recognized that special education for different groups may be less important than quality education for all children. Quality education implies facilities that are spacious and well furnished and teachers who know their children as well as the curriculum they teach. Quality education is always individualized and as such can assimilate children from diverse backgrounds. Disadvantaged children do not need a different education from advantaged children; they do need an education *as good as* that received by those who are more well off financially.

On the question of other minorities, such as homosexuals, the outlook is mixed. The new conservatism which may benefit heterosexuals by stabilizing relationships could work against a more liberal attitude toward homosexuals. While I do not believe that homosexuals will lose much of the ground they have gained in acceptance and recognition of their rights to freedom from discrimination, further progress in this direction is likely to be less rapid than it has been in the past decade.

In general, then, America in the late 1970s is more settled than it was in the sixties and early seventies. The new conservatism is likely to continue into the 1980s and overall will probably have

more beneficial than detrimental effects for children. Families
will be more stable, programs for minorities will be more balanced and less pressured, and probably will be more effective.
The danger in the coming years may be of another sort, namely,
complacency. If we become too relaxed, too settled, then neglected groups will rise to be heard once again.

THE FAMILY

In all probability, families will continue to be small, no more
than two children on the average, and the number of single
parent families will continue to be a significant portion of all
families in America. What does seem to be happening, however,
is that there is a much greater self-consciousness about parenting than ever before. Prior to the last decade, there were only a
few books published about raising children. But the past decade
has been witness to an ever growing number of books about
child rearing. This trend appears to be increasing.

The new demand on the part of parents to read about parenting can be seen in both positive and negative ways. From the
positive direction it could mean that parents are now more
aware of the importance of good parenting and are more desir-
ous of doing a good job than they were before. Television has
probably contributed to this inasmuch as many programs portray adults who are models of effective and constructive parenting. Some of the reason for the current upsurge in parent interest in books on parenting could derive from an attempt to emu-
late parenting that has been observed on television.

But the interest in books on parenting could also be looked at
in a more sinister light. It might be argued that parents today are
more insecure than ever before. Having grown up in nuclear
families, they lack direct experience with infants and children.
And, because we have become a society of experts and
specialists, parents look more and more to experts to help them
in their child rearing. Raising children "by the book" removes
from them the responsibility if anything should go wrong.

Accordingly, one can read the interest of parents in books on
childrearing as an index of strength—a willingness to learn to
improve and do better—or as a sign of weakness—an abnega-

tion of responsibility to an authority. My own impression is that probably both motives are operative and that the same forces that give some parents self-confidence undermine self-confidence in others. Whatever their motives for their turning to these books, however, most parents are less influenced by books than book sales might indicate. First of all, parents select books that coincide with their own philosophy of child rearing and which reinforce it. Secondly, parents are quick to find fault with an author whose suggestions don't work. In the end, parents today, like those of yesterday and those of tomorrow, always measure the merit of expert opinion against their own experience. The openness of contemporary parents to expert opinion in no way implies that they accept it unselectively or uncritically.

It is probably safer to predict that parents will continue to rear their children much as they themselves have been reared. Our own parents are the most powerful models we have when it comes time to parent our own children. There are variations in practices and material things, of course, but the more important parental attitudes toward children are resurrected when those children become parents themselves. So if parents become more conscious of their parenting and do a better job of it, this will have an impact not only upon their children but also upon their children's children.

THE SCHOOL

Education in America today is in a period of retrenchment. Children of the "baby boom" which reached its peak in 1957 are now out of high school, and school enrollments are shrinking, particularly at the lower grades where our contemporary low birth rates are beginning to be immediately felt. This means that schools are closing and that jobs in teaching are hard to find. School budgets, in the majority of places, are rather tight and choices have to be made as to which special programs are to be retained or dropped.

Philosophically, education is giving evidence of the new conservatism that is affecting American society in general. The "back to basics" movement and teacher "accountability" reflect this new conservative trend in education. Likewise, one hears little these days about alternative schools or innovative educators (like Holt and Kozol) and not even very much about "open" education or British primary schools. Rather than looking forward or outward, education is looking backward, in part at least, to a less turbulent educational era.

In some ways, the new conservatism in education reflects the new conservatism of parents. Today, more than fifty per cent of young people in America go on to college or university study. This means that the majority of parents have an academic orientation and are concerned, from the moment their child enters school, about their child's academic achievement. I discussed some negative aspects of this phenomenon in the chapter "Curriculum-disabled Children." The pressure on children for academic achievement is likely to continue at least for a while.

There may, however, be a generation of parents who will not press their youngsters so hard. Young people who are graduating today feel disheartened about job possibilities and the value of their years of working to get good grades. These young people, whom I talked about in the chapter "Exploitation and the Generational Conflict" may inculcate their children with a different set of values. But with the exception of this generation, I believe that parents will continue to focus upon academic achievement as a prime measure of their parenting skills and effectiveness. I hope, however, that this attitude will be more and more moderated by an appreciation and concern for the child's emotional well being.

For children, the retrenchment in education will have both positive and negative effects. If schools do not retrench too much, lower enrollments could mean smaller classes. And, other things being equal, smaller classes mean better education. With the shrinking market for teachers and with many different job opportunities open for women, the overall quality of teachers is likely to increase. This is true because now only those people who enjoy children and who want to teach are likely to enter the field. In the past it was one of the few professional job opportunities open to women and hence attracted people who taught school out of necessity rather than choice.

The new conservatism in education could, however, go too far. Educational philosophy and practice of necessity has to follow trends in the larger society but its adaptability in this regard is rather slow and cumbersome. While education is assimilating the new conservatism, society may be well on its way to a new liberalism. The inability of education to keep pace with trends in the larger society has been a cause of conflict in the past and, in all likelihood, will cause friction in the future.

Children, of course, are always caught in the middle of such conflicts. They suffered the "new" curricula of the 1960s and the "back to basics" of the seventies. If only schools could be kept open to continual innovation, there might be fewer swings between entrenched practices and revolutionary innovations that have always rocked American education in the past and that are likely to do so in the future. Children, unfortunately, always pay the price of education's inability to keep up with the pace of social change.

THE CLINIC

In many ways clinical theory and practice is much more conservative and resistant to change than is education. As I tried to argue in several of the chapters in this book, many forms of disturbed behavior in children are interpersonally produced and can be exacerbated by systemic factors like bad curriculum materials. But the tendency to look at learning problems or delinquency, as residing in the young person, rather than in his or her interpersonal relations, seems bound to continue.

I must say that I have little hope that so-called community psychology and psychiatry will alleviate this situation. Such programs are aimed at prevention rather than remediation, and this is what gives them their "community" flavor. But so long as emotional disturbance is conceived in traditional ways, preventive measures will be no more effective than remedial ones because the focus of prevention is misguided. To the extent that community psychology focuses upon the child, rather than the social forces that impinge upon him or her, it will perpetuate errors of clinical practice in the past.

Basically, what is needed is a new conception of mental illness and mental health that will take account of what we know about interpersonal and cognitive processes. A few efforts in this direction are to be found in the chapters on "Middle-class Delinquency," on "Egocentrism and Ego Defense," and on "The Curriculum-Disabled Child." Much, much more must be done in this domain before preventive efforts can really have any significant effects. Preventive efforts, after all, are only as good as the diagnosis of the illness being prevented. And contemporary diagnoses are rooted in dated conceptions of psychopathology.

The only real challenge to traditional clinical concepts has come from behavior modification. Behavior modification has the virtue of being pragmatic (if it works, it's good) and devoid of theoretical cant. But its view of the child as a completely maleable organism seems to me to deny the child's individuality and human intelligence. Behavior modification also seems to focus too much on the child and the material world and too little on the child's interpersonal relations.

I am afraid, therefore, that the new conservatism to be seen in other parts of society is simply a continuation of the old conservatism that has always prevailed in psychiatry and clinical psychology. Bizarre offshoots, such as EST, never really threaten the establishment, for even bizarre offshoots never really challenge the basic assumptions upon which clinical theory and practice are based, namely that mental illness, like physical illness, is isolated in the individual. Unfortunately, that is a viewpoint which perpetuates rather than ameliorates the suffering of emotionally troubled people.

But an interactionist position, such as the one that has been presented in this book, is a difficult one to take and to hold. Harry Stack Sullivan had it, but he never had the impact upon the larger clinical community that he should have had. And Piaget has it, but his work is not directly applicable to clinical practice. Any hope for a new liberalism in psychiatry and in clinical psychology will, I believe, have to come from building upon the conceptualizations of Sullivan and Piaget. Though different in training and research concerns, both have shown that we are interactional, not encapsulated, beings.

THE CHURCH

The liberalization of the church, like the liberalization of society, family, and school during the sixties, is also seeing a movement toward a new conservatism. This does not mean that the gains, particularly in Catholicism, of the past have been lost, but only that the pace of change has slowed considerably. The new religiosity that I suggested in "Culture, Change and Children" (written in the early seventies) is now manifest in the "born again" pietism and is still further evidence of a new religious conservatism.

For children, the new religiosity makes possible an alternative set of values that they should have the option of choosing. In effect, the denigration of religion, like its rigid espousal, deprives young people of an important alternative that should be open to them. To be most useful, for the adolescent, religion has to be presented as something to be examined, thought about, and decided upon. Young people should not be forced either to give up religious convictions or to maintain them. Religion is one of several repositories of human values that should be open to young people for examination, study, and possible commitment.

In general, then, America seems in the late nineteen seventies to be moving into a new conservatism that is, by and large, healthy. Gains in civil rights for minorities, changes in marital values, innovations in education, changes in clinical practice, and liberalization in religion have not been lost. Rather we seem to be moving into a more quiet time when some of these changes can be assimilated and digested.

By and large it should be a good time for children who thrive in social stability. It is likely, however, that in the next decade or two, a new period of instability will appear, particularly as natural energy resources begin to be depleted. Thankfully, the people who will have to deal with that new crisis will have grown up in stable times and will have the intellectual and personality resources to deal with it.

The relations between children and society, then, are dynamic rather than static. The same child growing up in different times would not be the same child. In working for child welfare, we need always to take account of the times as well as the child. But there are continuities as well as discontinuities. At any time in history, children need the love and care of their parents and the commitment to their well being of the larger society. In the end, children need society and society needs children. That is why it is so important that we in America make the health and welfare of children our first, and our most important, priority.

INDEX